Realism and the Cinema: A Reader

British Film Institute Readers in Film Studies

Realism and the Cinema:
A Reader/Edited by Christopher Williams

Routledge & Kegan Paul
London, Boston, Melbourne and Henley

in association with the British Film Institute
127 Charing Cross Road, London WC2H 0EA

First published in 1980
by Routledge & Kegan Paul Ltd
39 Store Street,
London WC1E 7DD
9 Park Street, Boston,
Mass. 02108, USA
296 Beaconsfield Parade,
Middle Park, Melbourne, 3206,
Australia and
Broadway House,
Newtown Road,
Henley-on-Thames,
Oxon RG9 1EN
Set in Sabon by
Oxprint, Oxford
and printed and bound in Great Britain by
T.J. Press (Padstow) Ltd, Padstow, Cornwall

British Library Cataloguing in Publication Data

Realism and the cinema. — (British Film
Institute. Readers in film studies).
1. Realism in moving-pictures—Addresses,
essays, lectures
I. Williams, Christopher   II. Series
791.43'0909'1208   PN1995.9.R3

ISBN 0 7100 0477 X
ISBN 0 7100 0478 8 Pbk

Contents

Acknowledgments

I would like to thank Edward Buscombe, Christine Gledhill, Jim Hillier, Alan Lovell, Angela Martin, Diana Matias and Stephanie McKnight for their help, in different ways and at different times, in the preparation of this book.

In addition, the editor and publishers gratefully acknowledge permission to reprint the following material: John Grierson, *Grierson on Documentary* (ed. Forsyth Hardy), reprinted by permission of Faber & Faber Ltd, London 1966, pp. 69–70, 86, 121–2, 126–8, 140–3, 146–7, 148–9; Sergei Eisenstein, *Film Form*, Harcourt Brace Jovanovich, Inc., New York 1949, pp. 3–4, 34–5, 183–5, and Dennis Dobson, London; Dziga Vertov, 'Kinok Instructions', Dziga Vertov: *Articles, journaux, projets* (translation and notes by Sylviane Mossé and Andrée Robel), 10/18 – Union Générale d'Editions, Paris 1972, pp. 97–106, English translation by Diana Matias, copyright © British Film Institute 1978; Cesare Zavattini, 'Some Ideas on the Cinema', *Sight and Sound*, vol. 23, no. 2, October–December 1953, pp. 224–5; Roberto Rossellini, 'A Discussion of Neo Realism – Rossellini interviewed by Mario Verdone', *Screen*, vol. 14, no. 4, Winter 1973–4, pp. 70–3 and *Bianco e nero*, no. 2; André Bazin, 'William Wyler or the Jansenist of *mise en scène*', *Qu'est-ce que le cinéma?*, Editions du Cerf, Paris, 1958, pp. 1–13, English-language copyright © 1967 by The Regents of the University of California, English translation by Angela Martin, copyright © British Film Institute; Eric Rohmer, 'Le celluloid et le marbre', *Cahiers du Cinéma*, vol. IX, 1955, (II) 'Le siècle des peintres', no. 49, pp. 10–15, (III) 'De la metaphore', no. 51, pp. 2–9, English translation by Diana Matias, copyright © British Film Institute, 1978; V. F. Perkins, 'Understanding and Judging Movies', *Film as Film*, Penguin Books Ltd, Harmondsworth 1972, pp. 121–33, copyright © V. F. Perkins; Frances Flaherty, *The Odyssey of a Film-Maker*, Beta Phi Mu Chapbooks, Princeton, New Jersey 1960, pp. 39–40; Helen van Dongen, *The Technique of Film Editing* (eds Karel Reisz and Gavin Millar), copyright © Focal Press Ltd., London and New York 1968, pp. 136–41; Siegfried Kracauer, 'Flaherty's "slight narrative"', *Theory of Film: The Redemption of Physical Reality*, copyright © Oxford University Press Inc., New York 1960, pp. 247–9; S. Tretyakov and V. Shklovsky, 'Lef and Film: notes of discussion', *Screen*, vol. 12, no. 4, 1971 and *Screen Reader*, SEFT, London 1977, pp. 305–10; O. Brik and V. Shklovsky, 'The Lef Arena; Comrades: Fight out your ideas!', *Screen*, vol. 12, no. 4, 1971 and *Screen Reader*, SEFT, London 1977, pp. 314–21; Yury Tynyanov, 'Foundations of the Cinema', *Poetika Kino*, Moscow 1927, English translation by Diana Matias, copyright © British Film Institute 1978; Colin MacCabe, 'Realism and the Cinema: Notes on some Brechtian Theses', *Screen*, vol. 15, no. 2, Summer 1974, pp. 7–17; Bertolt Brecht, 'Der Film braucht die Kunst', *Schriften aus Literatur*, Suhrkamp Verlag, Frankfurt 1967, copyright © Stefan S. Brecht, English translation by Diana Matias, copyright © British Film Institute 1978; Jean-Paul Fargier, 'Parenthesis or Indirect Route', *Screen*, vol. 12, no. 2, 1971, pp. 131–43, *Screen Reader*, SEFT, London 1977 and *Cinéthique*, no. 5, September–October 1969; Jean Epstein, 'Le cinématographe continue', in Marcel Lapierre (ed.), *Anthologie du cinéma*, La Nouvelle Edition, Paris 1946, pp. 239–42, English translation by Diana Matias, copyright © British Film Institute 1978; Patrick Ogle, 'Deep Focus Cinematography', an abridged version of an article that appeared in *Screen*, vol. 13, no. 1, 1972, pp. 45–56, 58, 59–62, and *Screen Reader*, SEFT, London 1977; Jean Renoir, *My Life and my Films*, Collins, London 1974, pp. 61, 62–3; Roberto Rossellini, 'A Panorama of History', interview by Francisco Llinas, and Miguel Marias with Antonio Drove and Jos Oliver, *Screen*, vol. 14, no. 4, Winter 1973–4, pp. 103–4 and *Nuestro Cine*, no. 95, March 1970; Allan King, 'Reactions to the Camera' in Alan Rosenthal (ed.), *The New Documentary in Action: A Casebook in Film-Making*, copyright © The Regents of the University of California, reprinted by permission of the University of California Press, Berkeley, 1971, pp. 29, 31, 32; Ed Pincus, in *Documentary Explorations: 15 interviews with film makers*, copyright © G. Roy Levin (ed.), reprinted by permission of Doubleday Company, Inc., New York 1971, pp. 334–5; Gianfranco Bettetini, *The Language and Technique of the Film*, Mouton Publishers, The Hague 1973, pp. 174–8; Jean-Louis Comolli, 'Détour par le direct – Un corps en trop', *Cahiers du Cinéma*, no. 278, July 1977, pp. 5–16, English translation by Diana Matias, copyright © British Film Institute 1978; Interview with Eric Rohmer, *Cahiers du Cinéma*, no. 219, 1970, English translation by Diana Matias, copyright © British Film Institute 1978.

Introduction

DISCUSSION of realism, in film as in other art forms, tends to be tortuous or circular. Does the real world exist? Most (though not all) people think it does. If it does, on what levels does it exist? On the level of the senses, perceptions and experiences of the people who live in it? On the level of the various theories – historical, political, sociological, economic, philosophical – which interpret it and make it comprehensible? Should these two levels be separated from each other, or should they be conflated? What are the relationships possible between forms of art and communication and the theoretical and practical accounts of reality that we have access to?

The problem of realism arises once we have accepted, even as a hypothesis, that the world exists, either as an objective fact for people to look at, or as a set of possibilities which they construct through their intelligence and their labour, or as the product of their imagination, or, most plausibly, as a combination of all three. Alongside this world, which does not stop changing, and arguably part of it, exists a range of artistic forms and practices, of which film is one. They have their own autonomies – which is to say, their own specific systems, rules, methods and materials – but they also stand in a complex relationship with the sets of practices, institutions and experiences which we have perhaps rather abusively summed up under the heading of 'the real world'. The problem of realism arises when we try to be specific about what the forms of these complex relationships are, and what they mean. Is art 'about' the real world, does it express it, or, more indirectly, does it act as at least an expression of certain themes and motifs in the real world? Or are its own

1

specific practices so forceful – at least in their own field – that it is always something *other*, even when its material seems to refer to things in the real world, or draws on its readers' or spectators' knowledge of the real world to be comprehensible?

Film has a special place in this debate, for several reasons. Historically, it first appeared in something like its present form in 1895, which is to say that it was about sixty years late for the modern industrial era, but just in time for the modern era in aesthetics. A part of its most obvious technical procedure, the mechanical recording of created or 'natural' images, it shares with still photography: a fact which the principal spokesmen for film realism have tended to make a great deal of, often without thinking very clearly about the other characteristics of film which strongly suggest its differences from photography. The area of people's responses (as spectators) to film is perhaps the one that least is known about, and correspondingly the easiest in which to make wild assertions, but it is at any rate arguable that for cultural reasons spectators of film have a strong inbuilt tendency to regard the sequences of images films offer them as 'realistic', or to want to understand them as such. The evidence for this argument lies partly in the fact that the initial popular impact of both photography and film centred on what nineteenth-century spectators saw as photography and film's almost 'scientific' accuracy in reproducing the visible circumstances of life. It is not clear how far-reaching or important this tendency is, but those who see it as having a determining importance in the subsequent development of film are not normally deterred by the argument that both media have also demonstrated that they have many uses other than the 'straight' reproduction or presentation of reality. Film is also important for its hybrid qualities: the fact that it combines elements drawn from the pre-existing forms of still photography, painting, the novel (and the written word in general), and the theatre, all welded together on a specific technological base. To add to this complexity, the hybrid form is then capable of further use within another form: television. And, lastly, film is pre-eminently both a popular and a mass-industrial medium: popular, in that with marginal exceptions it has always lived out of a direct relationship with the widest possible audience; industrial, in that it is organised like other industries and has known no other mode of production. These dimensions have often added a further emotional charge to the discussion of film, in that, along with other mass media, it has been seen as exercising power in political or semi-political fashions. The extreme form of this position sees control of the media as a substitute for political power.

Discussion of film, then, takes place in the confused but exciting arena which the preceding paragraph has attempted to delimit; an arena in which historical, technological, aesthetic and sociological factors constantly jostle with each other. Most of the well-established theories of film base themselves on a competence or a conviction in one of these factors, and then become interesting to the extent to which they also manage to incorporate thought about the others. As yet we have no over-arching or fundamental theory which deals convincingly with all the factors and their relations with each other, though the attempt to construct one must remain a concern of serious interest in film. Realism is one of the partial theories we have instead. As I think this book will show, it has plenty of deficiencies, yet it continues to occupy a central place because it is enmeshed in the problems outlined in the preceding paragraph.

The method of this book is to take a number of, I hope, fairly representative statements by film-makers, critics and theoreticians, and to place them side by side so as to bring out their similarities and contradictions. The commentary is meant to help in this process, but the reader should be warned that its approach is primarily conceptual rather than contextual. It is concerned with juxtaposing ideas rather than giving thorough accounts of the specific historical context in which the ideas were produced. In some cases, such accounts exist elsewhere, though they are frequently limited by their uncertainties about what the connections between contexts and artefacts are. Some of these accounts are indicated in the suggestions for further reading; in other cases they do not exist at all, and it was not within my power to create them.

In recent years, much teaching of the area has been carried out through the linked concepts of Realism and Anti-realism. To some extent, the structure of this book reproduces this pattern, since Part I: Realist positions, and Part II: Descriptions of the work of a realist film-maker, Robert Flaherty, could be seen as an anthology of the principal realist beliefs; while Part III: Forms and ideologies, and Part IV: Aesthetics and technology, offer the most interesting arguments against realism. Yet the pattern cannot be taken to the point where Realism and Anti-realism become strictly opposed polarities, glaring at each other across unfathomable aesthetic and political divides. The other structure of this book aims to make it clear that the two concepts have lived off each other, that if they are opposites they tend to be inter-penetrating opposites. The most committed realists call on some idea of aesthetics; the anti-realists are anti-realist because they believe it is more truthful, in one sense or another, to be so. It is clear that once you get down to studying the stylistic practices of particular films or groups of films, stylistic patterns can be detected which it may well be convenient to think of as 'realist' or anti-realist'. While study in these terms is a necessary part of any serious film education, we have to be aware that the terms themselves act as shorthand descriptions; they need to be explicated, broken down and further analysed in terms of both their relationships to each other and to the situations in which film is produced and consumed before they can serve as elements of a less partial theory.

This book aims to be of use in such a programme of elucidation. But its more important purpose is to serve as a fairly thorough introduction to the area of Realism and Anti-realism and the ways in which its practitioners and critics have seen it. The choice of texts is to some extent dictated by this introductory function, but I have included some unfamiliar material, and some relatively less familiar pieces by well-known names. I have also employed two further conventions, which need to be pointed out. The texts and extracts do not follow each other in chronological order. Such ordering might imply that we have a reliable history of the cinema, which at this stage we do not, and also that there has been an automatic progression of ideas from one generation to the next. The purpose of the book is to search for interesting ideas rather than to make such implications. The ideas have had lives that have been variable and recurrent; they too have formed patterns – the kinds of patterns which mean that it may well make sense to juxtapose an article written in the 1930s with one written in the 1970s. The actual year of writing is, however, clearly indicated at the end of each text. To be consistent with the focus on concepts rather than on history, in the commentary I refer to all the writers in the present tense. If in doubt as to whether a writer is physically alive or dead, the reader should consult the brief biographies at the end of the book.*

In each sub-area (i.e. historical movements, groups of films, etc.) to which the book refers, the reader is invited to extend his or her knowledge by following the suggestions of the texts back into the sub-areas that they come from. Indications of useful further reading are contained in the bibliography. The large number of films mentioned in the texts makes it clear that useful discussion of the ideas will best proceed in combination with the screening of a range of film material relating to them. A list of relevant films available in 16mm in Great Britain is added accordingly.

This introduction would not be complete without some discussion of the problems which many contributors do *not* engage with very systematically or completely, usually because of the dangerous combination of a focus on a particular set of films allied with a great generality of ideas. Such discussion may open up paths towards other kinds of film criticism, and make it clear that, with or without its anti-, realism – however inescapable – can never be the only, or even the principal, mode of film criticism. These problems concern the specific cinematic forms which have usually been thought of as realistic and to which our contributors have devoted much of their attention; the more general theories of realism deriving from philosophy and aesthetics, to which they have tended to allude only in passing; and the possible relations between both.

---

* For a greater sense of flow, I have tended to remove some of the notes by original authors and add my own explicative ones.

The first major realist function film has fulfilled consists of its ability to provide various kinds of documents, i.e. accounts of things outside itself. This function has a long and varied history, from its straightforward beginnings through the organised, 'public service' strand developed by Grierson and his followers, to a more modern variety of habits and styles summarised by Alan Rosenthal as 'working in looser and bolder forms'. In this field the ultimate dream is often of a film without any commentary, notionally without any language at all, so that the content may be left free to 'speak for itself'. But such films normally obey rules of structure, of tempo and sometimes of dramatic form; their aim is almost invariably presented as being to tell 'the truth', but it would, in fact, be more appropriate to say that they tell their truths within the framework of the particular set of languages available to them. It also seems clear that although their aim is to tell the truth or to say something about the truth, such films are invariably guided by a single basic concept about how to do either of these things – a concept which may be obvious or complicated. The concept sometimes requires events to be staged, since the things necessary to the realisation of the concept are not likely to occur in front of the camera of their own accord. The concept will also require a distinct process of selection out of the filmed material; the more demanding the concept, the more likely it is that material judged by the film-makers to be technically 'good' will in fact be left out of the finished film or severely adapted to fit the concept. Thus the editing process, though often thought to be difficult for films with documentary aspirations, is not usually seen as obstructive in itself; often, in fact, it is presented as an aid to the film-maker who wants to bring out the 'real truth' rather than 'mere appearances'. The process of filming itself, however, and the restraints it imposes, are often seen as an obstacle. Thus the BBC Television internal handbook on *Principles and Practice in Documentary Programmes*: 'the equipment is a constant obstruction between the producer and his subject, and a great deal of his skill is devoted to presenting his subject matter as if the equipment and the technical processes were not there.' This sense of the obstructiveness of equipment (camera, sound-recording, lighting, crew members) has led to large investments in ever smaller and more manageable equipment that can be handled by fewer and fewer people. This increased flexibility makes a quantitative difference, but not a philosophical one; the intervention of technology is always crucially important in documentary, and some modern film-makers believe that its operations should be acknowledged as part of the film itself, incorporated into the film's style. Interesting conflicts are sometimes generated between the characteristics of the material itself and the manner of filming it.

Some people would argue for a sub-category of the documentary film: the film that uses its material to present a specific socio-political argument or case. It seems to me that the difference between this kind of film and the apparently less 'militant', more orthodox type of documentary is only of degree and not of kind. The orthodox documentary makes a case too; but the very conventions it tends to use – objectivity, respect for the material, sense of 'real life', etc. – oblige it to some extent to appear to conceal its argument. The socio-political argument needs to be in a positive relationship with the film's basic production concept for the results to be interesting. This seems to be the rule for all documentaries whether they are overtly 'argumentative' or not.

The second area of form which is important in discussion of realism is the area of narrative. This is an area which has been quite scandalously neglected in film criticism, because traditionally a narrative was held to be merely the 'hook' on which the artist hung his more meaningful thoughts and patterns. More recently, since the development of semiotics, some attention has been paid to it, but usually from narrow, pre-judged positions, so that although the huge majority of films are cast in narrative forms we still know very little about how these forms work. To summarise what is known, it is clear that films have borrowed or adapted aspects of a story-telling tradition that goes back at least to Homer. The stylistic history of this tradition in literature is usefully described in Erich Auerbach's book *Mimesis*. It is often suggested that narrative films have parameters deriving from the nineteenth-century realist or naturalist novel. While it is true that films and novels share some of the same institutions – plots, characters, problems, resolutions – the methods film uses to handle and develop those institutions resemble novelistic methods in only a passing and tangential manner. When the forms of film narrative come to be studied in the detail they deserve, it is probable that they will be more usefully compared with the flexibility of the narrative tradition *as a whole*, rather than with any specific nineteenth-century form of it.

The difficult thing about film narratives is that they are both open and closed at the same time: closed in that every narrative organises its material so as to start at one point and finish at another; and however extensive the trials and tribulations in between, there is always a strong and structured relationship between the two points. The material that the narrative thus organises is of course shot through with conventions of all kinds, but it is at least arguable that the convention which holds all these events together is the most important convention of all. But in two senses the system is also open: first, because the spectator is aware of it as a system, as a piece of machinery (a large part of his/her pleasure in the film derives precisely from watching the unfolding of the mechanism of the narrative, through its subtle, or crude, or simultaneously subtle *and* crude patterns of repetition and variation), and second, because as with documentary there is a referent outside the film itself. This referent is not precisely 'the real world', nor is it the spectator's ideas about the real world, though it can partake of both. The pleasure of the film-text invites the spectator to think about what gives him/her pleasure, but perhaps more importantly it tries to give him/her pleasure at the same time. Hence the charge so often levelled at film, and at narrative film in particular, of being 'escapist' or narcotic. Traditional liberal high culture and marxist-influenced modernism agreed to recommend to the spectator that he/she should undertake hard and rigorous work, to avoid the danger of succumbing to the swamp-like fascinations of the narrative, whose manipulations are seen as deceiving by entertainment. No real progress can be made with narrative while this simple politico-psychological model prevails. The pleasures that narrative methods provide need to be recognised, and indeed shifted towards the centre of discussion, rather than deplored or condescended to.

It is obviously important to give the concepts of manipulation and closure positive senses, since they are central to narrative film construction even in the case of the most apparently 'natural' and/or 'open' films. But the question remains of what, if any, the relationship between these concepts and the realist/anti-realist spectrum may be. It has been argued that there is a meaningful parallel between the constraints and tensions internal to the film itself and the constraints and tensions experienced by the spectator in viewing it. Here I think one has to be cautious; the idea is that there is some kind of psychic connection between the world of the film and the world of the spectator. While it is clear that spectators of all kinds get involved-in/excited-by/interested-in the manipulations of films, and that some films attempt to play with the forms of this kind of involvement in their own narrative patterns (e.g. suspense), nothing very serious is known about the general demands viewers make of the film medium or the specific responses they have to it. Yet the area is one that certainly asks to be explored.

It is also true that the narrative film shows the spectator a 'world' which on one level has to be taken as 'real' or at any rate real-in-its-own-terms. Yet this *is* only one level; it cannot be read as implying a total mimesis or illusionism. As Thomas Elsaesser has suggested, 'the only element which is mimetic in even the most realistic film is the physical movement of the characters'; understanding of the other important elements, such as the characters themselves, the sets or location, the lighting and/or colour, and, on a different but related level, the articulation of the narrative, has to be based on a sense that they are only partially and variably mimetic, and that before being mimetic they are self-referential, which is to say that they refer back to themselves, or to their likes. One film protagonist-character refers to another, sets and lighting in one film refer to sets and lighting in others, and so on.

At the same time, it must also be recognised that films built around the institutions of stories and characters do, in indirect ways, make reference to the real world or to an idea of the real world, and the understanding that they do make such reference is a part of the way in which spectators themselves understand them. Thus love stories – even *Love Story* itself – are really about love itself; adventure stories and problem-dramas raise questions about personal performance and moral consciousness as well as satisfying the generic needs of the aesthetic systems they belong to. The power, for instance, of the way in which male-female relationships are organised in some of the best known films directed by Howard Hawks, derives from the fact that at some deep level the depiction corresponds to an aspect of the way in which people see relations of affection in the real world, and from the more general fact that in at least a large number of cultures people are preoccupied with the basic problems and criteria that surround sexuality, the taking of mates, and the sharing of lives. This does not mean that the spectator 'identifies' with the characters, though he or she may well 'recognise' the general parameters of the situation being depicted. What the film does is to reshuffle, through the operation of its self-referential characteristics, the basic data of human experience: basic data which are already conventionalised and often 'idealised' before the various modes of film-making re-manipulate and re-idealise them. This process of reshuffling *makes something different* of the basic data. Thus one can plausibly say that film uses or constructs images of human behaviour and institutions. But how these images relate to actual behaviour is problematic, since the forms specific to the medium crucially inflect the account of the behaviour offered. The term 'image' is a loose one, since films work through controlled sequences of multiple moving images, not single static ones. Naïve realists tend to demand that the 'image' should be adjusted so as to give a 'correct' picture of the conditions of life itself, transcending or escaping in one way or another the processes of the medium itself. While within a fairly narrow range the images do change over periods of time, the demand itself can never be met, because the processes of the medium cannot be transcended. The real world can never be 'restored' or 'correctly' rendered in the cinema.

The general question of the relations between the processes of the medium and the material, historical world in which they operate is a difficult one. Relatively speaking, film aesthetics has become a fairly advanced discipline, in which the realism debate figures as merely a part. What is needed to move towards a resolution of the general question is a more developed sociology of film. Without it we cannot begin to understand what the relations are; in its absence, there is a danger of substituting for it crude political slogans which assume the answers to problems rather than confronting them.

Philosophically, the debate about realism can perhaps best be grasped through the opposition between 'mere appearances', meaning the reality of things as we perceive them in daily life and experience, and 'true reality', meaning an essential truth, one which we cannot normally see or perceive, but which, in Hegel's phrase, is 'born of the mind'. In religious systems, the true reality is thought to derive from God; in liberalism, from the ethical or moral workings of the individual consciousness; in marxism, from the workings of class-consciousness. The opposition begins with Plato and has reappeared, in many different places and with many different re inflections, ever since. It reappears, for instance, in the marxist aesthetics of György Lukács, with his distinctions between the 'apparent form' of the art-work and its 'inner core' or essence, through which the conscious reader can gain access to the real truth of a historical situation, and between 'naturalism', which, albeit with great detail, shows only the appearances of situations, and 'realism', which by using devices like the historically typical character and action, functions in the same sort of way as the 'inner core'. 'Naturalism' describes events but without providing the reader with a key to understanding them; and thereby denies him/her access to the truth. . . .

How applicable to the cinema is the realism/naturalism opposition? The cinema has often been thought of as naturalist because it is at any rate partially concerned with the appearances of things, people, places, events. It arranges these appearances within a space – the cinema screen – which has often been thought of as being akin to the object of the human gaze. It has also been thought of as realist, though finally the term is so elastic in usage that a 'realist' film can either work in roughly the same way as a naturalist one or, apparently contradictorily, attempt to smash naturalism by using anti-naturalist devices. There is also a sense in which the cinema uses 'types', i.e. exemplary figures or characters, but this typicality seems fundamentally different in practice from the one Lukács envisaged, and to have more in common, for instance, with some kinds of theatrical typing.

While the terms of 'realism' and 'naturalism' would seem to have some virtue on the descriptive level, I doubt whether their opposition as theoretical concepts is helpful in thinking about film. Their meanings overlap too much; and there is also too strong a sense in which no film is realistic or naturalistic. Films do not tell us the truth about historical conflict, nor – though some films are highly decorated – do they pile up picturesque or intimate detail as naturalistic novels are supposed to do. I think this can be demonstrated by thinking about the highly developed ways in which films reshuffle time. In her book on *Realism* (1971) Linda Nochlin contrasts the idea about time of the nineteenth-century realist painters with those of their classical predecessors:

In pre-nineteenth century art, time was never a completely isolated instance but always implied what preceded and what would follow. In classical art and all schemata based upon it, the passage of time is condensed and stabilized by means of a significant kinetic summary. A Realist, like Degas, destroyed this paradigm of continuity in favour of the disjointed temporal fragment . . . [Degas] showed no interest in conveying any ideal image of movement but concentrated on creating the equivalent of a concrete instant of perceived temporal fact – an isolated moment.

Different realist theories of film imply both the uses of time that Nochlin describes – for instance, the implication of Rohmer's or Perkins's positions would be a condensed and stabilised, i.e. 'classical', time, whereas Bazin's positions tend towards the 'disjointed temporal fact'. Yet it would be more accurate to say that film conducts elaborate games with time which neither stabilise nor disjoint it. The organisation of time is an inescapable part of the construction of any film. This evidently relates to its narrative functions, but not only to them. In any case, it should put us on guard against general comparisons of film with media in which there is no equivalently necessary temporal structuring.

Film narrates, but there is no one person doing the narrating, nor is there one person receiving it, and the narration obeys complicated rules of its own. It shows 'documents', but the documents are only indirectly linked to the realities they are supposed to document. Realist and anti-realist theories attempt to resolve these paradoxes.

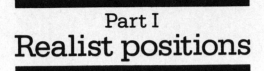

Part I
Realist positions

JOHN GRIERSON founded the British documentary film movement of the 1930s:

First principles. (1) We believe that the cinema's capacity for getting around, for observing and selecting from life itself, can be exploited in a new and vital art form. The studio films largely ignore this possibility of opening up the screen on the real world. They photograph acted stories against artificial backgrounds. Documentary would photograph the living scene and the living story. (2) We believe that the original (or native) actor, and the original (or native) scene, are better guides to a screen interpretation of the modern world. They give cinema a greater fund of material. They give it power over a million and one images. They give it power of interpretation over more complex and astonishing happenings in the real world than the studio mind can conjure up or the studio mechanician recreate. (3) We believe that the materials and the stories thus taken from the raw can be finer (more real in the philosophic sense) than the acted article. Spontaneous gesture has a special value on the screen. Cinema has a sensational capacity for enhancing the movement which tradition has formed or time worn smooth. Its arbitrary rectangle specially reveals movement: it gives it maximum pattern in space and time (Grierson, 1932).

Grierson's emphases on life and its interpretation express a basic tendency of documentary film. His own interests are clear from the ease with which he slips back and forth between the terms 'cinema' and 'documentary' as though they were interchangeable. It is not clear whether the notion of 'reality in the philosophic sense' is best understood in relation to the social purposes he saw as the cinema's proper sphere of operation, to

17

the aesthetic questions he was also concerned with, or to a combination of both. As we shall see, much realist thinking about film has ascribed specific realist effects to specific factors in film technology. Grierson's remark that the 'arbitrary rectangle' of the image serves to enhance, or rather to reveal, movement is perhaps best understood as a precursor of this tradition.

In the very different context of socialist Russia in the 1930s, parallel emphasis can be found in the writings of S. M. Eisenstein:

Without going too far into the theoretical debris of the specifics of cinema, I want here to discuss two of its features. These are features of other arts as well, but the film is particularly accountable to them. *Primo*: photo-fragments of nature are recorded; *secundo*: these fragments are combined in various ways. Thus, the shot (or frame), and thus, montage.

Photography is a system of reproduction to fix real events and elements of actuality. These reproductions, or photo-reflections, may be combined in various ways. Both as reflections and in the manner of their combination, they permit any degree of distortion – either technically unavoidable or deliberately calculated. The results fluctuate from exact naturalistic combinations of visual, interrelated experiences to complete alterations, arrangements unforeseen by nature, and even to abstract formalism, with remnants of reality.

The apparent arbitrariness of matter, in its relation to the *status quo* of nature, is much less arbitrary than it seems. The final order is inevitably determined, consciously or unconsciously, by the social premises of the maker of the film-composition. His class-determined tendency is the basis of what seems to be an arbitrary cinematographic relation to the object placed or found before the camera.

We should like to find in this two-fold process (the fragment and its relationships) a hint as to the specifics of cinema, but we cannot deny that this process is to be found in other art mediums, whether close to cinema or not (and which art is not close to cinema?). Nevertheless, it is possible to insist that these features are specific to the film, because film-specifics lie not in the process itself but in the degree to which these features are intensified (Eisenstein, 1934).

Again and again and again will all the advantages of the cinema flash out if we can picture the arts arranged according to the degree in which they are adapted to their chief task – the reflection of reality and the master of this reality – man.

How narrow is the diapason of sculpture which in most cases is obliged to tear man from his inseparable environment and society in order to hint – by his features and posture – at his inner world which is a mirror of the world around him. A diapason bereft of word, color, movement, the changing phases of drama, and progressive unfolding of events.

How frustrated have been those efforts by composers – Richard Strauss, in particular – to burden music with the task of conveying specific images.

How bound is literature, capable of penetrating into the most subtle coils of a man's consciousness, as well as into the movement of events and epochs, with speculative methods and melodic-rhythmic means, but can only hint at that amplitude of the senses, called for by every line and every page.

How imperfect and limited, too, is the theater in this respect! Only by external *'physical action' and behavior* is it able to convey to the spectator the inner content, the inner movement of consciousness and feelings, the inner world in which live the characters and the author himself. But this is not the material of representation alone.

Rejecting incidentals as well as the 'imitative limitations' of the arts as defined by Lessing,[1] and basing ourselves on the most important factors, we might describe the method of each of the arts:

The method of sculpture – patterned on the human body's structure.

The method of painting – patterned on the positions of bodies and their relations with nature.

The method of literature – patterned on the interrelations of reality and man.

The method of theater – patterned on the behavior and activity of people roused by outer and inner motives.

The method of music – patterned on the law of the inner harmonies of emotionally apprehended phenomena.

In one way or another, all of these – from the most external and lapidary, but more material and less ephemeral, to the most subtle and plastic, but less concrete and tragically ephemeral – with all the means at their disposal, strain towards a single aim.

And that is, through their structures and methods – to reconstruct, to reflect reality, and above all the consciousness and feelings of man. None of the 'previous' arts has been able to achieve this purpose to the full.

For the ceiling of one is – the body of man.

The ceiling of another – his acts and behavior.

The ceiling of a third – is the elusive emotional harmony that attends these.

The full embrace of the whole inner world of man, of a whole reproduction of the outer world, cannot be achieved by any one of them.

When any of these arts strives to accomplish this end, by venturing outside its own frame, the very base that holds the art together is inevitably broken.

The most heroic attempt to achieve this in literature was made by James Joyce in *Ulysses* and in *Finnegans Wake*.

Here was reached the limit in reconstructing the reflection and refraction of reality in the consciousness and feelings of man.

Joyce's originality is expressed in his attempt to solve this task with a special dual-level method of writing: unfolding the display of events simultaneously with the particular manner in which these events pass through the consciousness and feelings, the associations and emotions of one of his chief characters. Here literature, as nowhere else, achieves an almost physiological palpability. To the whole arsenal of literary methods of influence has been added a compositional structure that I would call 'ultra-lyrical.' For while the lyric, equally with the imagery, reconstructs the most intimate passage of the inner logic of feeling, Joyce patterns it on the physiological organization of the emotions, as well as on the embryology of the formation of thought.

The effect at times is astounding, but the price paid is the entire dissolution of the very foundation of literary diction, the entire decomposition of literary method itself; for the lay reader the text has been turned into abracadabra.

In this Joyce shared the sad fate of all the so-called 'left' tendencies in art that reached full flower with the entry of capitalism into its imperialist stage.

And if we examine these 'leftish' arts from the viewpoint of the tendency as described, we find an extremely curious explanation of this phenomenon.

On the one hand, there is a firm belief in the permanency of the existing order, and hence – a conviction of the limitations of man.

On the other hand, the arts feel a need to step beyond their limitations.

This frequently produces an explosion, but an explosion directed not outwards, towards the widening of the art's frame, which is only to be achieved by extending its content in an anti-imperialist and revolutionary direction, but inwards, towards *means*, not towards *content*. The explosion is not creative and progressive, but destructive

(Eisenstein, 1939).

Eisenstein stresses the intervention of the film-maker, in that he may choose the organisation of his 'photo-fragments'. This organisation may take the form of construction within the individual images and/or the construction of relations between different images. It proceeds without 'imitative limitations', i.e. it is not in itself naturalistic, and may thus appear arbitrary in relation to 'the *status quo* of nature'. Nature here is the same entity as Grierson's 'real world'. Technical resources – and in particular, for Eisenstein as for a whole generation of film-makers and critics, the resources of editing – take the activity of film away from the real world, propelling it towards 'art' and 'combination'. Many realists, Grierson among them, have rebuked him for this tendency. But for Eisenstein and others who have drawn on marxist ideas it is necessary to displace the real world, which is itself a construction of bourgeois ideology, and to replace it with a range of other possibilities.

This displacement, however, is itself carried out in the name of realism. The single aim of all the arts is 'to reconstruct, to reflect reality, and above all the consciousness and feelings of man'. Where they have failed to achieve this, the cinema will succeed. If the second extract above vibrates with revolutionary humanism, the first suggests a different route to reality: the organisation of the film is 'determined . . . by the social premises of the maker'. The mature Eisenstein's idea of a realist cinema is a compound of a correct ideological position and the technical means with which to reconstruct and reflect reality.

In the 1920s, his positions on construction were more ambiguous:

> The disproportionate depiction of an event is organically natural to us from the beginning. Professor Luriya, of the Psychological Institute in Moscow, has shown me a drawing by a child of 'lighting a stove'. Everything is represented in passably accurate relationship and with great care. Firewood. Stove. Chimney. But what are those zigzags in that huge central rectangle? They turn out to be – matches. Taking into account the crucial importance of these matches for the depicted process, the child provides a proper scale for them.
> The representation of objects in the actual (absolute) proportions

proper to them is, of course, merely a tribute to orthodox formal logic. A subordination to an inviolable order of things.

Both in painting and sculpture there is a periodic and invariable return to periods of the establishment of absolutism. Displacing the expressiveness of archaic disproportion for regulated 'stone tables' of officially decreed harmony.

Absolute realism is by no means the correct form of perception. It is simply the function of a certain form of social structure (Eisenstein, 1929).

By calling the proportionate representation of objects absolutist, Eisenstein confuses the issue. But his rejection of this kind of representation is typical of many avant-gardists of the 1920s, and his insight about realism being 'the function of a certain form of social structure' has been taken up, sometimes rather uncritically, by marxists for whom the social structure in question is the social structure of the bourgeoisie. Eisenstein reveals his penchant for the natural (the psychologically natural, if not necessarily the representationally natural) at the beginning of this extract, where he calls disproportion 'organically natural'. To understand this apparent contradiction, we have to remember that disproportion, as an aesthetic device, is of the greatest importance to Eisenstein, and that he seems genuinely confused as to whether its major import is to shatter our preconceptions of the world or, at some level which is below thought, to confirm them. At times his disproportion would appear to be another realist means, akin to Grierson's 'arbitrary rectangle'.

Despite their common concern for social premises and purposes, their humanism, and the fact that Grierson took a part of his aesthetic from the Russian cinema, it would be mistaken to associate Grierson and Eisenstein too closely. Grierson wants to see 'real man' on the screen, Eisenstein is perhaps more interested in the 'real man' as a spectator. His later thought, with its emphasis on feeling, and the moulding and drawing out of the spectators' responses, makes this clear. But both believe that through the cinema people will be able to see more clearly, to understand where before they did not. The formalist-documentarist Dziga Vertov believed this too.

An extract from his *Provisional Instructions to Kino-Eye Groups:*[2]

I Introduction

Our eyes see very little and very badly – so people dreamed up the microscope, to let them see invisible phenomena; they invented the telescope, to see and explore distant and unknown worlds; now they have perfected the cinecamera, to penetrate more deeply into the visible world, to explore and record visual phenomena, so that what is happening now, which will have to be taken into account in the future, is not forgotten.

But fate was unkind to the cinecamera. It was invented at a time when there was not a country in the world where capitalism did not reign supreme. And the bourgeoisie had the devilish idea of using this new plaything to distract the masses, or more exactly, to divert the attention of the working classes from their fundamental objective – the struggle against their masters. Sunk in the electrical narcotics of the cinemas, workers in various stages of hunger and the unemployed gradually unclenched their iron fists and unconsciously gave themselves up to the demoralising influence of the cinema of their masters. Theatre tickets are dear and hard to come by. Their masters are using the cinecamera to propagate theatre performances showing how the bourgeoisie love, how they suffer, how they are 'concerned' about their workers and in general, how these higher beings, the aristocracy, distinguish themselves from the lower orders (workers, peasants, etc.).

In pre-revolutionary Russia the cinema of the masters played a similar role. After the October Revolution, the cinema faced the difficult task of adapting to a new life: actors who had once played Tsarist officials, now began to play workers; actresses who once played court ladies, now pulled faces in the approved Soviet style. But very few of us as yet realised that all these affectations in many ways remain caught within the limits of bourgeois technique and the bourgeois theatrical model. There are many opponents of contemporary theatre who are nevertheless partisans of the cinema in its present form.

There are very few of us as yet who clearly understand that non-theatrical cinema (with the exception of the newsreel and a few scientific films) does not exist.

All theatrical performances and all films are constructed on the same lines: playwright or scriptwriter, then stage producer or film director, then actors, rehearsals, sets and a presentation to the public.

In the theatre, the fundamental element is the acting and *every film which is built on a script and on acting is a theatrical performance*, which is why there is no difference in productions by directors of various shades.

All this, considered overall or in detail, relates back to the theatre, independently of the trend and direction and independently of the attitude to the theatre as such. *All this falls outside the real purpose of the cinecamera, which is to explore living phenomena.*

'Kinopravda'[3] has made it very clear that *it is possible to work outside the theatre and in step with the revolution. 'Kino-Eye' is continuing the work of building a Red Soviet cinema, begun by 'Kinopravda'.*

II *The work of Kino-Eye*

On the basis of reports brought by cinema-observers, the Kino-Eye Council draws up for cinecameras a plan of direction and attack in the constantly changing living situation. The work of cinecameras is comparable to that of the GPU[4] who do not know in advance what they will encounter, but who have a clearly defined mission – to isolate and bring to the surface this or that question, this or that matter, from the complex tangle of life.

a) The kinok-observer[5] carefully examines the situation and the people around him and strives to link separate, heterogeneous phenomena in terms of general or specific characteristics. The kinok-observer is assigned his theme by the group leader.

b) The group leader or cinema-scout gives out themes to the observers and at first helps each of them to sum up his observations. When the group leader has gathered in all the summaries, he in turn groups them, arranging and re-arranging the individual facts until the structure of the theme emerges with sufficient clarity.

Themes assigned to an observer when he starts out can be divided into three categories:

1 *Observation of a place* (for example, the village reading club, the co-operative).

2 *Observation of a person or thing in motion* (for example, the observer's father, a member of the pioneer group, the postman, the tramway, etc.).

3 *Observations on a theme not dependent on a particular person or place* (for example, on the theme of water, bread, footwear, fathers and children, town and country, tears, laughter, etc.).

The group leader must make an effort to learn to operate a still camera (and then a cinecamera) in order to capture the most striking moments of the observation for the wall newspaper.

The 'Kino-Eye' wall newspaper comes out monthly or fortnightly; it illustrates factory or village life by means of photographs; it helps to raise support for various campaigns, gives as full as possible a picture of surrounding life, agitates, propagandises and organises. The group leader co-ordinates his work with the Red Kinok cell and takes orders directly from the Kino-Eye Council.

c) The Kino-Eye Council heads the whole organisation. It includes one representative from every kinok-observer group, one representative from the unorganised kinoks and provisionally, three representatives from the kinok-film makers.

The practical, day to day work of the Council is supported by the technical apparatus of the Red Kinok cell.

The latter should be seen as one of a number of factories where the raw material supplied by the kinok-observers is turned into film works.

The Red Kinok cell should also be regarded as a workshop for instruction and demonstration through which Pioneer and Komsomol[6] film groups will be drawn into the work of production.

All kinok-observer groups will be drawn, in particular, into the production of future Kino-Eye series. In fact they will be the author-creators of all future film works.

This transition from authorship by one person or a group of people to mass authorship will also, we believe, soon bring about the end of bourgeois art cinema and its attributes — the actor-poseur, the fairy-tale scenario, the expensive toys which make up the sets, and the director-high priest.

III *Basic watchwords*

1 The film-drama is the opium of the people.

2 Down with the immortal kings and queens of the screen! Long live ordinary, mortal people, captured in the midst of life going about their daily tasks.

3 Down with bourgeois fairy-tale scenarios! Long live life as it is.

4 The film-drama and religion are deadly weapons in the hands of the capitalists. By showing our revolutionary way of life we shall snatch that weapon from the enemy's hands.

5 Contemporary artistic drama is a hangover of the old world. It is an attempt to mould our revolutionary reality into bourgeois forms.

6 Down with the scripting of life: film us unawares, just as we are.

7 The scenario is a fairy tale dreamed up for us by the man of letters. We live our own lives and do not submit to anyone else's imaginings.

8 We all go about our daily work without interfering with the work of others and the task of film-workers is to film us in such a way that they do not interfere with our work.

9 Long live the Kino-Eye of the proletarian revolution!

IV *Kinoks and montage*

In art cinema the accepted meaning of montage is *the glueing together of separately filmed scenes* in terms of a scenario elaborated to a greater or less degree by the director.

The kinoks assign quite a different meaning to montage and see it as *the organisation of the visible world.*

The kinoks distinguish between:

1 *Montage during observation* – orientation of the naked eye in any given situation at any given time.

2 *Montage after observation* – mental organisation of the visible world according to certain characteristic features.

3 *Montage during filming* – orientation of the armed camera-eye in the place inspected under point 1. Adaptation to the now slightly modified conditions of filming.

4 *Montage after filming* – rough organisation of the material shot according to basic features. Determination of what fragments are lacking in the montage.

5 *Rapid sizing up by eye (hunt for montage fragments)* – swift orientation in any given visual context to catch the essential linking shots. Exceptional attention required – the battle rule: eye on target, quick reflex, pressure on the trigger.

6 *Definitive montage* – bringing the concealed, minor themes to the surface on a level with the major themes. Reorganisation of the material into the best possible sequence. Highlighting the core of the film. Tying together of similar situations and finally the numbering of montage groupings.

When filming takes place in conditions which do not allow for a preliminary inspection – let's say when the camera is shadowing its object or takes it unawares – the first two points drop out bringing up 3 and 5.

For the filming of short-footage scenes and filming under pressure of time, several points may be combined into one.

In all other cases, whether filming one theme or several, all points should be carried through. *Montage is an unbroken activity, from the initial observation to the stage of the finished film work.*

V *The kinoks and the scenario*

This is an appropriate place in which to mention the scenario. Literary scenarios hooked onto the montage system outlined above immediately cancel out its meaning and importance. This is because our works are constructed by montage, which is the organisation of material from life, as distinct from artistic dramas which are constructed by the pen of the writer of literature. Does this mean that we work in a random way, without thought or plan? Nothing of the kind.

But if we can compare our *preliminary plan* to the plan of a commission aimed at, say, the investigation of the housing of the unemployed, then we have to compare the *scenario* to an account of that investigation *written before* the investigation is carried out.

How does art cinema act in such cases, and how do the kinoks act?

The kinoks organise the film on the basis of real film-records of the investigation.

The *film director*, having polished and elaborated the literary scenario, proceeds to illustrate it with entertaining film scenes: two kisses, three tears, a murder, clouds scudding across the moon, and a dove. On to the end he tacks the words 'Long live . . .!' and everything finishes with 'The Internationale'.

Such, with a few exceptions, are our art film dramas.

When a film ends with 'The Internationale' the censors usually let it through, but audiences always feel a bit uncomfortable hearing the workers' hymn in such a bourgeois setting.

The scenario is the invention of one person or a group. It is a story which they want to see brought to life on the screen.

We do not find the desire criminal, but setting up works of that kind as the cinema's basic task, squeezing out true film work with such cine-stories, stifling all the remarkable possibilities of the cinecamera in order to pay homage to the gods of the art drama, is something we find totally incomprehensible and, of course, unacceptable.

We have not come into cinema in order to feed stories to NEP[7] lords and ladies lounging in the plush armchairs of our first-class cinemas.

We are not throwing off the art cinema in order to amuse the mass of workers and calm their consciousness with new trinkets.

We came to serve a determined class — the workers and peasants as yet not enmeshed in the sugary web of the art drama.

We came to show the world as it is and to reveal its bourgeois structure to the workers.

We want to bring into the worker's consciousness a clear awareness of the things that affect and surround him. To give every worker at the plough or the workbench a chance to see all his brothers, working together with him in various corners of the world, and all his enemies, the exploiters.

We are taking our first steps in the field of cinema, which is why we call ourselves kinoks. Existing cinema, cinema as a commercial object and cinema as a field of art, has nothing in common with our work.

Even in the field of technique we overlap with so-called 'art cinema' only partially, since the fulfilment of the tasks set by us calls for a different technical approach.

We have absolutely no need of enormous studios and grandiose sets, any more than we have of 'grandiose' directors, 'grand' stars and 'fantastic' photogenic women.

But we do need:
1 rapid means of transport
2 highly sensitive film stock
3 light hand-held cameras
4 equally light lighting equipment
5 a crew of super-swift cinema-reporters
6 an army of kinok-observers.

In our organisation we make a distinction between:
1 kinok-reporters
2 kinok-cameramen
3 kinok-constructors
4 kinok-montage specialists (men and women)
5 kinok-laboratory technicians.

We teach our film work processes only to the members of the Komsomol and Pioneer groups, transmitting our knowledge and our technical experience into the sure hands of a growing generation of worker youth.

We dare to assure respectable and unrespectable film directors that the cinema revolution has only just begun.

We shall persist, not yielding a single one of our positions, until such time as we are relieved by the iron strength of youth, and then together we shall advance, over the head of bourgeois art cinema, towards a cinema of the Soviet Union, a universal cinema – towards October (Vertov, 1926).

The rejection of acting and the various artificialities held to go with it, recurrent in realist thinking about the cinema, and expressed in Grierson in terms which combine morality with aesthetics, is here given an emphatically political turn. For

Vertov, the educational purpose of discovering the visible world, for which the film-camera is by technical definition suited, is perpetually threatened by the survival of such bourgeois institutions as fiction, narrative, actors and the 'high-priest' artistic director. Vertov's methods in film-making rested on a combination of observation of visible 'realities' and the reorganisation of these observations by editing. He was never able to articulate the principles of this editing with sufficient clarity to give them a theoretical bite. On a more modest level, his description of editing as concerned with the inter-relationships of movement, distance, angle and light has become part of the technical stock-in-trade of most film editors throughout the world. In his own work, his concern with these same inter-relationships, perhaps best embodied in *The Man with the Movie Camera*, is inflected towards the systematic exploration of the technical possibilities of the material *données* of film. This led to his being attacked for formalism by critics in Russia and elsewhere, and, after 1937, to his not being able to make films at all.

The doctrine of socialist realism set out by Zhdanov and officially adopted in Russia after 1932 produced no significant texts in the field of cinema, though we should note that much of Eisenstein's later writing represents a kind of response to it. After the Russian movement of the 1920s and the British documentary school of the 1930s, the next national movement to base itself on the primary notion of realism is the Italian neo-realist school of *c.*1940 to *c.*1955. One of its foremost spokesmen is Cesare Zavattini:

The cinema should never turn back. It should accept, unconditionally, what is contemporary. *Today, today, today.*

It must tell reality as if it were a story; there must be no gap between life and what is on the screen. To give an example:

A woman goes to a shop to buy a pair of shoes. The shoes cost 7,000 lire. The woman tries to bargain. The scene lasts, perhaps, two minutes. I must make a two-hour film. What do I do?

I analyse the fact in all its constituent elements, in its 'before,' in its 'after,' in its contemporaneity. The fact creates its own fiction, in its own particular sense.

The woman is buying the shoes. What is her son doing at the same moment? What are people doing in India that could have some relation to this fact of the shoes? The shoes cost 7,000 lire. How did the woman happen to have 7,000 lire? How hard did she work for them, what do they represent for her?

And the bargaining shopkeeper, who is he? What relationship has developed between these two human beings? What do they mean, what interests are they defending, as they bargain? The shopkeeper also has two sons, who eat and speak: do you want to know what they are saying? Here they are, in front of you. . . .

The question is, to be able to fathom the real correspondences between facts and their process of birth, to discover what lies beneath them.

Thus to analyse 'buying a pair of shoes' in such a way opens to us a vast and complex world rich in importance and values, in its practical, social, economic, psychological motives. Banality disappears because each moment is really charged with responsibility. Every moment is infinitely rich. Banality never really existed.

Excavate, and every little fact is revealed as a mine. If the gold-diggers come at last to dig in the illimitable mine of reality, the cinema will become socially important.

This can also be done, evidently, with invented characters; but if I use living, real characters with which to sound reality, people in whose life I can directly participate, my emotion becomes more effective, morally stronger, more useful. Art must be expressed through a true name and surname, not a false one.

I am bored to death with heroes more or less imaginary. I want to meet the real protagonist of everyday life, I want to see how he is made, if he has a moustache or not, if he is tall or short, I want to see his eyes, and I want to speak to him.

We can look at him on the screen with the same anxiety, the same curiosity as when, in a square, seeing a crowd of people all hurrying up to the same place, we ask, What is happening? What is happening to a real person? Neorealism has perceived that the most irreplaceable experience comes from things happening under our own eyes from natural necessity.

I am against 'exceptional' personages. The time has come to tell the audience that they are the true protagonists of life. The result will be a constant appeal to the responsibility and dignity of every human being. Otherwise the frequent habit of identifying oneself with fictional characters will become very dangerous. We must identify ourselves with what we are. The world is composed of millions of people thinking of myths (Zavattini, 1953).

What Zavattini adds to the realist spectrum is the element of questioning, the direct involvement of the spectator in the process of questioning the realities shown, on a one-to-one equal basis: as though the screen could not only show the spectator 'facts' but also afford him access to them. With hindsight, it is clear that very few neo-realist films go far into any such process of questioning, but assumptions such as Zavattini's underlie most of their makers' positions. In this version of realism questions of aesthetics are downgraded or not discussed at all. The important notions are responsibility, warmth, understanding. The film-maker Roberto Rossellini, interviewed by Mario Verdone:

. . . historical precedents aside, Italian post-war films have a certain air of realism which would have been quite inconceivable before the war. Can you give a definition of it?

I'm a film-maker, not an aesthete, and I don't think I can give an exact definition of realism. All I can say is what I feel about it and what ideals I've formed about it. Perhaps someone else would be able to explain it better.

It involves a greater interest in individuals. Modern man feels a need to tell of things as they are, to take account of reality in an uncompromisingly concrete way, which goes with today's interest in statistics and scientific results. Neo-realism is also a response to the genuine need to see men for what they are, with humility and without recourse to fabricating the exceptional; it means an awareness that the exceptional is arrived at through the investigation of reality. Lastly, it's an urge for self-clarification, an urge not to ignore reality whatever it may be.

This is why I have tried in my films to reach an understanding of things, and give them their true value. It's not something easy or lightly undertaken, but a highly ambitious project, because to give anything its true value means grasping its real universal meaning.

You give a clear meaning for the term neo-realism – or more simply realism – but do you think that everyone who discusses it or works on it is as clear?

I think there is still some confusion about the term 'realism' even after all these years of realist films. Such people still think of realism as something external, as a way out into the fresh air, not as the contemplation of poverty and misery. To me realism is simply the artistic form of truth. If you re-establish truth you give it expression. If it's a dead truth, you feel it is false, it is not truly expressed. With my views of course I cannot accept the 'entertainment' film, as the term is understood in some business circles, especially outside Europe. Some such films may be partially acceptable, to the extent that they are capable of giving partial expression to reality.

What object does a realist film have that you would counterpose to the usual kind of 'entertainment' films?

The realist film has the 'world' as its living object, not the telling of a story. What it has to say is not fixed in advance, because it arises of its own accord. It has no love of the superfluous and the spectacular, and rejects these, going instead to the root of things. It does not stop at surface appearances but seeks out the most subtle strands of the soul. It rejects formulae and doesn't pander to its audience, but seeks out the inner motives in each of us.

What other characteristics do you think a realist film has?

To put it briefly, it poses problems, poses them to itself as well. An American paper wrote an attack on my film *Il Miracolo*[8] saying that the cinema is for entertainment and ought not to raise problems. But for me a realist film is precisely one which tries to make people think.

In the post-war period we were faced by this task, and none of us wanted to make what you might call an 'entertainment' film. What mattered to us was the investigation of reality, forming a relationship with reality. For the first so-called 'neo-realist' Italian directors it was undoubtedly a genuine heartfelt act. Then after the real innovators came the popularisers – who were perhaps even more important, as they spread neo-realism everywhere, and possibly with greater clarity. They didn't have to change anything and were perhaps better able to express themselves, making neo-realism more widely understood. But then deviations and distortions crept in, with fatal consequences. But by this time neo-realism had accomplished the main part of its work.

Do you think you have remained faithful in all your films to this concept of realism as you've now spelt it out?

If I have been faithful to it it has been spontaneously and without effort on my part. I don't think that one should preserve one's consistency at any price. Anyone who does so isn't far from being mad. In so far as I had respected certain principles in which I firmly believe, and which are very deep-rooted in me, then you can say that I have been consistent. And I think perhaps I have, since there is a single line you can trace through all my various works – the documentaries, the early war films, the post-war films and those of today. For example it's undeniable that you find the same spirituality in *La nave bianca*, *L'uomo dalla croce*.

Do you regard Francesco Giullare di Dio *as a realist film?*

Of course – even in imagining what St Francis might be like as a man, I never abandoned reality, either as regards the events which are strictly historical, or in any other visual aspect. The costumes, for example, are part of the 'reality'. They are so true to life that you scarcely notice them.

What I have tried to do in this film is to show a new side of St Francis, but not one which lies outside reality: to show a St Francis who is humanly and artistically credible in every sense.

What do you think have been the constant elements in your films?

I don't go by formulae and preconceptions. But looking back on my films, I certainly do find that there are things which have been constant features, recurring not in a planned way, but as I said, quite naturally – in particular, their human warmth. The realist film in itself has this quality. The sailors of *La nave bianca* count as much as the people hiding in the hut at the end of *L'uomo dalla croce*, the population of *Roma, città aperta*, the partisans of *Paisà* or the monks in *Giullare*.

La nave bianca is such a film – from the first scene, with the sailors' letters to their sweethearts, to the battle itself and then the wounded going to Mass or playing and singing. It also shows the ruthless cruelty of the machine; and the unheroic side of men living on a battleship, acting almost in the dark, surrounded by measuring instruments, protractors and steering-wheels – a side of them which appears unlyrical and unheroic, and yet is overwhelmingly heroic.

Again, there is the *documentary* style of observation and analysis, which I learned in my first shorts – *Fantasia sottomarina*, *Ruscello di Ripasottile*, *Prélude à l'après-midi d'un faune* – and took up again in *Paisà* and in *Germania anno zero* and *Stromboli*.

I constantly come back, even in the strictest documentary forms, to *imagination*, because one part of man tends towards the concrete, and the other to the use of the imagination, and the first must not be allowed to suffocate the second. This is why you find fantasy at work in *Il Miracolo, La Macchina ammazzacattivi* and *Paisà*, as well as in *Giullare*, with the rain at the beginning, the young monk being knocked about by the troops, and Saint Clare standing by the hut. Even the finale in the snow was meant to have an air of fantasy.

And then again there is the religious quality – I don't mean the invocation of divine authority by the woman in the finale of *Stromboli*, so much as the themes I was dealing with even ten years ago.

Do you think then that this human warmth has always been a characteristic of your work?

I definitely began by stressing this above all. The war itself was an impulse to me: war is a heartfelt experience. If then I moved on from this to the discovery of personality and a deeper study of character, as with the child in *Germania anno zero* or the woman running away in *Stromboli*, this was part of my natural evolution as a director.

Is it true to say that in your films there is often a break between a particularly good episode like the scene with the child running through the city in Germania anno zero, *and other parts which are inexplicably left incomplete or at least much more hastily sketched in?*

That's right. As a matter of fact every film I make interests me for a particular scene, perhaps for a finale I already have in mind. In every film I see on the one hand the narrative episodes – such as the first part of *Germania anno zero*, or the scene from *Europa '51* that you just saw me shooting – and on the other the *event*. My sole concern is to reach that *event*. In the other narrative episodes I feel myself hesitating, alienated, absent.

I don't deny that this is a weakness on my part, but I must confess that scenes which are not of key importance weary me, and make me feel quite helpless, I only feel sure of myself at the decisive moment. *Germania anno zero*, to tell the truth, was conceived specifically for the scene with the child wandering on his own through the ruins. The whole of the preceding part held no interest at all for me. It too was thought up around the scene with the cans of milk. And when I made *Paisà* I had in mind the last part with the corpses floating on the water, slowly being carried down the River Po with labels bearing the word 'Partisan' on them. The river had those corpses in it for months. Often several would be found on the same day (Rossellini, 1952).

Rossellini's ideas have an explicitly Christian-humanist cast, but in invoking 'truth' as a critical category he speaks for all the realists, including the Marxists. Perhaps the most interesting answer in the extract above is the last. In describing the construction of *Germania anno zero* (*Germany Year Zero*) he seems to admit a degree of manipulation of the 'events' whose 'truth' we might expect the film to be displaying; he also admits that one event may be more important than others. Such admissions are rare in neo-realism. What Verdone here calls the 'hasty sketch' aspect of parts of Rossellini's work has produced interesting discussion. Some see it as reinforcing the realistic pretensions of the work, in that human perception can be described as operating in the same broad way. Others have seen it as the distinctive stylistic hall-mark of Rossellini in particular, or by extension, as typical of neo-realism in general. Still others have suggested that the apparently unorganised nature of the sketch-fragments might be related to Brechtian strategies of distantiation.

Zavattini's 'fact', Rossellini's 'event' are both categories taken up by the French critic André Bazin, who is at once the most substantial international defender of neo-realism and the most thoughtful and sophisticated writer about film realism in general. Bazin's sophistication is evident in the range of possibilities he offers the reader. He begins by re-stating the traditional relationship of film to still photography. Both have the primary function of showing the spectator the real world. We have already seen versions of this position in Grierson and Eisenstein. For Bazin, this starting position means that film is either 'a recreation of the world in its own image', or, more complicatedly, the making of 'an ideal world in the likeness of the real world'. But the question is further complicated by the importance of techniques and styles. Films can only be understood through an understanding of their styles. Bazin attempts to fuse this newer position with the initial one: the Italian cinema 'has reminded us once again that there has been no "realism" in art that has not basically been profoundly "aesthetic"'. Or, more trenchantly: 'realism in art can only be achieved in one way – through artifice'.

Through which artifices, then, is film to fulfil its destiny of remaking the real world? For polemical purposes, Bazin establishes a kind of heroic line of realist film-makers, beginning with von Stroheim, Murnau and Flaherty in the silent period, represented by Renoir in the 1930s, and culminating in the 1940s with a (theoretical, not actual) coalition of the Italian neo-realists and certain American film-makers whose use of specific techniques made them pre-eminently realist whether they were aware of it or not. The Italians are realistic because their main aim is to show the world and to do it as directly and limpidly as possible. Their aesthetic is one which 'integrates reality' into the film; the realistic material (provided by reality) permits the artist to discover realistic 'means of expression'. The Americans (principally Orson Welles and William Wyler, with the help and influence of the cameraman Gregg Toland, who worked with both of them) are realistic because they use deep-focus cinematography, a technical device which enables film-makers to show foreground, middle ground and background simultaneously in one shot with equal clarity. In this way, the camera 'takes in with equal sharpness the whole field of vision' and, Bazin holds, promotes a respect for 'the continuity of dramatic space and its duration'. The ideal world of the film finds, through the use of this and other techniques, the aesthetic equivalent of human perception in the real world. Some of these issues are explored in the following essay entitled 'William Wyler, or the Jansenist[9] of *mise en scène*':[10]

Wyler's directing

A detailed study of Wyler's mise en scène reveals very clear differences between each of his films,[11] as much in the use of the camera as in the quality of the photography. Nothing is further from the pictorial values of *The Best Years of our Lives* than those of *The Letter*. One realises that the dramatic material is very varied, and the directorial ingenuity deployed in presenting it to the best possible advantage takes very different forms in all of them. The highlights of Wyler's films: the red ball-dress in *Jezebel*, the dialogue during the shaving sequence or the death of Herbert Marshall in *The Little Foxes*, the death of the sheriff in *The Westerner*, the tracking shots across the plantation at the beginning of *The Letter*, or the scene in the junked bomber of *The Best Years of our Lives* do not reveal that lasting predilection for themes that we find in John Ford (the rides on horseback), Tay Garnett (the brawls) or René Clair (the marriages and chases). No favourite décors or locations. At the very most one recognises a clear preference for psychological scenarios against a social background. But if Wyler is a past-master in the treatment of this type of subject, whether it is taken from a novel like *Jezebel* or from a play like *The Little Foxes*, if on the whole his work leaves us with the somewhat tart and austere flavour of psychological analysis, it does not detract from those sumptuously eloquent images which leave behind an indelible impression of formal beauty inviting retrospective contemplation. We cannot define a director's style simply by his preference for psychological analysis and social realism, especially when he does not use original scenarios.

And yet I don't think it's more difficult to recognise Wyler's signature in some shots than it is John Ford's, Fritz Lang's or Hitchcock's. It's even certain, citing only these names, that the director of *The Best Years of our Lives* is amongst those who have made the least use of technological tricks to cover up an absence of style. Whereas Capra, Ford or Lang have occasionally parodied themselves, Wyler has only ever erred through weakness. He has, on occasion, given less than his best, his taste is not infallible and one sometimes feels he is capable of a sincere admiration for Henry Bernstein[12] or his peers, but no-one would be able to catch him perpetrating a formal sleight of hand. There is a John Ford style and a John Ford manner. Wyler has only one style; that is why he is safe from imitation, even by himself. Imitation would not pay, for it would not be definable by any precise form, any specific lighting or special camera angle. The only means of imitating Wyler would be to espouse that ethic of mise en scène of which *The Best Years of our Lives* offers us the purest results. Wyler canot have imitators, only disciples.

If one tried to characterise the film's mise en scène, starting from the 'form', one would necessarily have to give a negative definition. It is an intentionally self-effacing style; the corresponding positive proposition being that when the mise en scène is at its most inconspicuous the dramatic structures and the actor appear with maximum power and clarity.

The aesthetic meaning of this asceticism will perhaps become clearer if we take an example of it in *The Little Foxes*, because here it is pushed to the point of paradox. Lillian Hellman's play has scarcely been adapted: the film respects the text almost integrally. Under these conditions one imagines it was difficult to insert the exterior scenes, which most other directors would have judged indispensable in order to add a bit of 'cinema' to this mass of 'theatre'. As a rule good adaptation consists precisely of 'transposing' the maximum of what is not irretrievably pre-formed by the literary and technical constraints of the theatre into specifically cinematic forms. For example, it would not be exactly reassuring to hear from someone that M. Berthomieu[13] had just brought M. Henry Bernstein's latest play to the screen without changing a line. If the bearer of ill-tidings further added that 9/10 of the film took place in the same setting as in the theatre, it might well prompt the reflection that the cynicism of filmed-theatre merchants was even more bottomless than one had supposed, but if, in addition, he announced that the film's découpage accounted for no more than 10 camera changes and that the camera was for most of the time placed immobile in front of the actors, one would definitely conclude that the bottom had been reached. However, it was from this paradoxical base that Wyler directed one of the most purely cinematic works there is.

The essential action takes place in the same, totally neutral setting: the ground-floor drawing-room of a vast colonial-style house. At the back, a staircase leading to the first floor bedrooms, Bette Davis' adjoining that of Herbert Marshall. There is not a single picturesque detail to add any individualising touch of realism to the 'scene of action' which is as impersonal as the antichambers of classic tragedies. The protagonists have a credible but conventional pretext for confronting each other as they come in from outside or downstairs from their bedrooms. They can also linger there. The staircase at the back of the room plays precisely the role of a stage prop: it's a pure element of dramatic architecture which will serve to situate the characters in vertical space. Let us take the principal scene of the film, Herbert Marshall's death, which takes place precisely in this décor. An analysis of it will clearly reveal the secrets of Wyler's style.

Bette Davis is seated, in mid-shot, facing the camera, her head in the centre of the screen: very harsh lighting accentuates the sharp white patch created by her heavily made-up face; Herbert Marshall is caught in close-up partly turned towards the camera. The relentless retorts between husband and wife are thrown back and forth without any change of shot, then comes the heart attack which makes the husband beseech his wife to go and look for his drops in the bedroom. From this instant, all the dramatic interest resides, as Denis Marion has rightly noted, in the way the director uses the camera's immobility. Marshall is obliged to get up and fetch the medicine himself. He dies of the effort on the first steps of the staircase.

In the theatre this scene would visually have been constructed in the same way. A spot-light could be directed onto Bette Davis, and the spectator would have felt the same horror at her criminal refusal to move, the same agony at following her victim's staggering steps. But in spite of appearances, Wyler's mise en scène makes the maximum use of the means offered him by the camera and the frame. Bette Davis' place in the centre of the screen confers on her a privileged position of power in the dramatic geometry of space, the entire scene revolves around her, but her frightening immobility is forcefully manifested only through Marshall's two exits, in close-up to the right, then in long-shot to the left. Instead of following him in this lateral movement, which would have been the reaction of a less intelligent eye, the camera stays imperturbably immobile. When Marshall finally comes back into shot for the second time and goes upstairs, Wyler has taken great care to ask his cameraman, Gregg Toland, not to give complete depth of focus, so that Marshall's fall down the stairs and his death could not clearly be distinguished by the spectator. The vagueness of the image increases our feeling of unease. We have to strain in order to see the outcome of the drama which takes place at a distance, over the shoulder of Bette Davis, who is turning her back on the protagonist.

We can see just how much the cinema adds to the resources of the theatre here but, over and above this, there is the remarkable fact that the maximum cinematographic coefficient coincides paradoxically with the minimum mise en scène possible. Nothing could have augmented the dramatic power of this scene better than the absolute immobility of the camera. The least movement, which to a less prudent director would have seemed just the cinematographic element to introduce, would have caused the dramatic voltage to drop. Here the camera does not take the position of a spectator, but rather organises the action itself with the help of the frame provided by the screen and the ideal co-ordinates of its dramatic geometry.

During my student days when I was doing mineralogy, I remember being struck by the structure of certain fossil shells. Whereas limestone was distributed in the living animal in thin layers parallel to the surface of the valves, a slow working of the material had regrouped the molecules into fine crystals perpendicular to the initial layers. Apparently the shell was intact; one could still distinguish the original stratification of the limestone; but, if one broke it with a finger, the fracture revealed that its form was fallacious; it was completely belied by this minute interior architecture. I apologise for this comparison, but it illustrates perfectly the invisible molecular work which changes the aesthetic structures of Lillian Hellman's play while respecting, with a paradoxical fidelity, its theatrical appearances.

In *The Best Years of our Lives*, the problems presented themselves quite differently. It was, to all intents and purposes, an original scenario. McKinlay Kantor's novel in verse certainly was not treated with the same respect as Lillian Hellman's play.[14] The nature of the subject, its actuality, its social value called for, in the first place, a quasi documentary of meticulous accuracy. Samuel Goldwyn and Wyler wanted to make a social rather than an artistic film. It was a question of exposing one of the most distressing social problems of post-war America with all the necessary breadth and subtlety through a, no doubt fictionalised, narrative, though scrupulously truthful and exemplary. In one sense, *The Best Years of our Lives* relates closely to those didactic productions of the US army film department which Wyler had just left. The war, and the awareness of a particular notion of reality which it has brought about, had as we know profoundly influenced the European cinema; its consequences had been less perceptible in Hollywood. However, several directors had been involved in it, and something of the inundation, the cyclone of realities which it had unfurled on the world, were able to find interpretation there too, through an ethic of realism. 'We had all three (Capra, Stevens and Wyler) taken part in the war. It had a profound influence on each of us and without this experience I would not have been able to make my films as I did. We learned to understand the world better . . . I know George Stevens has never been the same since he saw the corpses at Dachau. We have had the recognition forced upon us that Hollywood hardly reflects the world and the times we live in at all.' These few lines of Wyler's are sufficient to illustrate his purpose in making *The Best Years of our Lives*.

One knows from elsewhere the considerable attention he devoted to the preparation of this, the longest and without doubt the most expensive film of his career. Nevertheless, if *The Best Years of our Lives* was only a socially propagandist film, however skilful, honest, moving and effective it was it wouldn't merit very serious attention. The scenario of *Mrs Miniver* is not, all things considered, so inferior to this one, but it was well enough made without Wyler's facing particular stylistic problems. The result is rather disappointing, whereas it is precisely in the mise en scène of *The Best Years of our Lives* that the meticulous ethical concern for truth finds its aesthetic medium. There is nothing more false or absurd than to set '*realism*' and '*aestheticism*' in opposition to each other, as was frequently done in regard to the Russian or Italian cinemas. There is not, in the true sense of the word, a more *aesthetic* film than *Paisà*. Reality is not art, but a *realist* art is one capable of creating an aesthetic which integrates reality. Thank God! Wyler has not limited himself to respecting the psychological and social truth in the scenario (in which moreover he didn't succeed all that well) and in the performance of the actors. He has tried to find aesthetic equivalents in mise en scène. In concentric order of value, I will first of all cite the realism of the décor, built in actual dimension and in its entirety (which I suspect would complicate the shooting since it would be necessary to raise the 'sections' to give the camera proper perspective). The actors wore clothes exactly like those their characters would have worn in reality, and their faces were no more made up than in any town. No doubt this quasi-superstitious but scrupulous regard for the truthfulness of the everyday is uncommonly strange to Hollywood, but its true importance rests perhaps not so much in its tangible convincingness for the spectator, as in the disruptions it must inevitably introduce into the mise en scène: the lighting, the camera-angle, the direction of the actor. It's not by starting from pieces of meat on the set or Antoine's real trees[15] that one can define realism, but by the means of expression which realistic material permits an artist to discover. The *realist* tendency has existed in the cinema since Louis Lumière and even since Marey and Muybridge.[16] It has been through many mutations, but the forms in which it has appeared have survived only in proportion to the amount of aesthetic invention (or discovery) – conscious or not, calculated or innocent – involved. There is not one, but several realisms. Each era looks for its own, that is to say the technique and the aesthetic which can best capture it, arrest and restore whatever one wishes to capture of reality. On the screen, technique naturally plays a much more important role than in a novel, for example, since the written language is more or less stable while the cinematographic image has been profoundly modified since its beginnings. The panchromatic plate, sound, colour, have constituted genuine transformations of the image. The syntax which organised this vocabulary has itself been subjected to revolutionary changes. Construction by 'montage' which above all corresponds to the silent period, has today been almost totally succeeded by the logic of editing. These shifts can undoubtedly be due in part to the existence of fashion in the cinema as elsewhere – but all those which have a real importance and which enrich the cinematographic heritage are in close liaison with technique: and this constitutes the infra-structure.

To produce the truth, to show the reality, all the reality, nothing but the reality is perhaps an honourable intention, but stated in that way, it is no more than a moral precept. In the cinema there can only be a *representation* of reality. The aesthetic problem begins with the means of this representation. A dead child in close-up is not a dead child in long-shot any more than a dead child in colour. Indeed our eye, and consequently our consciousness, has a different way of seeing a dead child from the camera's way of seeing it – as an image placed in a certain relation to its rectangular frame. Thus the 'realism' does not consist only of showing us a corpse but, also, in such conditions as respect certain given physiological or mental facts of natural perception or, more precisely, by finding the equivalents of them. Classical editing which analyses a scene by a certain number of elements (the hand on the telephone, or the door-knob which turns slowly) corresponds implicitly to a certain natural mental process which makes us accept the sequence of shots without being aware of their technical arbitrariness.

In reality, in fact, our eye adjusts spatially, like a lens, to the important point in the event which interests us; it proceeds by successive investigation, it introduces a kind of temporalisation on a second level by analysis of the space of a reality, itself evolving in time.

The first lenses of the cinema were not varied, their optical qualities naturally gave a great depth of focus which conformed to the editing, or rather the quasi-absence of editing, in the films of the period. It wasn't a question then of cutting a scene into 25 shots and adjusting the focus with the shifting of the actor. The optical improvements are in close liaison with the history of editing, at the same time cause and effect.

To bring back into question the technique of shooting, as Jean Renoir in 1933, and a little later Orson Welles, had done, it was necessary to have discovered how much illusion was concealed in the apparent psychological realism of analytic editing. If it's true that our eye perpetually changes its focal point under the impulse of interest or attention, this mental and physiological adjustment comes into effect a posteriori. The event, in its entirety, is there all the time, demanding to be looked at; it is we who decide to choose such and such aspect, to pick this rather than that one according to the demands of action, of feeling or of reflection, but someone else would perhaps choose differently. Whatever the circumstances we are *free* to do our own mise en scène: there is always another possible choice which can radically modify the subjective aspect of reality. Now, the director who chooses for us, exercises, in our place, the discrimination with which we are faced in real life. We unconsciously accept his analysis because it is consistent with the laws of attention; but it deprives us of the privilege, no less grounded in psychology, which we abandon without realising it, and which is, at least virtually, the freedom to modify our method of selection at every moment.

The resulting psychological and then aesthetic consequences are important. This technique tends in particular to exclude the immanent ambiguity of reality. It 'subjectivises' the event in the extreme since each tiny fragment is a result of the director's bias. It doesn't only involve a dramatic choice, affective or moral, but also, and more seriously, a clear standpoint on reality as such. It would no doubt be excessive to revive the quarrel over universals in discussing William Wyler. If nominalism and realism have their cinematographic mode of expression they cannot be defined solely in terms of a technique of shooting and of découpage; but it's certainly not a fluke if Jean Renoir, André Malraux, Orson Welles, Rossellini and the William Wyler of *The Best Years of our Lives* are of the same mind in their frequent use of deep focus or at the very least 'simultaneous' mise en scène; nor if from 1938 to 1946 they have left their stamp on everything that actually counts in cinematographic realism, in the use of a technique which proceeds from an aesthetic of reality.

With the help of deep focus, which can often complement the simultaneous movement of actors, the spectator has the possibility himself of the final operation of découpage.[17] I quote Wyler: 'I had long discussions with my cameraman Gregg Toland. We decided to strive for as simple a realism as possible. The gift Gregg Toland has for moving without difficulty from one shot of the scene to another . . . allowed me to develop my own technique of direction. Thus I can follow through a piece of action and avoid cuts. The resulting continuity makes the shots more alive; more interesting for the spectator, who studies each character *as he pleases* and makes his own cuts.'

The terms employed by Wyler clearly indicate that he was pursuing an appreciably different goal from those of Orson Welles or Renoir. The latter used simultaneous and lateral mise en scène above all to make perceptible the intercrossing of intrigues, as we can clearly see in the party at the chateau in *La Règle du Jeu*.[18] Orson Welles sometimes strives for a sort of Dos Passos-like tyrannical objectivism, sometimes for a kind of systematic stretching of reality in depth. It is as though he had drawn reality on an elastic band, and was stretching it out to revel in our alarm, and finally, to let it go in our faces. Orson Welles' vanishing perspectives and low-angle shots are well-aimed slings. It's not Wyler's way at all. Of course, he is still aiming to integrate the maximum reality into the découpage and the image, to make the setting and the actors totally and simultaneously present in such a way that the action is never a subtraction. But this constant summation of the event in the image is aiming at the most perfect neutrality. There is no place in *The Best Years of our Lives* for Orson Welles' sadism and Renoir's ironic uneasiness. It's not a question of provoking the spectator, of drawing and quartering him. Wyler wishes solely to allow him: 1) to see everything; 2) to choose 'to his liking'. It's an act of trust in the spectator, a will to dramatic honesty. He is showing all his cards. Indeed, it really seems, looking at this film, that the customary découpage here would have been quite unsuitable, like a permanent conjuring-trick: 'Look over here' the camera would have told us, 'now over there'. But between the shots? The frequency of long-shots and the perfect sharpness of the focal depths contribute enormously to reassuring the spectator and leaving him the means of observing and making choices, and even, thanks to the length of the shots, the time to form an opinion, as we shall see in the following section. William Wyler's deep focus endeavours to be liberal and democratic like the consciousness of the American spectator and the heroes of the film!

Style without style

Considered in terms of narrative, Wyler's deep-focus is almost the cinematographic equivalent of what Gide and Martin du Gard declared to be the ideal in writing fiction: perfect neutrality and transparency of style which must interpose no colouration, no refraction between the reader's mind and the story.

Thus, in agreement with Wyler, Gregg Toland has here utilised an appreciably different technique from the one he used in *Citizen Kane*.[19] First, in the lighting: Orson Welles strove for contrast, simultaneously both violent and subtle, the large masses of semi-darkness split by shafts of light, which he subtly interplayed with the actors. All that Wyler asked of Gregg Toland was that the lighting be as neutral as possible, not aesthetic, not even dramatic, simply an honest light which would adequately illuminate the actor and the surrounding set. But it's in the difference between the lenses employed that we can best grasp the opposition of these two techniques. The wide-angle lenses of *Citizen Kane* greatly distorted the perspectives, and Orson Welles' sets created an effect of vanishing perspectives. Those of *The Best Years of our Lives*, conforming more to the geometry of normal vision, tended rather to squash the scene because of their long focus, that is, to spread it out on the screen. Thus, in order better to respect reality, Wyler denied himself, again, certain resources of mise en scène. It seems moreover, that this exactingness complicated Gregg Toland's task; deprived of the help of optics, it was necessary for him to stop down further, it appears, than anyone had ever had to on any film in the world.

Sets, costumes, lighting and above all, photography, all so far tend towards neutrality. It seems that this mise en scène is defined, at least in those elements we have studied, by its absence. Wyler's efforts are systematically concentrated on obtaining a cinematographic universe, not only rigorously consistent with reality, but also as little modified as possible by the optics of the camera. By means of paradoxical technical feats like the use of full-size three-dimensional sets and the lens diaphragm, Wyler manages to get just the section of a parallelepiped on the screen, which keeps as closely as possible, within the inevitable residue of conventions imposed by the cinema, to the scene which the eye would be able to see through a homothetic mask of the type used in photography.

This experimentation could not take place without also modifying the découpage. Firstly for quite obvious technical reasons the average number of shots generally diminishes in the cinema in relation to their realism. One knows that sound films have fewer shots than silent films. Likewise colour further diminishes the number, and Roger Leenhardt,[20] taking up a hypothesis of George Neveux's, was able to propose with some probability that a 3-D film's découpage in relief would naturally assume the number of scenes of Shakespeare's plays: about 50. Indeed one understands that the closer the image comes to reality the more complex becomes the psycho-technical problem of making the film fit together. Sound has already complicated montage (which, to be truthful, has almost disappeared in favour of the découpage), deep-focus makes each change of shot a technical tour de force. It is in this sense that we must understand Wyler's homage to his cameraman. His talent does not in fact lie in a particularly thorough knowledge of the resources of film, but, beyond his understanding of framing, about which we will speak later, in the faultless movement from shot to shot, not only in the habitual precision of the photograph, but in the way the whole mass of decor, light, and actors, are embraced in one limitless, unified field.

But the determinism of this technique served Wyler's intentions perfectly. The cutting of a scene into shots is a necessarily artificial operation. The same aesthetic calculation which made him choose deep-focus shooting must have led him to reduce the number of shots to the minimum necessary for the clarity of the narrative. In fact *The Best Years of our Lives* has no more than 190 shots an hour — approximately 500 shots in a film of 2 hours 40 minutes. Let's recall, for reference, that modern films comprise on average some 300–400 an hour, approximately double that number, and for the record, that *Antoine and Antoinette*,[21] which surely represents the exactly opposite technique, counts some 1200 joins in 1 hour 50 minutes' projection. Shots of longer than 2 minutes are not rare in *The Best Years of our Lives*, without even a slight re-framing to reduce their static nature. In reality, there is no longer any trace of the resources of montage in such mise en scène. Even the découpage, considered as an aesthetic of the relation between shots, is singularly reduced: the shot and the sequence tend to become one and the same. Many of the scenes of *The Best Years of our Lives* merge together with Shakespearian dramatic unity and are treated in a single fixed shot. Even in this, the comparison with Orson Welles' films illuminates clearly the different aesthetic intentions, though based on partly comparable techniques. Deep-focus must equally, by the same realistic logic, have led the auteur of *Citizen Kane* to merge shot and sequence. Remember, for example, the poisoning of Susan, the scene of the breach between Kane and Joseph Cotton and, in *The Magnificent Ambersons*,[22] the admirable love-scene in the cab, with that interminable tracking shot which the final pulling-out of the camera reveals not to be back-projection, or again, the kitchen scene where the young George is stuffing cakes while chatting to Aunt Fanny. But Orson Welles uses it with extreme variety. The long-shots correspond in his aesthetic to a certain systematised crystallisation of reality, to which he opposes other crystallisations such as *The March of Time* newsreel[23] and above all the temporal abstraction of the series of fades which summarise long sections of narrative. The rhythm and structure, even of reported facts, are modified by the dialectic of Orson Welles' narrative. With Wyler, nothing of the kind. The aesthetic of découpage remains constant, the process of the narrative only aims at assuring him the maximum of clarity and, through this clarity, of dramatic efficacy.

At this point in our analysis the reader is perhaps wondering where the mise en scène can be found in *The Best Years of our Lives*. It's true that our analysis has up to now endeavoured to demonstrate its absence. But before finally coming to the positive aspects of such a paradoxical technique, I would like to avoid a misunderstanding. If Wyler has systematically searched, occasionally at the cost of technical difficulties never solved before, for a perfectly neutral dramatic universe, it would be naive to confuse this neutrality with the absence of art. Just as the respect for theatrical forms in the adaptation of *The Little Foxes* hid subtle aesthetic transmutations, the laborious and erudite conquest of neutrality here implies multiple previous neutralisations of customary cinematographic conventions. It required that much more courage and imagination to do without the help of almost inevitable technical conventions (implying also, somewhat inevitably, certain aesthetic conventions) or of methods of découpage imposed by fashion. It's quite normal to praise a writer for his pared-down style and one admires Stendhal's writing in the style of the Code Civil[24] without suspecting him of intellectual laziness. Earlier on I compared Wyler's ideals to those of Gide and Roger Martin du Gard[25] when they defined the perfect style for the novel! It's true that this preliminary paring-down only takes on sense and value from the works which they make possible and which are paradoxically their specific terrain. This is what we now have to explain.

Wyler had made no secret, in the long article quoted above, of the confidence he had in Gregg Toland's ability to carry out découpage while on the set. He has moreover personally confirmed it to us and it is easy to believe on close examination of the shots. The working conditions, exceptional in a French studio, are without doubt firstly explained by the fact that Gregg Toland had already made six films with Wyler, and so they understood each other.

Wyler was so certain of his cameraman's judgement and of their artistic accord, that he did not write a shooting script. The film was practically made from a dramatic découpage according to which the technical solutions for each scene had to be solved on the set. The preparatory work before shooting each shot was very long but didn't affect the camera. Wyler's 'mise en scène' proper was thus wholly concentrated on the actor. This space, vertically sectioned and limited by the frame on the screen, had only been cleared of all inherent interest to better allow for the drawing of the dramatic outline, polarised through the actors.

Nearly all Wyler's shots are constructed like an equation; perhaps to put it in a better way, according to a scientific dramatic technique by which the parallelogram of the forces can almost be drawn in geometric lines. That is doubtless not an original discovery, and any director worthy of the title organises the positioning of his actors within the co-ordinates of the screen, according to still obscure laws, the spontaneous perception of which is part of his talent. Everyone knows for example that the dominating character must be higher within the frame than the one who is dominated.

But apart from Wyler's ability to give his implicit constructions an exceptional clarity and force, his originality resides in the discovery of several laws which are his alone; above all, in this film, the utilisation of deep-focus as a supplementary co-ordinate. The analysis outlined above of Marshall's death in *The Little Foxes* clearly reveals Wyler's ability to hinge a scene entirely on the actor: Bette Davis held, transfixed like an owl, in the centre by a spotlight, and Marshall staggering around her, a second, mobile, point of reference, the movement of which out of the foreground carries off with it all the dramatic emphasis, with the astonishing added tensions due to his two disappearances off to the side and to the imperfect focussing on the staircase. One sees how in this connection Wyler utilises deep-focus. The purpose in *The Best Years of our Lives* was to keep it constant, but he didn't have the same reasons to systematically respect this in *The Little Foxes*; thus he preferred Gregg Toland to make the dying figure of Marshall somewhat blurred, so that the spectator experiences an added disquiet and almost the desire to push the immobile Bette Davis aside to see more clearly. Thus the dramatic evolution of this shot really follows that of the dialogue and of the action proper, but its cinematographic expression superimposes on it an appropriate dramatic evolution; a sort of second action which is, as it were, the actual narrative of the shot from the moment when Marshall gets up to his fall down the staircase.

Here, from *The Best Years of our Lives*, is a dramatic construction on three characters: the scene of the break between Dana Andrews and Teresa Wright. The sequence takes place in a bar. Fredric March has just persuaded his friend to break with his daughter and compels him to go and telephone immediately. Dana Andrews gets up and moves towards the telephone box which is situated near the door, at the other end of the room. Fredric March leans his elbow on the piano in close-up and feigns interest in the musical exercises of the disabled sergeant, who is learning to play with his hooks. The range of the camera goes from the piano keyboard in close-up, includes Fredric March in mid-shot, takes in the entire bar-room, leaving Dana Andrews in the telephone box at the back, very small but noticeably in view. This shot is neatly constructed on 2 dramatic points of reference and 3 characters. The foreground action is secondary, though interesting and unusual enough to claim our attention, all the more vigorously since it occupies a privileged place and surface on the screen. The real action, on the other hand, which at this precise moment constitutes a decisive turning-point in the intrigue, unfolds almost clandestinely in a tiny rectangle at the back of the room, i.e., in the left corner of the screen.

The link between these two dramatic areas is formed by Fredric March, alone, with the spectator, in knowing what is happening in the telephone box, and who is himself also, according to the scene's logic, involved in the feats of his disabled friend. From time to time, Fredric March turns his head away slightly and his glance, across the diagonal of the screen, anxiously scrutinises Dana Andrews' gestures. Finally he hangs up, and without turning back, disappears suddenly into the street. If we reduce the real action to its elements, it's basically only composed of Dana Andrews' phone call. Only the telephone conversation interests us immediately. The only character whose face we wish to see in close-up is precisely the one which the distance and the telephone-box window prevents us from seeing clearly. As for his words, they are naturally imperceptible. The true drama is unfolding in the distance in a sort of small aquarium, which permits us to see only the banal gestures and rituals of the public call-box. Deep-focus is utilised to the same end as that which, conversely, made Wyler resort to soft-focus for Marshall's death, but the relative distance is sufficient for the laws of perspective to produce the same effect as the soft-focus.

The idea of the call-box at the back of the room and the subsequent obligation the spectator feels to imagine what is happening, was already in itself an excellent piece of directorial ingenuity, but Wyler clearly felt that that alone would destroy the spatial and temporal equilibrium of the shot. It was necessary at the same time to counterbalance and reinforce it. Hence the idea of a diversionary action *in close-up*, secondary in itself, but whose interest as an image would be in inverse ratio to the dramatic importance. A secondary piece of action, but not an insignificant one, and one which the spectator cannot ignore because he is also interested in the face of the disabled sailor and does not see someone play the piano with hooks every day. Forced to wait for the hero to finish phoning, without seeing very well, the spectator is moreover obliged to divide his attention between the hooks and the public call-box. Thus Wyler has killed two birds with one stone: the diversion with the piano allows him firstly to make a shot last for the time necessary, which would have been interminable and inevitably monotonous, but it's above all the introduction of this redundant pole of action which dramatically organises the image and literally constructs it. On the real action is superimposed the appropriate action of the mise en scène which lies in dividing the spectator's attention against his will, in directing it where it's necessary, when it's necessary, and thus in making the spectator participate for himself in the drama created by the director.

For greater precision, I will point out again that this scene is twice cut by a close-up of Fredric March looking at the call-box. Wyler was no doubt afraid that the spectator might be too interested in the piano exercises and gradually forget the action at the back. He prudently took several shots as a safety-measure, completely isolating the principal action: the dramatic line between Fredric March and Dana Andrews. The editing doubtless revealed that two inserted shots were necessary and sufficient to recapture the audience's possibly wandering attention. So much prudence moreover is characteristic of Wyler's technique. Orson Welles would have contrived for the very distance of the call-box to stress it violently and would have given the shot as much time as necessary. So, for Orson Welles, deep-focus is, in itself, an aesthetic end; for Wyler, it remains subordinate to the dramatic demands of the mise en scène and quite particularly to the clarity of the narrative. The two inserted shots are equivalent to a sort of setting in bold type: to a reinforcement of the reference.

Wyler particularly liked to construct his mise en scène on the tension created in a shot by the coexistence of two pieces of action of unequal importance. One again sees it clearly in the still taken from the last sequence of the film (the wedding ceremony).

The characters grouped on the right, in mid-shot, apparently constitute the principal dramatic pole since everyone is gathered in the room for the marriage of the disabled man. In reality, as this action has henceforth been established, and is, as it were, virtually at an end, the spectator's attention turns to Teresa Wright (in long-shot, wearing white) and Dana Andrews, in close-up on the left, who are meeting for the first time since their break-up. Throughout the entire marriage sequence Wyler manoeuvres his actors with consummate skill to gradually disengage from their mass the two protagonists who the spectator feels never cease thinking about each other. The still reproduced corresponds to the intermediate stage. At this point the two poles, Dana Andrews-Teresa Wright are still apart, but the shift of positions of the other actors which is carefully calculated to be natural makes the Andrews-Wright relationship appear very clearly. Teresa Wright's white dress draws a sort of dramatic break down the middle of the shot such that we need only to cut the image in two, in relation to the angle of the walls, to divide the action equally into its two elements. Alone of all the people present in the scene the two lovers are plastically and logically set aside in the left section of the screen.

One will notice also in this still the importance of the direction in which people look. With Wyler, this always constitutes the skeleton of mise en scène. The spectator only has to follow them like a pointing finger in order to fulfil all the director's intentions. It's sufficient to concretise them all together in the image, to permit us to see all the dramatic currents crossing the screen, as clearly as the pattern made in iron filings by a magnet. All Wyler's preparatory work consists of simplifying the mechanics of the mise en scène to the maximum, assuring him the greatest effectiveness and clarity possible. In *The Best Years of our Lives* he arrives at an almost abstract paring down. All the points of dramatic articulation are of such a sensitiveness that a shift of some degrees in a look is not only legible to the most obtuse spectator, but also, through the manipulation of an ideal invisible lever, capable of tilting the balance of a whole scene.

It's perhaps the nature of a consummate science of 'mise en scène' that it avoids following a pre-established aesthetic. In this too Wyler embodies the opposite of Orson Welles, who set out in the cinema with the intention of drawing certain effects from it. Wyler spent some time working on obscure westerns of which no-one remembers the name. It was by learning the trade, not as aesthetician but as a craftsman, that he became the skilled artist who is revealed by as early a work as *Dodsworth*. When he speaks of his mise en scène it's always in terms of the spectator; it is his first care to make the spectator understand the action exactly and in the strongest way possible. Wyler's immense talent resides in this science of clarity produced by the paring down of the form, by his humility towards the subject and the spectator. In Wyler there is a sort of craftsmanlike genius, a perfect understanding of what cinema is which allows him to push the economy of means towards, paradoxically, inventing one of the most personal styles in today's cinema. But in order to try to describe it, it's been necessary for us to make it appear first of all like an absence.

Cinema is in one way like poetry. It's folly to imagine it as an isolated element which one could gather on a sheet of gelatine and project onto a screen through an enlarger. Pure cinema exists quite as much in combination with sentimental drama as with Fischinger's coloured cubes.[26] Cinema is not an indescribable independent entity whose crystals must be isolated at any price. It is rather an aesthetic state of matter. A modality of the narrative-spectacle. The experience sufficiently proves that it's necessary to keep oneself from identifying the cinema with such and such a given aesthetic, or still less with some style, some solidified form which the director is compulsorily required to use, at last like pepper or cloves. The 'purity', or better still, in my opinion, the cinematographic 'coefficient' of a film must be calculated from the efficacity of the découpage.

In the degree that Wyler has never endeavoured to distort the romantic or theatrical character of the greater part of his scenarios, he makes the cinematographic act the more clearly apparent in all its purity. Never has the auteur of the *Best Years of our Lives* or *Jezebel* said to himself that he must a priori 'make cinema'. Nevertheless, no-one knows better how to tell a story through 'cinema'. The action, for him, is primarily expressed through the actor, and it's in terms of the actor that Wyler, just like a theatrical producer, conceives his task of producing the maximum effect from the action. The décor and the camera are only there to allow dramatic intensity without parasitically turning it to their advantage to produce an extraneous meaning. But if this is also the intention of the theatrical director, he has only very limited means at his disposal due to the architecture of the modern stage and above all to the position of the footlights. He can play with his material, but in these conditions it's fundamentally the text and the actor's playing which constitute the essence of theatrical production.

Cinema does not start at all, as Marcel Pagnol would naively wish, with the binoculars of the lady in the balcony. Size and time have nothing to do with the matter. Cinema begins when the frame of the screen or the proximity of the camera and the mike serve to present the action and the actor to the best possible advantage. In *The Little Foxes* Wyler changed practically nothing in the play, the lines or even the décor: one could say that he had confined himself to producing them as a theatre man would have liked to be able to do, arranging the screen's frame to hide certain parts of the décor, and the camera to bring the stalls closer. What actor would not dream of being able to act sitting on a chair immobile before 5000 spectators who would not miss a movement of his eyes? What theatre director would not wish to be able to compel the spectator in 'the gods' to understand clearly the characters' movements, to read their intentions easily at each moment of the action? Wyler has chosen nothing more than to realise through cinema that which constitutes the essential of theatrical mise en scène; better still of a theatrical mise en scène which even denies itself the help of lighting and décor to add something to the actor and the text. But without doubt there is not a shot in *Jezebel*, in *The Little Foxes*, or *The Best Years of our Lives*, not a minute in these films which is not of pure cinema (Bazin, 1948a).

Perhaps the single most controversial notion in this essay is the focus on the freedom of choice of the spectator: freedom to construct his own *mise en scène*, his own meaning. It is in fact quite easy to argue that devices such as depth of field, minimal editing, or the 'geometry of looks' which Bazin discerns in Wyler are quite as limiting, constraining and directorial as the montage style he was concerned to reject and the 'classical editing' style he was concerned to transcend. It can be argued that they merely set up different stylistic parameters – ones which Bazin's commitments to the freedom of the spectator within realism lead him to ignore. Bazin's contention that 'composition in depth means that the spectator's relationship with the image is nearer to that which he has with reality' is also easily disprovable, in that human visual perception is capable of adjustment according to different situations. It is, however, quite possible that the use of a stylistic device such as deep-focus may set up or be part of the operation of a set of conventions, and that one of these conventions may well be the notion that such a (deep-focus) representation or image has 'more in common with reality'. That Bazin is aware of the existence of such conventions is clear from this paragraph in his general essay on Italian neo-realism:

Cinematographic styles can be grouped, though not in a hierarchy, in terms of the added reality they represent. We shall thus call *realist* any system of expression or narrative procedure tending to make more reality appear on the screen. Naturally, 'reality' must not be understood in terms of quantity. The same event, the same object is capable of several different representations. Each of them discards or retains some of the qualities that lead us to recognise the object on the screen, each of them introduces, to didactic or aesthetic ends, more or less corrosive abstractions which do not permit the original object to subsist in its entirety. At the end of this inevitable and necessary chemistry, an illusion of reality made up of a complex of abstraction (black and white, plane surface), of conventions (the laws of montage for example) and of authentic reality has been substituted for the initial reality. It is a necessary illusion, but it leads rapidly to a loss of consciousness of reality itself, which is identified in the spectator's mind with its cinematographic representation (Bazin, 1948b).

If Bazin is valuable in that he thinks in terms of style, he disappoints by not being able to develop the ideas of convention and abstraction to a point where they become a part of thought about style or a reshaping of it. Meaning for him is always 'there', waiting to be revealed; it cannot be constructed. The realism to which he is so attached, and through which he seems to discover style, blocks his path in any further theoretical development.

Another set of conventions that Bazin describes without being able to think through is that pertaining to acting and what he calls 'dramatic structures'. Here we can at least note a significant difference from the realisms of Grierson and Vertov: acting is tolerated, even welcomed in some circumstances, though it is restricted to the function of clearly bringing out the narrative-dramatic structures. In the Wyler essay, the final reference to 'pure cinema' and the earlier use of terms such as the 'maximum cinematographic coefficient' can best be understood in reference to a notion that has haunted aesthetic discussion about cinema since around 1920: the belief that the aesthetic 'secret' of film might lie in some quality specific to film in itself, and not significantly present in any other medium. This quality is variously known as 'pure cinema', 'the essence of film', 'cinematic specificity', etc.

Bazin associates this idea with what he thinks of as the built-in characteristic of the photographic – and, by extension, the cinematographic – image. The film image is objective; it rescues moments of the real world as they are, preserving them from the corruption of time. Such is its specificity.

Bazin was one of the founding fathers of the journal *Cahiers du Cinéma*. The concerns for individual authorship, for *mise en scène*, and for the attempt to produce some kind of definition of formal beauty which are visible in the Wyler essay, became the core of *Cahier*'s work in the 1950s and early 1960s. A whole generation of critics, many of whom later became film-makers, felt and reformulated Bazin's influence through *Cahiers*. One of them was Eric Rohmer. In the two articles that follow, taken from a longer but uncompleted series called *Celluloid and Marble*, Rohmer attempts to establish the relationships of film first with painting, then with poetry, writing and language:

There is good reason why the painter has rubbed shoulders with the poet in recent times. The two muses, previously fairly alien to each other, have discovered common concerns, one major concern in fact – *style*.

This is the sole perspective that concerns me in examining these two departments of art, with which the cinema sustains some highly ambiguous relations, calling above all for clarification.

There are many respectable minds, more than one might think, for whom the cinema is an art only insofar as it imitates the other arts. But the experienced viewer to whom this is addressed flatters himself on having long ago passed that stage. He casts a half-indulgent, half-bored eye at all those *film poems* and *experimental* films which are indeed well-named if the point is that there is a lesson to be drawn from their failure. We ought really to put our trust in the general public, that excellent judge with whom these works have never found favour. In all too many critics and professionals, cameramen and scriptwriters, I discern a paralysing admiration for the pen, pencil or palette, a feeling that the cinematic imagination is no more than the respectful offspring of pictorial or poetic invention.

I would never claim that the film-maker does not care about plastic forms. I would almost say that poetry is his supreme goal and concern. But still, we have to fix our line of approach very clearly. The cinema is an art of space. It does not follow that it must look for help in that particular branch of the formal arts represented by painting as it has been understood since the Renaissance. In its highest ambitions, the cinema attains a kind of lyricism. It does not follow that it needs to borrow the highly formal schema of poetry proper, the poetry of words.

'We are just photographers', said Jean Renoir recently. A piece of conventional modesty? Not at all. His words state the obvious, an axiom we have to accept at all costs if we are not to risk falsifying our researches. What does it matter if a thousand of the cinema's defenders crumble at one blow as a result! It is up to us to construct a different defence. I know a great deal of effort has gone into devising a proof that the camera is not a simple recording instrument, that the world of the screen differs from perceived reality. How many pages have been devoted to that particular theme! And what a futile undertaking it is! What need is there to prove the self-evident? Even its greatest detractors will admit that the cinema is an art, in the humblest sense of the term, i.e. a creation of man. Once it has been explained to you that such and such a shot resembles a painting by Vermeer or Lautrec, you are quite at liberty to prefer Vermeer or Lautrec, and you would be right. I have often been tempted to say of certain films that they are 'almost as beautiful as paintings'. But it is the *almost* which is the rub. I'm simply dealing with the ersatz. I am prepared to put it bluntly. The most beautiful photograph will never equal the least brush stroke, the least fragment of a phrase. If the ambitions of the new art were confined to producing a skimped version of what its elders have brought to perfection, I wouldn't really give much for it. . . .

It has been dinned into us that the cinema is an art *although* it rests on a mechanical mode of reproduction. I would assert the direct opposite: the ability to reproduce exactly, simply, is the cinema's surest privilege. But then, the objection will be raised, how does the creator intervene, what constitutes his freedom? His freedom is there throughout and it is very great. What a film-maker worthy of the name wants to make us share is not his admiration for museums, but the fascination which objects themselves exert over him.

All right, it will be argued. Clearly the cinema can't exercise the same freedom in relation to the model as painting. But isn't this just a simple difference of degree? Didn't painting too once have that same respect for the real? Wasn't reproduction its original goal?

The objection is such a serious one that it forces me to improve on my argument. Not just 'once'; it still does, probably. I firmly believe that all the experiments of modern painting are born of a more rigorous need to grasp the essence of things. Manet, the Impressionists, Van Gogh, Cézanne, the Fauves, the Cubists, Paul Klee . . . did they not all lay claim to greater truth? That plate on the table, according to the painter André Lhote[27] is not a circle, as a child would draw it; nor is it an ellipse as we are taught at school; it is a curve, swelling or shrinking according to the intensity of colour and light in the surfaces it touches. Our practised eye hardly even notices these 'deformations' any longer, but they incensed Cézanne's contemporaries who attributed them directly to the astigmatism of the painter.

What, then, are the criteria of accuracy? By refining and changing the way we look, Art has set out to change the world. Seen in passing, a reproduction of a late Matisse in some shop-window seems to pour down a light so true that the Paris street we are walking in suddenly seems as unreal as an old print. Far from denigrating modern art, I would say that more than one of the works of the masters of the 20th century has taught me to see, and, via detours of varying length and violence, finally brought me back to things themselves. It is not so much the style, the quality of line, the human hand, or the man himself and the tortuous impetuosity of his moods that I admire in the canvases of a Cézanne, a Bonnard, a Matisse, a Picasso, or a Klee. I love them for what they have led me to discover, because they bring me back to a reality which is not themselves. In other words, because they are true.

Such is the homage I want to render to the regal art of the 20th century, and I can think of none higher. The genius of its ten or twelve most brilliant representatives seems to me to have no parallel in other fields. The past offers no lack of examples of such exclusive flowerings. Who would dare to compare the best painter of the 18th century with Bach or Mozart, or the greatest of the polyphonists[28] to Michelangelo or da Vinci? And the beginning of this century was just such an exceptional period which saw painting suddenly soar so high, imposing its laws on the other arts. However forearmed people may have been against its advances, it was impossible not to cast an envious eye on so much youth, and such extraordinary fertility. Calmly and surely it took its place at the head of the column. The standard it unfurled was not for anarchy and rejection, but for a freedom firmly and consciously bound to the old order. All this did not come about without a certain amount of noise and breakages. But generally, the progress of modern art was relaxed, occasionally smiling; it indulged the luxury of preferring joy to pain, harmony to chaos. Classical in affinities if not in intention, it flooded the soft Paris skies with the full glory of its pure colours. It provoked never-ending discussion and, through the breach thus made, the imposing mausoleum of Art released one of its most jealously guarded secrets.

Swansong? Rebirth? Certainly a dazzling blaze for which a thousand enticing explanations beckon, but I doubt if they could be made to cohere. The simplest is, I think, that as the most objective of arts, the one most reluctant to start by exploiting our instinctual responses, our mental and emotional excitement, it inevitably experienced a particular upsurge in a century like this one, so devoted to the intellect and to amiable forms of anarchy. The arts which excite the emotions like music, dance and poetry wilt when cut off from their native soil, but painting is by instinct curious, a wanderer, retaining its bloom and its traditions in any environment. Because it lacks movement and is elaborated spatially, its first function is to soothe, and this allows and justifies any kind of audacity. Because it sets itself the task of copying and the existence of the model or motif acts as a break and an authority, it uses its freedom to the hilt.

This is what I was thinking about one night when a November rainstorm stopped me under the awning of an art bookshop. Matisse had just died and I was able to contemplate one of his last works in the shop-window: a paper collage incorporating vegetable motifs. An inexplicable fascination flowed from that vermilion, green and mauve, that theme at once seascape and woodland, those flat, stable surfaces which looked as if a gentle flick of the finger might suddenly swell and animate them, so rich were they in latent movement and dimensions. It was if a drug was seeping into me through the channels of my eyes; a spell held me, as imperious as that inspired by a musical phrase. I yielded to the highest and most violent visual pleasure possible; I understood, and approved the frenetic pride of the modern painter, our religion of line, touch and personal style. . . . But even as my contemplation was at its most intense, I was seized by a doubt, not about the quality of that pleasure, but about the purity of my look. Was it really fastened on the naked work? Or wasn't it rather lingering along the complicated network which linked this painting to a hundred, a thousand others by the same painter, by his contemporaries, his precursors? I thought I was enjoying the work as an amateur, but my admiration was that of a scholar. For how could a naive eye evaluate such a painting? It would see, understandably, only childishness and barbarism.

Painting was born of a need, precisely the thing that bothers it least at the moment, which explains the innumerable sophisms we are prepared to swallow unquestioningly. This or that young painter, writer or musician takes it upon himself to liquidate a material which he decrees has been used to death. Let him follow his own argument through to its logical conclusion and challenge the very existence of the art he practises. So he wants to efface the object, replace the word by the syllable, sound by noise. But who is forcing him to paint, compose poems or sonatas, if he has such a distrust of visible things, language or musical instruments? Does the world's greatest chef carry refinement to the point of concocting inedible dishes to titillate jaded palates? Forgive the incongruous comparison. I am only trying to assert a very simple fact, so simple that it scarcely holds the attention. Our predecessors taught us to cover particular rectangles with canvas. Why? Was it just a game, like cards or chess? We learned to congregate in concert halls. Was it to sacrifice to some baroque superstition?

We omit to ask ourselves the question. In any case we find it extremely vulgar. 'Art must at least be based on certain conventions.' A curious response from intellects so feverishly set on denouncing convention of any kind. For my part, I think that the painter's original aim was to reproduce a fraction of the real world which, for one reason or another, be it simple pleasure, fetishism, or religious belief, we should like to have before our eyes. It is a disturbing fact that today the majority of great works are, with rare exceptions, no longer produced for the intimacy of a room, but for the draughtiness of museums, or worse still, for the sinister storehouse of the collector. The artist's ambition is no longer the modest one of pleasing his client. Rather he wishes to enrich the human heritage. I'm not saying that the enterprise lacks grandeur, but simply, that it is contradictory and makes me think of those children's toys which are so perfectly finished that children are forbidden to touch them.

I doubt whether the lucky owners of canvases by Matisse are able to follow the painter's advice to 'contemplate them calmly, from a comfortable armchair'. Were they able to, their pleasure would be spoiled by the regret that they possessed only one or a few specimens from a complete work, severed from which the single canvas stands for very little. And even the complete work itself—would we value it at all if it were to surge up in front of us suddenly unless we knew something of the history of art? It is the very grandeur of the Old Masters which authorises us to savour the Moderns. If the Mona Lisa hadn't existed, could we decently look upon those faces where only the outline is shown by a light stroke? Up until the present, other centuries threw a thick veil over the monuments of preceding ages, occasionally obscuring them altogether. Would we be prepared to live exclusively in the close company of abstract artists and atonal musicians? The catalogues of record companies and art book publishers would give the answer and it is no, we would not.

Let us look again at the attractive notion that Art changes nature, an idea we almost appropriated a moment ago. If art did so modify our view of things would we be so sensitive to the masterpieces of the past? The paradoxes set by certain painters should be approached with caution. They doubtless paint as they see and teach the public to see as they do, but that kind of seeing is a luxury, we know how to resume our everyday eyes. However, that raises the question – what is ordinary vision? Is photography really to be the yardstick?

'Photography . . . or almost', I would say, without false modesty. It is no coincidence that since its invention, art has taken a completely new direction. No painter could better satisfy the desires it fulfils – for example the desire to preserve the image of something dear, a facial expression, the uniqueness of an event 'caught unawares'. A need which I consider noble even if its origins are not aesthetic. Painting did fulfil that need once: today the results would be called gross or mediocre. I can understand such a response on the part of an artist. But we all have the right to reserve our interest for the face deliberately ignored by the contemporary artists if we wish. If photography is, precisely, a minor art, it is not because it can only reproduce exactly. I would rather reproach it with inexactness, the flatness of its surfaces. the harshness of its contrasts, the rigidity it imposes on what is supple and lively. But the greatest of painters could not claim that the face he had painted was *truer than the one we see on the screen*. And he can't take refuge in phrases like 'but it's not *beautiful*' or 'it's not art'. I intend to show that it can be just as beautiful and that *it certainly is art* for those who will just agree to a change of viewpoint.

If there are phases where our love of art is sectarian and exclusive, there are others when, on the contrary, it is in perfect harmony with our other passions. This is not meant as homage to the Fine Arts. On the contrary, it is something of a slight; to see the evolution of the Fine Arts as a natural and continuous process, a simple reflection, an epiphenomenon, the thermometer of a civilisation, the fruit of a world view, of a sensibility which differs today from what it was yesterday, is not to pay homage to them; it is to underestimate them. Art as an autonomous organism grows of its own accord. Like a living creature, it is endowed with childhood, maturity and age. While each period has its own charm, the early ones seduce us with the promises they carry, the late ones because they tap memories. And it is only right that we should have a prejudice in favour of the mature, classical period.

I don't know how many hundreds, millions of years our civilisation is destined to continue. But I am sure that while the artist's inspiration is perhaps drying up, it doesn't follow that we may one day see the sensitivity to beauty of form and colour, which we prize so highly today, as a symptom of mediocrity. If art has to die, it will be crushed by the same internal force which today gives it life. Every pencil line, every brush stroke, by a painter worthy of the name, opens up new paths and at the same time, closes a door behind. I find it difficult to explain how it works, but those doors cannot be opened in reverse direction and the number of new paths is not infinite. Any retracing of steps is impossible and already – terrible sign – the young painters who want to be so bold in their march forward are beginning to perceive that their immediate precursors *went further than they have*.

Today, one art stands at the summit of that *classicism* we spoke of, in the full flush of a health the other arts have lost forever. It reassures us by the very fact of its existence, shows us that the cause of civilisation and that of certain art forms are not so closely linked as we believed, that man is less deeply engaged on that perilous adventure into which he was swept by aesthetic passions not so long ago. All our old desires, our traditions and our established ideas have faithfully kept the appointment in front of the new screen – despite all our scepticism, our taste for revolt, we haven't rejected them too much. All that we frenziedly tried to destroy has suddenly been given back to us by an invention, but in a rejuvenated form, washed clean of the patina which justified our former disaffection. We realised that the saga of modern art had delighted only a few of us. Were we going to love it the less for that knowledge? A little bit less I'm afraid [. . .] (Rohmer, 1955a).

[. . .] The first theoreticians of the cinema were interested solely in formal expression. The past ten or fifteen years have seen a growing tendency towards a consideration of the notion of *language*. As a new language, film was seen as capable not only of showing, but of naming and designating. Thus it would contain elements of two forms of art, themselves at opposite poles: painting and poetry.

The line I am following, for all that it is not inspired by any particular Fine Arts system, is nevertheless not arbitrary. Poetry takes its natural place after painting as its exact antithesis. Painting addressed itself to the senses and sought to reproduce material form. Poetry only uses signs, that is, words as signs and, which is more important, deflects them from their everyday meaning. Poetry sets out to mask the arbitrary nature of words by introducing another arbitrary element. It names things, but wrongly. It uses deliberate approximations and its constant recourse is to metaphor. While the painter, and I am not excluding the moderns, has always sought to be a faithful witness, the poet from the beginning has always delighted in disguising the truth. The writers of classical antiquity showed the way and we have simply followed. And are there really degrees in lying?

Three thousand years, or nearly, separate the 'vast hump-backed sea' and 'iron-clad sky' from the 'earth as blue as an orange'. The surrealists did not discover anything new, they simply pushed poetic arbitrariness to its extreme.

What is the source of the sickness which is killing poetry today? Have we indulged in excessive lying? Or is it rather that we are slightly more reticent about lying than our ancestors? Both explanations are valid. And total freedom is even more difficult to work with. Poetry went up in smoke as soon as an attempt was made to relieve it of its framework of conventions. And the real could not serve it as a safety net since it is a flight outside of the real. When everything can be compared to everything else, comparison itself loses its essential purpose.

It is the second explanation I want to follow up today. Our age has its good aspects. If it rejects the artifices of language, surely this is from scruples about sincerity? If we are honest, is there not something rather ridiculous and a little indecent about a man in a city suit designating surrounding objects other than by their prosaic, everyday name? For us the moon is no longer 'queen of the night', nor is the sun the 'clear beacon of the world' and we should give up dressing them up in other trappings.

For some years many respectable thinkers have taken a stand against the present decline of language. They denounce the taste for vulgarity or, worse still, for abstraction in present-day writers. I can only agree with them. Pseudo-scientific jargon has even contaminated children's books. But the cause of the evil needs to be sought beyond the modern combination of permissiveness and pedantry. The verb is losing its efficacity and daily yielding ground to the *noun* because our contact with the ready-made objects of the modern world makes the notion of *becoming* less and less useful and favours the notion of *end-product* instead. The old terms, like the hand of the craftsman, preserved the actual shape of things moulded into their crevices. Present-day neologisms on the other hand offer as unlikely an image of the real as the dashboard of a luxury car does of the complex mechanism concealed under the bonnet.

Limiting their effort to tapping a keyboard, our fingers escape getting scratched but the sensitivity of the fingertips is dangerously blunted. The price of science which, for all our emotional misgivings, we do not hesitate to pay.

We live in a world without mystery and rather than manufacture false mysteries, let us make a clean break with poetry. Nothing is more irritating to me than the kind of preciosity in modern prose and verse which offends commonsense. I am not saying that from now on the use of any figure of style is forbidden; the language of the scientist itself is strewn with images, but these – *current, tension, resistance,* for example – are simply matters of convenience and have nothing to do with art. What the writer is losing a little each day is not his freedom to manipulate words according to his wishes, a right he arrogated to himself on his own authority, but the right to pretend this arrangement is anything other than a façade behind which one would search in vain for any profound conviction or philosophy.

About Metaphor

Balzac is not one of the great stylists and yet I would give up pages of some more rigorous prose writer, or a line of verse by the most celebrated poet, for just one of his master strokes. For this reason a short passage from *Père Goriot*[29] long excited my admiration without my being able to uncover the precise reasons for the charm it exercised over me. I leave it to others to denounce a certain tendency to bourgeois mediocrity, characteristic of the reign of Louis-Philippe,[30] which in no way detracts from my argument. The passage has Rastignac visiting Madame de Restaud and surprising the Countess still in her morning gown:[31]

> Her perfume filled the air; she had probably just come from a bath and her beauty seemed, as it were, softer and more voluptuous; her eyes had a liquid brilliance. Young men's eyes see everything; their spirit reacts to the charm a woman radiates just as plants breathe in the substances they need from the air: so Eugène did not need to touch this woman's hands to feel their freshness.

I will not linger over the phrase 'beauté assouplie' (in the English translation 'her beauty *seemed . . . softer*') – a combination of words that might well rouse the jealousy of many of our modern writers. It is the didactic and naive nature of the two final sentences which delights me and even more, that 'so' which underscores their serious tone. The opposition of science to poetry is unjustifiable, quite the contrary; since Homer, Virgil and Lucretius, poets have sought the framework of their symbolic systems in the science of their time. A comparison is either purely a mental exercise or it rests on a conviction subscribed to by its author.

The former heresy was committed by the sixteenth and seventeenth century writers who, having over-indulged a praiseworthy admiration for the writers of classical antiquity, claimed to be returning the classical armoury of rhetorical and poetic devices to their rightful place of honour while at the same time they rejected the classical world view. And that is why I have preferred to use Balzac rather than Racine to illustrate my thesis. What I admire in him is his recovery of that simple knowledge of the ancient world, in exchange for which the greatest of our poets, from Ronsard to Baudelaire or Rimbaud, offer only knowing simplicities. The symbolism of western poetry draws on three main currents which in any case interconnect: the classical, the Christian and finally, the notion of a universal magnetism which the author of *Louis Lambert* and *Séraphita* borrowed from Swedenborg. It is not for me here to challenge the scientific or philosophical value of such a system. I simply note its literary richness; from the German Romantics to Edgar Allan Poe, the whole first half of the nineteenth century turned to it for inspiration. Established science regarded it with justifiable suspicion, although it rested on the same theory of universal attractions as established science, as Poe's *Eureka* shows.[32] But the appeal is to notions so familiar to us, so profoundly rooted since earliest antiquity, that our emotions urge us to accept just as strongly as reason tells us to reject. It is not, therefore, science in its most widely accepted sense of theoretical knowledge which is incompatible with poetry, but the specific notion of science which in these romantic times has managed to substitute itself for the classical ideal of finality. The transition has come about so unobtrusively that our poets failed to notice that they were preaching not just against their age, but against themselves; they lacked the power to replace the old belief in finality with a renewed spiritualism.

In a world where everything is reducible to a relationship of cause and effect, there is no place for poetry, not even for fine style. The sentences from *Père Goriot* are no longer 'possible' in our day. That kind of assimilation of plant life into the life of the soul is not among the propositions of modern science. Of course, for Balzac himself, the question was simply one of a comparison, but, you must agree, there is a *seriousness* there which our contemporaries are no longer capable of, a seriousness which, precisely because it shows the comparison to be necessary and useful, also gives it its beauty. Without this seriousness I would readily agree that the image is precious, heavy, ridiculous. Let me offer another example, taken from the same work, some pages further on:

> Rastignac arrived at his lodgings in a state of admiration for Madame de Nucingen's charms. He remembered how slender she was, as clean-lined and graceful as a swallow. The intoxicating sweetness of her eyes, the delicate silky texture of her skin under which it seemed to him he could perceive the flow of the blood, the enchantment of her voice, her fair hair, he recalled them one by one; and perhaps the exercise of walking by quickening his blood enhanced her fascinations.

Well, you may say, that's all very materialist and in no way conflicts with contemporary medicine. 'Quickening his blood' sounds a bit dated of course, but the effect of walking on the workings of the mind is a fact no one would wish to dispute. But it is precisely the 'quickening blood' which to me seems essential and the *direct* effect (as Balzac thought) which that quickening action can have on the action of the intellect, without having to pass via the intermediary of this or that complex physiological process. Supermaterialism? No, rather we are dealing once again with that same theory of analogy founded on the belief in the finality of the universe. I would even hazard the guess that without this basis, the beauties of the beginning of the sentence – 'graceful as a swallow' or 'skin under which it seemed to him he could perceive the flow of the blood' – would not have such a powerful effect. When Balzac, and the same might be said for the writers of classical antiquity, proposes a comparison, for example that of a human being with an animal or a natural object, you can sense behind it all the density of the theory of 'social species', which Balzac himself proposes as the key to his work and which is essentially the offspring of the classical theory that preceded it. It is one of the mysteries of art that all the ideas he develops abstractly seem at the very heart confused and unlikely to inspire conviction. But as developed in the course of episodes of the novels they constitute a continuous and coherent substructure from which each particular stylistic effect draws its impact. I could equally have taken Virgil or Goethe as my example, but I deliberately chose a prose writer in order to make it clear that the present decline of poetry is not to be imputed solely to the verse form, but to an actual depreciation on the level of language.

You probably know already what I'm leading up to. By exempting us from the need to name things, the cinema makes any form of literary metaphor useless. The beauty of a wave caught in colour on the wide screen makes all stylistic artifice more than ever superfluous. The greatest goal of poetry was to *render* the movement which painting was by its essence incapable of expressing. But when the sea, just as it is, can be delivered at will in cans of film to the deepest countryside or dusty towns, there is nothing more to be said. I want to take the point further, however, to show that the power of metaphor, whose secret has been lost by poetry, is now a kind of prerogative of the cinema and that this is the main reason why the newest of the arts is the sole legitimate refuge of poetry.

The scorn customarily poured on the cinema stems from the fact that its poetry is always seen as something superimposed and non-intrinsic. True, the times when this or that heavily explicit symbol

provoked ecstasies of admiration are past, but a film-maker's strain-
ing after the esoteric in the way of subject matter is still taken as
evidence of poetic intention. I should like to assert the opposite. I am
satisfied with the most banal gesture, provided it suggests something
other than its utility, its immediate purpose, and carries within itself
a kind of secondary meaning. The style of the greatest film-makers, a
Murnau, a Vigo, a Renoir, a Hitchcock, a Rossellini, abounds in
metaphor; rather than deny their presence we would be better employed learning how to uncover them.

All original poetic expression is founded on an abstract framework
of quasi-mathematical rigour, a development of the mysterious and
sacred power of numbers. For some of my colleagues the term
mathematician is a reproach when directed at Hitchcock, but would
be a term of praise if applied to Virgil or Poe. If Virgil or Poe has some
superstition centring on the number two or the colour white, well that
is fine. If the author of *Rear Window*[33] yields to the same fascination
the result is deemed a mere formal exercise! Just as it is impossible to
imagine a poet insensitive to rhythm, so every great cinematic work
constantly reveals the presence of a certain vigorous geometrical
structure which is not superimposed like some vain decoration, but
absolutely consubstantial with the work. It is as if every gesture, every
look, whatever its immediate function, must at the same time insert
itself into a system of lines of force carefully constructed in advance.
This is how I conceive of stylistic device in the cinema. It has nothing
to do with bringing one form into some arbitrary relation with
another by means of editing or some other external process. On the
contrary, the fully metaphoric is that which suggests or even, more
precisely, uncovers the presence of primary universal laws within the
particular. And I do not have in mind the totally abstract notions
proposed by science, but the pre-established harmony and constant
parallelism, celebrated by classical antiquity, between the phenomena
of the various natural orders: vegetable, mineral or human, solid or
liquid, celestial, spiritual or material. And suddenly, the theory of
analogies, which we rejected earlier, emerges endowed with a new
foundation. It seems it was not so much to be despised after all,
because it carried within itself some measure of the truth. The cinema,
most positive of all arts, insensible to all that isn't caught raw, pure
appearance, is therefore a long way from leading us down the road of
determinism, as might justifiably have been suspected. On the contrary, it presents us with the idea of a hierarchical, ordered world
with a final end. We are not led to look for the existence of atoms
behind what the film shows us, but for something that reaches beyond
phenomena, a soul, or some totally other spiritual principle. Have you

noticed how, on the screen, a space is drawn between human behaviour and that of the animal, how the sight of a machine disturbs us, that of our peers reassures? The poetry lies above all in that revelation of a spiritual presence which I am proposing you set out to find.

I have already tried to clarify the classical aspect of cinema. Now I want to put the emphasis on its modern side. And the two go together: being modern does not mean systematically rejecting all tradition, burning everything that you previously worshipped – a futile and petty enterprise. The cinema is modern because it gives a new basis and an original translation to beliefs we have no reason to reject, towards which we are always carried by the same deep feelings. To be modern is not necessarily to glorify confusion on the grounds that the ancients extolled order and harmony. It does not mean taking pleasure in shadow because they praised the light, belittling man because they exalted him. The film-maker who, from the outset, is endowed with a marvellous capacity for making his matter out of the presence of the world, has no reason to abandon the optimism of the classical period. He is at ease in his age and only in him does the age find a singer worthy of it. We are very far from the antiquarian bric-à-brac beloved of Breton.[34] Our so-called modern poets evince a very dubious taste for the most faded material; they have always shown themselves incapable of accepting into their work the manufactured objects which are our daily companions in the modern world. If they ever do name them, these objects take on the obsolescent quality of a magic lantern, or a gramophone in some old loft. In the cinema, aeroplanes, cars, telephones, firearms are not transformed into monsters. They are what they are in their everyday usage; like the bow, the chariot, and the galley of antiquity, they seem to merge with the décor which surrounds them, the gesture which controls or manipulates them. The thought that presided over their creation seems to animate them still, their movements are the extensions of those of man, whose power they multiply tenfold, exalting his basic nobility.

It would never occur to us in judging a poem to first put it in prose. But how many of our film critics go in for this strange exercise! Our aesthetic categories, produced by the practices of a decadent literature, become sterile or dangerous when the question is one of evaluating the merits of a film-maker. We should rather, like the ancients, concentrate purely on inventiveness, effectiveness and other qualities much despised today. The truth is, the majority of the pseudo-connoisseurs want only a wink in the direction of the audience, to show that the film-maker is not taken in by the game he is playing, that he himself is what's important – as for the film, it can be disposed of as quickly as possible. During the last century we have got too used to considering an art product solely from the point of view of its creators' self-expression. I am willing to admit poems have always, more or less, been outlets for completely individual excitement or anxiety, but I refuse to believe that that is all they can be. If as Jacques Rivette has said 'the highest thought of our time chooses to express itself through cinema', it is because the essential modesty of the film-maker gives him the capacity to translate the universal, something others can no longer flatter themselves they attain.

I have talked about the cinema in general and I would not try to claim that all films bend equally easily to my definition. So I will conclude with a few examples. There are few film-makers who do not confuse true poetry with an anxious search for the esoteric. For most of them there is no such thing as a happy accident, everything has to be noted down in minutest detail in the script. Nothing irritates me more, for example, than the moment in *La Blé en Herbe* when the bicycles topple over to give dramatic punctuation to a fairly feeble kiss. What a strange idea, as Boileau[35] would have said. At the very least it's rather laborious. Intention is betrayed so quickly on the screen that it is impossible to warn film-makers strongly enough against any conscious striving after effect. I would be just as severe on that shot in *Umberto D* where the little maid stretches out her leg to push the door shut. A graceful note and easy on the eye, but if the cinema were no more than 'that' sort of thing, we would have every right to consider it a minor art. *La Strada*, which I like a lot, is crawling with similar ideas, to which I am rather afraid the film owes its success. On the other hand, what about an example of a fine shot, rich in poetry? The scene in *Tabu* where the old priest cuts the rope to which his pursuer is clinging. By means of the wave which momentarily brings the boat closer before carrying it irrevocably away, nature seems to sanction the man's act. With it that Destiny whose mysterious weight has made itself felt throughout the film explodes to the surface. In a recent George Cukor film, *A Star is Born*, there is a similar wave, coming in to splash and then carry out the dressing gown left on the beach by James Mason. The idea would be questionable if the film-maker's sole intention had been to indicate thereby the suicide of his hero. But there is in the very motion of the wave so much grandeur and splendid indifference that I could never begrudge the author such a successfully realised effect. There is in any case no need for a nudge from the film-maker to make us aware of the inter-action between the world of matter and the world of spirit. The greatest privilege is to be able to achieve this without the slightest recourse to symbol, ellipse or allusion. When the couple in *Viaggio in Italia* are coming back from their walk across the ruins, the décor is simply there, but its presence is more eloquent than the most beautiful of classical pronounce-ments on the frailty of man and the eternalness of nature (Rohmer, 1955b).

Behind the almost feline delicacy of Rohmer's argument lies a series of quite simple propositions. Painting is somewhat controversially assimilated to its representational aspects; twentieth-century modernist art would be incomprehensible without the history of representation which precedes it. And in any case the great modern painters are also pursuing truth. The basic representational function of painting is better performed by cinema. (This opinion is one shared by many modernists, but they tend to draw an opposite conclusion: that it is unfortunate for the cinema to have been saddled with this function at the very time that the other arts appear to be giving it up.) As for poetry and literature, they are concerned not with representing, but, through metaphor, with naming. Naming is a process which involves language, not reality. Here lie the roots of Rohmer's dualism: art is a compound of matter and spirit. Film is concerned both with 'brute facts' and 'pure appearances' and also with the 'great universal laws' that lie behind them. Its harmony with both matter and spirit is what allows film to breathe new life into the traditional forms of classical art. Rohmer's 'great universal laws' may seem rather capricious alongside Grierson's 'interpretation of the modern world', Eisenstein's 'ideological reality' or Bazin's 'consciousness of reality itself', but perhaps their formulation may serve to emphasise the fact that however diffuse its manifestations, realism always aims to be a system. Both in theory and in expressive practice, it has something of the force of a law, purporting to explain and codify the materials that it uses. In practice, it imposes formal constraints, and these constraints, which differ from school to school and style to style, shape the works themselves. For Rohmer, over and above his inherent classicism, these constraints would seem to be epitomised at the level of particular sequences of images by what he calls the 'geometrical rigour' of a 'system of force-lines carefully constructed in advance'. In Bazin the equivalent pressure is the need to fabricate aesthetically satisfactory representations of reality which do not destroy the 'truth' of that reality. Both attempt to construct a visual, representational culture within the wider culture they inherit. Eisenstein is more complicated: the system he is interested in constructs itself out of the search for dynamic relations between content (of the material) and consciousness and feelings (of the spectator) — these relations being mediated, in the earlier work at least, through the 'play' of montage.

The notion of formal constraints has been further explored by the English critic V. F. Perkins:

On one level cinematic credibility is no different from that which we demand of other story-telling forms. It depends on the inner consistency of the created world. So long as that is maintained, the premises are beyond question: people can express their feelings in impromptu song, with or without instrumental backing; inanimate objects can be self-willed and malevolent; Death can be a devotee of chess. But the created world must obey its own logic. There is no pretext, whether it be Significance, Effect or the Happy Ending, sufficient to justify a betrayal of the given order. In a fictional world where anything at all can happen, nothing at all can mean or matter.

This fact has specific implications for the movie. It gives the criterion of credibility a *physical* dimension which it has not had elsewhere in art since the decline of representational painting. Faced with the camera's obstinate literal-mindedness (which means our literal-minded approach to the camera's products), the film-maker follows Conrad's advice to the drowning man: 'In the destructive element immerse . . .' Conquest through submission: since the image insists on its relationship with visual reality the film-maker takes that as one of the starting points for his organization and works through it to achieve reality for his imagined world. In this sense even the fiction movie is a documentary — the Authentic Record brought back from a fictional universe.

Here too it is important that we avoid confusing credibility with authenticity. The question of authenticity simply does not arise when we enter a fictional world. There is no actuality against which we can check images derived from *One Million Years B.C.*[36] or *2001*. But the image must be credibly derived from the created world in order to maintain its reality.

A very basic demonstration of the two levels of credibility is provided by Hitchcock's *The Birds*. On the first level, we can make no difficulty about the fact that the feathered kingdom is seen to declare war on humanity. That is given. But it is also given that the attackers are ordinary, familiar birds. Nothing in our experience or in the film's premises permits them to develop intermittent outlines of luminous blue as they swoop, or to propel themselves in a manner that defies the observable laws of winged flight.

While it was scarcely Hitchcock's fault if his movie's central hypothesis was weakened by the fallibility of Special Effects, other directors have voluntarily incurred a similar breakdown, more often by forcing their actors into unconvincing postures or movements in order to fit a preconceived image. The more aspiring among inept film-makers frequently do this in pursuit of Dramatic Impact, which is like cutting off one's nose to beautify one's face.

Nothing the *camera* does can offer any threat to the credibility of the imagined world. It has complete freedom, within that world, to seek its most revealing image. It can hang from the ceiling, look through kaleidoscopes, coloured filters or distorting lenses, and register with varying degrees of definition, grain and focus.

But we make sense of the movie image by *relating* it to our common knowledge and experience of the visible world. The relationship cannot be one of simple correspondence. In the colour movie, for example, the prominence or absence of particular tones may be thoroughly abnormal or designedly unnatural: no part of the greatness of a Western like *Johnny Guitar* or a musical like *The Pirate* could be traced to the likelihood of their colour-schemes. An apparent artificiality of décor in no way undermines the kind of belief assumed by *The Wizard of Oz*.

In *Moulin Rouge* John Huston established (and exploited with, for the most part, enthralling results) a system of colour based on the palettes of the Impressionists and therefore owing nothing to naturalism. Yet he had not created a world whose reality could tolerate a room that changed colour in sympathy with its occupant's moods. When the director characterized his hero's jealousy by flooding the set with, in the film's own terms, inexplicable green light, he broke down the essential structure of his picture's relationships and thus destroyed the world within which his hero *existed*. A minor, momentary relationship between the hero's temper and a literary convention of colour ('green with envy') was surely not worth achieving – or, more strictly speaking, capable of being achieved – at the sacrifice of the fundamental pattern [. . . .]

No game worth watching changes its rules at the players' convenience. From the spectator's point of view, part of the function of the narrative discipline is to prevent the story-teller's making things easy for himself at the expense of his work. But while a coherent principle of organization is essential, it is not in itself enough. A game may be played in strict accordance with a consistent body of rules yet remain a dull game. The rules provide a basis, not a substitute, for skilled and exciting play.

In like manner the disciplines of credibility adopted by the film-maker can be of only partial help to our understanding and judgement. By enabling us to explain why some part of a movie's structure is incoherent they allow us to indicate that the work is flawed; how seriously flawed will depend on how marginal or central the incoherence proves to be. But when we've said that a film is credible, we've not said much. We have established the soundness at only one end of its balance.

I have now described both sides of this balance, credibility as well as significance, in terms of coherence. But as the *Moulin Rouge* example has shown, the relationships concerned are of different kinds. The problem of balance arises because different relationships may make incompatible demands. When that happens opposed strains lead not to productive tension but to breakdown.

The image too has its givens. Like the created world, and in harmony with it, the image retains its sense and validity so long as it follows the logic of its premises. We can adjust to any scheme of selection provided that it is appreciable as a scheme. In coming to terms with the cinema's artifice we need to be able to sense which elements of our common experience apply and which are in suspension. The credibility of an artificial world, the reliability of an artificial eye, depend on the consistency of their relationship with our reality and on a system of deviation from the norms of our experience.

In the photographic film tension is applied whenever the image is required to act not just as representation but also as a significant structure. The relationship between image and thought may conflict with or reinforce that between image and object. As the weight of meaning carried by the image increases, so does the strain placed on this balance. At any point short of collapse, the tension is a source of strength and energy. Up to this point, the greater the force of expression which the image can be seen to bear, the more illuminating will be the interlock between what is shown and the way of showing it.

The movie's technical conventions allow the film-maker himself to define the principles of organization which are to control this relationship. When we enter the cinema we have to accept the implications of a controlled viewpoint. Since the camera has no brain, it has vision but not perception. It is the film-maker's task to restore the selectivity of the cinematic eye. In this process he may control our perception so that *his* vision and emphases dominate our response to the created world.

A scene in *Rope* demonstrates how extensively the controlled viewpoint may heighten our response to action without making our awareness of control a barrier to imaginative involvement. The two murderers have placed their victim's corpse in an unlocked chest. At their dinner party refreshments are served from the top of the chest-coffin. The books which are usually kept in the chest have been placed in the next room. After dinner the housekeeper begins to clear the chest. When she has finished doing so she will want to replace the books. She makes three journeys to and from the dining-room, taking away empties and bringing back books. Throughout this deliberately extended scene the camera stands fixed so that we can watch her going about her perilous business. We know where the young criminals and their guests are standing, we can hear their conversation, but we can see only the back of one of the guests at the very edge of the screen.

Hitchcock has deliberately chosen an angle which prevents us from seeing either of his guilty heroes. The suspense of the scene depends on our being made to wait for the moment when the housekeeper opens the chest. It is heightened by the frustration of our desire to know whether either of the heroes is in a position to observe what is happening and so intervene to prevent catastrophe. The effect depends on a calculated refusal of desired information.

A similar refusal of information occurs in William Wyler's *The Loudest Whisper*. We are shown a schoolgirl telling her straitlaced grandmother a scandalous lie about the relationship between two of her teachers. However, we do not hear the accusation because at the moment the child begins to speak Wyler cuts in a shot from the front seat of the car in which they are travelling. The glass panel behind the chauffeur prevents our hearing the rest of the conversation. The obvious intention is to heighten the menace of the scene, to emphasize the 'unspeakable' nature of the charge. There is no need for us to hear the actual words spoken since we are well enough aware that the accusation is of homosexuality.

Both Hitchcock and Wyler in these scenes are exploiting the opportunities created by the necessity of a controlled viewpoint to heighten our response by providing only a partial 'view' of the action. In each case the alert spectator is likely to be aware of the device employed to secure the effect. Yet I would maintain that there is a great disparity between the strength and validity of the two devices.

When Wyler changes our viewpoint he quite clearly does so at his own convenience and at our expense. The camera changes position only in order to explain the silence; the effect is scarcely more subtle than a simple cut-out on the sound-track. The change of angle covers the silence, but gives us no new or interesting information which would justify the change itself. There is, literally, no excuse for the device: we are deprived of what we expected to hear and offered no compensatory distraction. We are thus encouraged to notice the nature of the device, at the expense of the response which it was too clearly designed to provoke.

But in *Rope* the effect of the restrictive viewpoint is in no way damaged by our awareness of the director's design. What we are prevented from seeing is fully covered by what we do see and know. The position of the guests at one side of the room was established naturalistically *before* the housekeeper began her clearing up; as so often in Hitchcock's work, the fact is initially offered as a piece of neutral, more or less irrelevant information so that it is not questionable later, when it takes on its more threatening aspect. We could still object to the camera device if Hitchcock had not employed his décor so cunningly. He has placed his actors in such a way that within this setting there is no angle from which the camera could embrace both the corner where the heroes are standing and the housekeeper's passage from sitting-room to dining-room. In order to stand back far enough to include both points the camera would have to travel, and see, through the wall opposite the sitting-room door. If this episode occurred early in the film we might suspect that the wall, like Wyler's glass panel, served only the purpose of restricting our knowledge. But the camera has explored the apartment so freely in the preceding sequences that by the time Hitchcock begins to exploit his décor for dramatic effect we have come to accept its reality and the limitations which it imposes. We cannot, at this stage, see the décor as something which exists purely at the director's convenience in order to inhibit the camera and limit our access to the action.

Hitchcock's cunning makes him seem to be a victim of the situation at just the point where he is most completely its master. The scene has been moulded so that, whatever happens, we shall be able to see only *one* of the focal points of its drama: *either* the housekeeper and the chest *or* the heroes. If the camera were to move to show the heroes we would lose sight of the housekeeper; as long as its eye remains fixed on the housekeeper we are unable to see the heroes. Hitchcock's camera is obsessively concerned with the menace of the housekeeper's actions. It 'can't take its eyes off her'. But the same presentation, just as skilfully integrated, would seem ridiculous applied to an event of less gravity: if, for example, the chest was known to contain only the evidence of some minor indiscretion and not the corpse of a man who was son, nephew, pupil, best friend and fiancé of the various guests.

The emphasis provoked by Hitchcock's confined viewpoint is consonant with the dramatic import of the action it shows. This cannot be claimed for Wyler's glass silencer; the action here is not sufficiently 'charged' to bear the weight of meaning which the scale of the device asserts.

Emphasis depends on the establishment of a norm. In the fictional film the norm is given by the nature of the spectator's relationship to narrative. Our relationship to stories is that of an interested observer – the satisfaction they offer depends upon the extent to which they arouse concern. Once our interest in a story is aroused our drive is to discover *what happens*. So it is the structural information, the facts which indicate possibilities of development and resolution, that we grasp first and with most ease. When we have grasped the available structural information our perception of less specifically functional information increases.

With reference to this characteristic the film-maker establishes his norm, a base from which he can move in order to assign degrees of importance to objects and events within his world. While each film-maker establishes his own base, he does so by reference to a standard expectation. As 'interested observers' we expect the image to be the ideal record; freed from human contingencies, its attention is devoted to the matter of greatest moment for *us*.

Since the spectator expects the image to operate as a clear presentation of necessary facts, he is able to comprehend its other functions by sensing the import of deviations from the norm. The anticipation of relevant information in the image provokes close attention, in part at least because despite the 'perfection' of the record we can never be certain whether information which appears merely contingent may turn out to be structurally vital. When the amount of clearly relevant information is reduced, our attention may be directed towards a more intense scrutiny of the less extensive and less active images. We are provoked to assume an enhanced relevance in what we *do* see because it is given a special status in the film's world, an emphasis that implies heightened significance.

The degree of deviation from the norm indicates the scale of emphasis assigned by the film-maker. The less completely the image is committed to offering us information about developments in the film's world, the more it asserts its own significance either as a particularly revealing view of that world or as a presentation of a particular significant aspect.

The controlled viewpoint presupposes a continuous quest for the most revealing presentation of events. But it remains open to the film-maker to heighten or subdue our awareness of his control. We can be made more or less conscious that we are seeing the world through a particular 'eye'. That is why it is possible for the film-maker to establish emphasis from his own base and in his own way. For Otto Preminger[37]

the ideal picture is a picture where you don't notice the director, where you never are aware that the director did anything deliberately. Naturally he has to do everything deliberately — that is direction. But if I could ever manage to do a picture that is directed so simply that you would never be aware of a cut or a camera movement, that, I think, would be the real success of direction.

This 'real success' is unattainable, at least so far as the alert spectator is concerned. Ironically, one of the major pleasures of a Preminger movie is the grace and fluidity of his camera movements. But Preminger's ideal picture makes sense as an aspiration which reflects one attitude to the spectator and one type of viewpoint. Preminger uses means of emphasis which do not draw our attention to the image as an image but rely on arranging the action so that the scale of significance is established *there*. In *River of No Return* the symbolism is so completely absorbed into the action that it may easily pass unnoticed. When the heroine drops most of her belongings into the water as she is lifted from a raft grounded on the rapids, the camera does nothing to emphasize the meaning of the incident. It could be seen, at best, as a demonstration of the dangerous power of the current (her bag hurtles away downstream); at worst, it might look like mere padding designed to keep the action moving along for a few extra seconds. In either case a claim that the event has symbolic significance would seem an absurd and pretentious exercise in 'reading-in'.

Still, the claim is made. The loss of the bag is the first in a series of events which, in the course of her journey, strip the heroine of the physical tokens of her former way of life. This process parallels the character's moral development from fatalistic acceptance towards a degree of self-conscious decision. The two movements are united in the final shot of the movie: the heroine herself removes and throws away a pair of flashy red shoes, her last remaining item of 'uniform'.

The fact that the bag is lost to the rushing waters is itself significant. Contrasted attitudes to the river point up different attitudes of life; the heroine initially regards it as an irresistible force of nature, but to the hero it is a force which must be mastered, used and, when necessary, defied. The first time we see Robert Mitchum in relation to the river he is riding along the bank in the opposite direction to that of the current. But our first sight of Marilyn Monroe on the river shows her as its victim, swept along helplessly on a raft she cannot control.

Preminger reveals significance by a dramatic structuring of events which his camera seems only to follow – never to anticipate. Moreover, the image appears to attempt always to accommodate the entire field of action so that it is the spectator's interest which defines the area of concentration.

At the other end of the scale Hitchcock is prepared to indicate areas of concentration very forcibly. The chest-clearing scene from *Rope* impresses on us the fact that our view is partial and that the area of our concentration has been defined by the director. Hitchcock allows us no independent selection. Moreover, he is fully prepared to use a camera which anticipates the action. The shot which follows the heroine's plea for help in *Marnie* is a camera movement towards a door, the very deliberation of which predicts an event of crucial significance.

The distinction between these two approaches is necessarily one of degree. Hitchcock's ability to impose an area of interest is contingent upon that area's being or quite rapidly becoming as important to us as his treatment assumes. Preminger's open image imposes on us *his* sense of foreground and background; obviously a certain anticipation of events is inherent in the movement from sequence to sequence. While neither of these tendencies can be observed in a pure state, in Hitchcock the norm is a base for meaningful deviation while Preminger works by accumulation, enriching the basic structure by the addition of detail whose significance the spectator is free to observe or ignore. The contrast between their methods is further reflected in their narrative styles. Hitchcock tells stories as if he knows how they end, Preminger gives the impression of witnessing them as they unfold. Employed without skill, Preminger's method would be dull and unrevealing; Hitchcock's would be bombastic.

What matters to our judgement of the 'Hitchcock tendency' is not that an assertion of significance is made, but that we can feel it to be justified. Then the correlation of emphasis assigned with importance perceived maintains the authority of the image. It creates stress without strain by winning our acceptance of the given viewpoint.

The fictional world is not some inert matter to be galvanized into significance by the rhetorical manipulation of the movie's language. The trouble with Wyler's usage in *The Loudest Whisper* is that it places too great a reliance on the independent value of a technical device as a source of impact and meaning. We can claim that it 'uses the medium', but larger claims for a productive relationship of viewpoint and event can be advanced only when the film-maker maintains the correspondence between stylistic and dramatic weight.

In his own interest the film-maker must protect the channel through which his personal vision becomes communicable, the terms from which it derives its sense, strength and clarity. The more urgent his desire to communicate, the more persistently is he likely to be tempted to go beyond those terms in order to heighten meaning and impact. But when he disrupts his established discipline, in however worthy a cause, he is like a mason digging away his foundations to quarry stone for a steeple.

The hallmark of a great movie is not that it is without strains but that it absorbs its tensions; they escape notice until we project ourselves into the position of the artist and think through the problems which he confronted in his search for order and meaning. The more each element is not just compatible with, but an active contributor to, the network of significant relationships, the more value we can claim for the synthesis achieved [. . . .]

The great film approaches an intensity of cohesion such that its elements do not operate solely to maintain or further the reality of the fictional world, nor solely to decorative, affective or rhetorical effect. Of course this is a counsel of perfection, even though it is one derived from existing movies. *Exodus, Johnny Guitar, Letter from an Unknown Woman, Psycho, La Règle du jeu, Rio Bravo, Wild River*: these are among the films which I recall as approaching this condition most clearly. Yet each of them *does* contain actions and images whose sole function is to maintain the narrative. In most cases these moments are to be found during the initial exposition; in *Psycho*, notably and on account of its peculiar construction, they occur at the end. But these masterpieces allow us reasonably to hope for the next best thing to total cohesion: minimum (credible) redundancy. And they remind us that the minimum can be minute.

To hope for the fewest possible one-function elements in a film is not to demand that every element be of *equal* significance. There is a modulation of scale within each image just as there is throughout the whole movie. While we may expect each action to be relevant, only some will be climactic. One of the advantages of the narrative 'frame' is that the relevance of details to theme and viewpoint is a variable; it may occasionally be relaxed without threatening the overall coherence of the film.

Yet the movie that contains too much material serving only to maintain its reality pays the penalty of slackness and dullness, occasional or total. An even higher price is paid for unattached decoration, emotion or assertion: in vacuity, sentimentality or pretension. If I have said little in this chapter about such traditional failings – or about the traditional qualities like inventiveness, wit and economy – it is not because I think them unimportant. Rather, because they result from defects or achievements of balance and integration, and are most clearly defined in those terms. What, after all, is sentimentality if not a failure of emphasis, a disproportion between pathos asserted (in music, say, or image or gesture) and pathos achieved, in the action? What is pretension other than an unwarranted claim to significance, meaning insecurely attached to matter? And what inventiveness, but the ability to create the most telling relationships within the given material?

How can economy be defined unless by parity between energy expended and effect conveyed? 'Energy' itself is a matter of scale: a fast camera movement will *claim* most in a predominantly static movie; a big close-up will hit hardest in a picture mainly composed of more distant images. Consider again the *Psycho* slaughter. I have already talked of the concentration of imagery that Hitchcock's fragmented treatment allowed. It is equally valid to remark that without such concentration, the treatment would have fallen quite flat. If the emotional intensity of the scene's action *permits* extreme imagery, it is also largely a consequence of it. The correspondence between action, image, meaning and effect is so tight that each maintains the others. In theory, for example, Hitchcock could have given a more detached image at a number of points by moving the camera back through the open door of the bathroom. But the more distant view would have been quite inapposite to our experience of the action. The limitation of space was not entirely physical; it corresponded also to a psychological-emotional enclosure.

Hitchcock's achievement here represents as well as may be the achievement of any fine film-maker working at his peak. He does not let us know whether he is finding the style to suit his subject or has found the subject which allows him best exercise of his style. He builds towards situations in which the most eloquent use of his medium cannot emerge as bombast.

At the level of detail we can value most the moments when narrative, concept and emotion are most completely fused. Extended and shaped throughout the whole picture, such moments compose a unity between record, statement and experience. At this level too, sustained harmony and balance ensure that the view contained in the pattern of events may be enriched by the pattern of our involvement. When such unity is achieved, observation, thought and feeling are integrated: film becomes the projection of a mental universe – a mind recorder.

Synthesis here, where there is no distinction between how and what, content and form, is what interests us if we are interested in film as film. It is that unity to which we respond when film as fiction makes us sensitive to film as film (Perkins, 1972).

For Perkins, film is primarily an illusion, but it is essential that through the dextrous use of credibility, coherence and balance the film should appear to be a *truthful* illusion. As with Bazin, the film creates or re-creates an ideal world; but Perkins' originality is to involve the spectator crucially and explicitly in the process. Both films and spectators offer certain conventions; the play of credibility, coherence and balance of elements has to satisfy both parties. Realism is redefined as coherence; the internal truth of varying sets of conventions.

Is it possible, at this stage, to summarise these basic realist positions? The voices we have heard reflect differing film-making practices, differing critical practices. The only idea on which they seem to agree is that film should in some sense be truthful or tell the truth. If some notion of Truth lay at the centre of the realist system, the system could only lose its power – its force in people's minds – at the point where publics, critics and film-makers no longer require of films that at some crucial stage of their operation they appear to reflect or reflect on 'the Truth'. The answer to this problem, or rather the next stage of thinking about it, has to be an uneven one. It is clear that audiences for some kinds of films – for instance, the very various films frequently described as 'mass-entertainment', 'popular', 'commercial' or 'classic Hollywood', on the one hand, or specialist avant-garde films on the other – do not make a pronounced 'realist requirement' of their films. Not very much is known about the reasons for these abeyances, but it seems possible that the 'popular' audience comes to the cinema with quite different expectations from the earnest seeker after Truth – in other words, it never expected the damn things to be realistic in the first place – and that the avant-garde audience has learned through education to suspend belief. In this hypothesis, the popular audience might primarily be concerned with entertainment, pleasure, escapism (all terms which need to be stripped of the pejorative connotations theory, criticism and culture have allowed them to retain), the avant-garde one with self-cultivation (eminently acceptable, alas).

If we looked merely at this side of the question, we might decide that 'the realist moment' was past. But such a judgment would be mistaken, for two clear reasons. First, it is also clear that despite the kinds of abeyances described above, a sizeable part of the justifications advanced by theorists, critics, film-makers, intellectuals or moralists for all films, including Hollywood or avant-garde ones, continue to draw on realistic and/or truthful criteria. The maker of a fiction film wants his fiction to be perceived as 'real', however fantastic its parameters. Some avant-gardists believe their work to be real even if the film does not show a single human being or recognisable object – in their eyes it is *more real* precisely because it does not show these things. Second, we have also to take into account the wide range of films, principally forms of documentary and fiction films operating within primarily 'realistic' modes and styles, which do in fact seem to operate within the systems laid out by our realist voices. What else do these systems involve over and above the reference to the varying Truth? They involve the play of sets of (again varying) conventions; conventions which operate, as we have seen already, with the force of formal constraints. So it might be fair to say that after the philosophical appeal to Truth, aesthetic realism constructs itself out of certain usages of formal conventions.

On this question of convention, realism itself tends to have rather little to tell us. For obvious reasons: the 'pure', more naïve versions of realism are concerned either to deny conventions utterly or to fight them root and branch, to pretend that they do not exist or to deplore them. Thus, of the voices already heard, Grierson, Zavattini, Rossellini have little to tell us explicitly – though, for instance, Grierson's notions of 'capacity for getting around', 'original actor and scene', and 'materials and stories taken from the raw' can be turned around and usefully seen as themselves contributing to formal conventions.

But the others – Eisenstein, Vertov, Bazin, Rohmer, Perkins – in so far as they are aware of questions of style, do open up useful avenues of investigation. The rest of this book will be concerned with exploration of the conventional constraints which define realism(s) and its/their operation(s). They are all ideas which have been mentioned in the texts reprinted in this first section, but often not explicitly, and all require further elaboration. They are ideas about movement, about narrative and its organisation, about the authorship of films, about the relationships of film with more traditionally established forms of art, about entertainment, about manipulation and the role it plays in the construction of film works, about technology and techniques, and about ideology and its relations with film forms. With some of these ideas realism seems obliged to co-operate if it is to function as a system; others seem to contest realism.

Notes

1 In his *Laocoon* the German critic G. E. Lessing (1729-81) argued that artists should respect the specific limitations of the media they worked in, while exploring all the potentialities of those media. The visual arts he thought best suited to the representation of idealised human beauty in repose.

2 According to *The Oxford Companion to Film,* Kino-Eye is the 'term invented by Vertov to describe both his ideology of film and the group of film-makers who shared it'. This text obviously means to appeal to groups wider than Vertov's immediate collaborators, but I have not been able to discover whether such groups actually came into existence in the USSR.

3 A popular series of newsreels produced by Vertov's group between 1923 and 1925.

4 *Gosudarstvennoe Politicheskoe Upravlenie* (State Political Admini-stration) – the Soviet political police, which replaced the Cheka in 1922 and was reorganised in 1923 as OGPU, or Unified State Political Organisation.

5 Kinok = film eye.

6 The Pioneers is a children's organisation, the Komsomol (the Communist League of Youth, established in 1918) an organisation for young people aged fourteen and over.

7 NEP, the New Economic Policy, was introduced by Lenin in 1921 to conciliate the peasantry, encourage small-scale private industry and stabilise the economy:

> It began . . . as an agricultural policy to increase the supply of food by offering fresh inducements to the peasant; it developed into a com-mercial policy for the promotion of trade and exchange, involving a financial policy for a stable currency; and finally . . . it became an industrial policy to bring about that increase in industrial productivity which was a condition of the building up of a socialist order. . . . Everyone, once the first shock of surprise was over, accepted NEP as a necessity. But it was accepted by some willingly, by others with an uneasy conscience (E. H. Carr, *The Bolshevik Revolution 1917–1923,* Macmillan, 1952).

Vertov's 'lords and ladies' is a reference to those members of the business class whom the policy made 'respectable' again.

8 Films directed by Rossellini and referred to in this extract: *Il miracolo* (The miracle) is the second part of *L'amore* (Love, 1948), a two-part film celebrating the talents of the actress Anna Magnani; *La nave bianca* (The white ship, 1941) and *L'uomo dalla croce* (The man with the cross, 1943) both deal with wartime Italian heroism; *Francesco, giullare di Dio* (Francis, God's jester, 1950) is about St Francis of Assisi; *Roma, città aperta* (*Rome Open City,* 1945) and *Paisà* (1946) established Rossellini's international reputation; the powerful *Germania anno zero* (Germany year zero, 1947) was less well received; *Fantasia sottomarina*

(Underwater fantasy, 1939), *Il ruscello di Ripasottile* (The stream at Ripasottile, 1941) and *Prelude à l'après-midi d'un faune* (Prelude to the afternoon of a faun, 1938) are all early shorts; *Stromboli* (1949) is the director's first film with the actress Ingrid Bergman; *La macchina ammazzacattivi* (The machine for killing wicked people, 1948) is a fantasy about all kinds of confusion, which Rossellini abandoned before completing it.

9 Jansenism was a minority movement within the seventeenth-century Catholic church. The movement, eventually proscribed, was strongly opposed to Jesuit worldliness and sophistication, and believed a form of predestination. Some of its French adherents renounced careers in law, administration, the church and similar fields for a life of relative austerity and self-denial. In literature, Jansenism inspired aspects of the work of the philosopher Pascal and the playwright Racine (see Lucien Goldmann, *The Hidden God*, Routledge & Kegan Paul, 1964). Bazin uses the term Jansenist in a loose sense connoting austerity and self-denial.

10 *Mise en scène* means literally 'putting on the stage'; in a French theatre programme the normal credit for 'directed by –' would be '*mise en scène de –*'. It has been loosely adapted for use with reference to the cinema, to cover such areas as visual style, movement of camera and/or of actors, disposition of actors in relation to décor, uses of lighting and colour, etc., with the overall connotations of production-style, style or direction. In spite or perhaps because of its problematic nature it is still a living term.

11 Films directed by Wyler and referred to in this text: *The Best Years of our Lives* (1946), story of three war-veterans returning home which won several Oscars; *The Letter* (1940), sex-drama on a Malayan plantation; *Jezebel* (1938), ups and downs of a spoilt Southern belle; *The Little Foxes* (1941), adaptation of Lillian Hellman's stage play about financial intrigue in a Southern family (these three films all starred Bette Davis); *The Westerner* (1940), a classic Western starring Gary Cooper; *Mrs Miniver* (1942), melodrama about Britain in wartime; *Dodsworth* (1936), based on a novel by Sinclair Lewis.

12 French playwright (1876–1953), successful in 'Boulevard' or 'West End' styles.

13 André Berthomieu, French film director (1903–59), with a reputation for prolixity and commercialism. His most interesting film is said to be *La Femme idéale* (The ideal woman, 1934).

14 Kantor (1904–) is an American writer specialising in historical fiction. Commissioned by the producer Samuel Goldwyn to write a story about returning war-veterans, he submitted it in the form of a novel in blank verse titled *Glory for Me*. The novel was then adapted into film-script form by Robert Sherwood.

15 André Antoine (1858–1943) was a pioneer of naturalism in the French theatre. As director of the Théâtre Libre (1887–94), the Théâtre Antoine (1897–1906) and the Odéon (1906–14), he produced works by Ibsen, Strindberg, Hauptmann, Brieux and many others. He was influential in changing styles of acting and scenic design. Real trees seem to have

figured in several of his productions between 1902 and 1906; in 1888 he used real sides of meat in a play called *The Butchers*.

16 Louis Lumière (1864–1948), French inventor and pioneer realist film-maker, invented the cinematograph (1894) which led to the first public, commercial film-shows (1895). Etienne-Jules Marey (1830–1904), French scientist and inventor, developed the chronophotograph camera (1882), patented a camera using celluloid film (1890). Eadweard Muybridge (1830–1904), British-born photographer, invented the zoopraxinoscope, a primitive form of film projector.

17 The nearest general equivalent in English to the French term *découpage* is 'shooting-script'. However the term can also be used to mean either the division and structuring of a film story into scenes, sequences or episodes at the scriptwriting stage, or the subsequent breaking down of the scenes (at or before the stage of filming) into individual shots. It is in the last of these three senses that Bazin uses it here.

18 *La Règle du jeu* (The rules of the game, France, 1939), directed by Jean Renoir. Bazin's note:

Actually, in *La Règle du jeu* Renoir makes more use of simultaneous actions in the same shot than of deep-focus. But the intention and the effect are the same. It is a kind of lateral deep-focus.

Here one can point out a psychological paradox: deep-focussing the lens allows projection on the shot, of a uniformly sharp parallelepiped of reality. No doubt this sharpness at first appears to be that of reality: a chair is not fuzzy simply because we're not sitting on it; so it's right that it should stay in focus on the screen. But the actual event has three dimensions; it would be physiologically impossible for us to see with simultaneous sharpness the bottle of poison on Susan Alexander's night-table in close-up and the bedroom door right at the back of the perspective. In reality we would be obliged to change the focus of our crystalline lens as Henri Calef naïvely does in the scene at the municipal council in *Jericho*: so one could maintain that the realism of representation is on the same side as analytical découpage. But this would be to disregard the mental factor, more important here than the psychological factor of perception. In spite of the mobility of our attention, the event is perceived in a continuous manner.

Moreover, the accommodation of the eye and the resulting 'changes in focus' are so rapid as to be equivalent, by an unconscious adding-up, to the reconstruction of an integral mental image: a little like the illusion of continuity given by television due to the sweeping across the screen of the cathodic brush.

One can add that for the spectator in the cinema, continually focussing on the screen and thereby compulsorily and steadfastly perceiving the event in all its sharpness *without having the resources* to get away physiologically by looking at something nearer or something further off, the event is compulsorily made perceptible (its ontological unity before even its dramatic unity).

That is to say that the slight trickery implied in the uniformly sharp cinematographic image is not in opposition to realism, but that on the contrary it reinforces it, confirms it and is faithful to its essence of ambiguity. It concretises physically the metaphysical affirmation that all reality is *on the same level*. The slight physical effort of accommodation often masks, in perception, the mental operation which corresponds to it and which, alone, is important. In the cinema, on the contrary, as in the Quattrocento portraits where the landscape is as sharp as the face, the spirit cannot escape the purity of its act of choice, the reflexes are destroyed and the attention is returned to the responsibility of consciousness.

19 *Citizen Kane* (USA, 1941), directed by Orson Welles. See also Part IV, pp. 186–97.

20 Roger Leenhardt (1903–), French film producer, director and critic. Georges Neveux (1900–), French playwright and film script-writer.

21 *Antoine and Antoinette* (France, 1947), directed by Jacques Becker.

22 *The Magnificent Ambersons* (USA, 1942), directed by Orson Welles.

23 *The March of Time* was a monthly current affairs film magazine, produced by Louis de Rochemont between 1935 and 1951. It combined archive and stock material with newly shot actuality material and staged scenes with actors. In *Citizen Kane* it is parodied under the title *News on the March*.

24 Promulgated by Napoleon Bonaparte in 1804, the Civil Code set out in straightforward terms the legal rights and duties of the individual and the state in post-revolutionary France.

25 Roger Martin du Gard, French writer (1881–1958), best known for his panoramic series of novels *Les Thibault* (1922–36).

26 Oskar Fischinger (1900–67), German-born animator, best known for his abstract short films (1921–34) and later work in film and advertising in America.

27 André Lhote, French painter and art critic (1885–1962) influenced by cubism.

28 Polyphony was the dominant form of European music between about 1450 and 1600. Almost completely choral, its main interest lies in the harmonic relationships between the different vocal parts rather than in their individual contents.

29 Novels by Balzac referred to in this text: *Le Père Goriot* (*Old Goriot*, 1835); *Louis Lambert* (1832); *Séraphita* (1835). All form parts of his *Comédie Humaine* cycle.

30 Louis-Philippe I, King of France from 1830 to 1848.

31 Translations from *Le Père Goriot* are from the Penguin edition, translated by Marion Ayton Crawford.

32 *Eureka* (1848), a prose poem in which Edgar Allan Poe (1809–49) set out his theory of a harmoniously ordered universe in which science, literary criticism and ethics all played essential roles.

33 Films referred to in this text: *Le Blé en herbe* (*Ripening Seed*, France, 1954), directed by Claude Autant-Lara; *Umberto D* (Italy, 1952), dir.

Vittorio de Sica; *La Strada* (Italy, 1954), dir. Federico Fellini; *Tabu* (USA, 1931), dir. F. W. Murnau and Robert Flaherty; *A Star is Born* (USA, 1954), dir. George Cukor; *Viaggio in Italia* (Italy, 1953), dir. Rossellini; *Rear Window* (USA, 1954), dir. Hitchcock.

34 André Breton (1896–1966), leader of the French literary surrealists. Best known for the three Surrealist Manifestos of 1924, 1930 and 1942.

35 Nicolas Boileau-Despréaux (1636–1711), French poet and critic, whose *Art poétique* (1674) established the conventions and criteria of literary classicism for the next sixty years.

36 Films referred to in this text: *One Million Years B.C.* (GB, 1966), directed by Don Chaffey; *2001* (GB, 1968), dir. Stanley Kubrick; *The Birds* (USA, 1963), dir. Alfred Hitchcock; *Johnny Guitar* (USA, 1954), dir. Nicholas Ray; *The Pirate* (USA, 1948), dir. Vincente Minnelli; *The Wizard of Oz* (USA, 1940), dir. Victor Fleming; *Moulin Rouge* (GB, 1952), dir. John Huston; *Rope* (USA, 1948), dir. Hitchcock; *The Loudest Whisper* (US title, *The Children's Hour*, USA, 1962), dir. Wyler; *River of No Return* (USA, 1954), dir. Otto Preminger; *Marnie* (USA, 1964), dir. Hitchcock; *Exodus* (USA, 1960), dir. Preminger; *Letter from an Unknown Woman* (USA, 1948), dir. Max Ophuls; *Psycho* (USA, 1960), dir. Hitchcock; *Rio Bravo* (USA, 1959), dir. Howard Hawks; *Wild River* (USA, 1960), dir. Elia Kazan.

37 *Movie*, no. 4, 1962.

Part II
Descriptions of the work of a realist film-maker
Robert Flaherty

ROBERT FLAHERTY (1884–1951) is a film-maker who has been described as a poet and as a story-teller. Both of these categories are important for the notion of realism in general, though 'poetry' is a term that has been used with great imprecision. In writing about film it is often linked with 'movement': another term which is difficult to define. Grierson on Flaherty's sense of movement:

Before Flaherty went off to the Aran Islands to make his *Man of Aran*,[1] I had him up in the Black Country doing work for the E.M.B. [Empire Marketing Board]. He passed from pottery to glass, and from glass to steel, making short studies of English workmen. I saw the material a hundred times, and by all the laws of repetition should have been bored with it. But there is this same quality of great craftsmanship in it which makes one see it always with a certain new surprise. A man is making a pot, say. Your ordinary director will describe it; your good director will describe it well. He may even, if good enough, pick out those details of expression and of hands which bring character to the man and beauty to the work. But what will you say if the director beats the potter to his own movements, anticipating each puckering of the brows, each extended gesture of the hands in contemplation, and moves his camera about as though it were the mind and spirit of the man himself? I cannot tell you how it is done, nor could Flaherty. As always in art, to feeling which is fine enough and craft which is practiced enough, these strange other world abilities are added (Grierson, 1932).

Frances Hubbard Flaherty also evokes potters:

That life is movement we all know. But we can see how deeply this is so in a beautiful film[2] which shows us under the microscope the rhythmic

89

flow, the measured movement, in protoplasm, the primordial stuff of which we are all made. When this movement stops, the measure that measures it still goes on unbroken, and when movement begins again, we see it come in, like music, on the beat. The beauty of this film is its simple and profound approach to this rhythmic mystery, taking us on the one hand into physics and chemistry, and on the other into the realm of philosophy, religion, poetry. Leonardo da Vinci says, 'Where there is warmth there is life, and where there is life there is the movement of love.' The movement of love, the mysterious rhythm of life – this is the life of film. Take, for instance, the hands of the potter as he molds the clay. The motion-picture camera can follow these movements closely, intimately, so intimately that as with our eyes we follow, we come to feel those movements as a sensation in ourselves. Momentarily we touch and know the very heart and mind of the potter; we partake, as it were, of his life, we are one with him. Here, through those nuances of movement we found in *Moana*,[3] we come again to that 'participation mystique' we found in *Nanook*. Here is the 'way' of the camera, of this machine: through its sensitivity to movement it can take us into a new dimension of seeing, through the mysterious rhythmic impulses of life and love take us inward into the spirit, into the unity of the spirit.

Robert Flaherty let the camera see everything, avid as a child, filled with a childlike wonder. His pet word was 'marvellous'. Everything was marvellous, and his enthusiasm was equalled only by his patience. Patient as a scientist, he let the camera see everything exhaustively, and then, you remember, he brought all this to the screen, and screened and screened it, and went out and shot again, for one reason only: to give the camera a chance to find that 'moment of truth,' that flash of perception, that penetration into the heart of the matter, which he knew the camera, left to itself, *could* find. The point in this process was that it was purely visual. Words played no part in it; it went beyond words. It was simply a degree of seeing. As ice turns to water and water to steam, and a degree of temperature becomes a transformation, so a degree of seeing may become a transformation (Flaherty, 1960).

It seems clear that realist film-making, in its most naïvely advanced forms, implies a kind of mysticism. An osmosis is believed to take place between the spectator and the material shown. The intermediaries in this process are the camera (on the spectator's side) and the movement-in-the-material (on the material's side), with emotion acting as another link. At extreme points the process is believed to transcend linguistic constraints. This notion of the possibility of a 'purely visual' perception is still common, particularly in milieux where film is considered to have most in common with traditional or modern arts like painting and photography. To achieve some escape from the mysticism of this vision it may be useful to consider Helen van Dongen's account of the editing of the first sequence of Flaherty's film *Louisiana Story*:[4]

For *Louisiana Story* we did not have a shooting script indicating what individual scenes to shoot or where to place them in the final story. Instead we had a visually and cinematically written script, the main aim being that the story be readable. For instance Flaherty wrote the opening sequence as follows:

'We are deep in the Bayou Country of Lower Louisiana. It is the high-water time of the year – the country is half drowned. We move through a forest of bearded trees. There are wild fowl everywhere, in flight and swimming on the water. We are spellbound by all this wild life and the mystery of the wilderness that lies ahead . . .'

To cover this sequence an enormous amount of miscellaneous material was shot, not only when going out to make shots for this specific sequence, but all during the shooting period, whenever something was sighted that might eventually be used to express the atmosphere and geography of the country. (200,000 ft. of material were shot for the film which was in the end 8,000 ft. long.) Almost anything could cover this theme and almost anything was actually shot. Like everything living in the swamp, our images grew abundantly. We had scenes of alligators sitting on their nests, slithering through the water, basking in the sun or rearing their ugly heads from a mud-patch in the swamp-forest; strange and magnificent birds perched on tree-tops or sitting on branches sticking out of the lily-pond; snakes sliding up trees, lotus-leaves reflected in the clear water, dewdrops on the leaves, little flies skimming the water, a spider spinning its web, spanish moss dangling from huge oak trees, fishes, rabbits, fawns or skunks, and others too numerous to mention.

Such a great quantity and variety of material, all temporarily filed under the heading 'scenes for introduction' – all of it covering the theme 'atmosphere of the swamp and forest' – of course presents its own difficulties in editing. At the first screening all this material looks incoherent. Where, in this welter, is the main theme that must be developed?

The editor had no precise shooting script to follow which told him:

'We open with a close-up of a lotus-leaf silhouetted against the water, followed by a shot of an alligator climbing upon a raft . . .' Instead, there was only a general description of the locale and of the atmosphere the feeling which should be expressed ('We are spellbound by all the wild life and the mystery of the wilderness which lies ahead . . .').

The editor has to discover and disclose the director's design and use as further guides:

1. the indication that he has to portray a mysterious wilderness as yet untouched by civilisation;

2. that he has to portray this in a lyrical mood to conform to the style and balance of rhythm in the rest of the film and that this wilderness has to be seen through the magic eyes of a twelve-year-old boy (the editor has to watch that this particular sequence does not unfold like an epic or become a glorified travelogue);

3. though each shot already possesses the inherent qualities of the mysterious wilderness, each shot in itself is still neutral in content and remains so until it is brought into proper relationship to another shot — when it will at once become alive and acquire a deeper meaning;

4. last but not least: the screening and discussions with the director.

The dominant factor in the selection and continuity of the scenes should be their emotional content, their inner meaning. Once the desired feeling and atmosphere are conveyed throughout the sequence and the balance and unity have been achieved between form and content, the metric and rhythmic values will take care of themselves.

Here is how the opening sequence looked, when finished:

LOUISIANA STORY

The opening sequence
The film is 'an account of certain adventures of a Cajun (Acadian) boy who lives in the marshlands of Petit Anse Bayou in Louisiana.'

Feet

1   After a *very slow fade in*   *Music begins.*   13
    (eight feet) during which
    the *camera pans upwards*
    slowly we open on an
    enormous lotus-leaf undu-
    lating slowly. The leaf
    itself and some mud-
    patches form black reflec-
    tions in the water-surface

Ft

in which also bright white
clouds are reflected. Tiny
bugs skim over the water-
surface.

2   *L.S.*[5] Black, silhouette-like   11
form of an alligator swim-
ming very slowly. Again
clear white clouds are
reflected in the water.

3   The surface of the water   8
with reflections of several
lotus-leaves and branches
with a bird on it. *Camera
pans upward,* revealing
what we have seen before
in the reflections.

4   The surface of the lily-   12
pond, lotus-leaves here
and there in the water. An
alligator crawls slowly on
a cypress-log.

5   *C.U.* Lotus-leaf, the   3
shadow of unseen
branches on it. In the
foreground of the leaf:
dewdrops.

6   *C.U.* Dewdrops on the   3
lotus-leaf.

7   *M.L.S.* Magnificent bird,   8
perched on the branch of
a tree.

8   *L.S.* of the forest in the   72
swamp. The trunks of
trees are standing in the
dark water, silvery
spanish moss dangles
from the branches. *(Shot
from a floating raft*

Ft

*which moved slowly
along, while the camera
itself pans very slowly in
the opposite direction,
thus creating an almost
three-dimensional effect.)*
After approximately 25 feet
we discover from very far
behind the trees a little boy
paddling his pirogue. He
disappears and reappears
again far behind the enormous trees in the foreground.

9   Forest, low-hanging spanish   17
     moss in the foreground.
     Camera moves farther in
     through the moss, as if
     passing through a
     Japanese screen.

10   *C.U.* Swirl in the water-   6
     surface caused by the boy's
     paddle *off-screen.*

11   *M.C.S.* Boy in his canoe,   *Commentator:*   41
     back to camera. He is pro- His name is Alexander –
     ceeding cautiously, stop-   Napoleon – Ulysses –
     ping at times, looking   Latour.
     around.

                                   Mermaids – their hair is
                                   green he says – swim up
                                   these waters from the
                                   sea. He's seen their
                                   bubbles – often.

12   *C.U.* Bubbles coming up   10
     to the surface, disturbing
     the tiny little leaves.

13   The boy bends low to pass   And werewolves, with   15
     underneath the low-   long noses and big red
     hanging spanish moss. He   eyes,
     paddles away from camera.

Ft

14 Forest. The boy is very small in the midst of the huge oak-trees. He paddles forward *towards camera.* come to dance on moonless nights. 12

15 The boy now closer, paddling from right to left and *out of frame.* 13

16 Some trees, surrounded by water. The sunlight here penetrates the forest and reflects in the water. The slight movement of the water projects the sunlight in turn against the trees. 6

17 The water surface and overhanging branches, reflected in the sunlight. 5

18 A fish gliding along just below the surface of the water. 4

19 *M.S.* Boy in his canoe, bending very low to pass underneath the spanish moss and moving aside an enormous lotus-leaf. 15

20 *C.U.* Alligator slowly raising his head. 9

21 *M.S.* Boy, holding the canoe with his paddle. He looks around but does not see the alligator *off-screen.* 13

22 The dark surface of the swamp-water. Nothing is visible but some reflections of tree-trunks. 5

23 *M.L.S.* Boy, partly hidden by the branches, moving away. 9

24	*L.S.* Boy in his pirogue, travelling slowly *away from camera.*		7
25	*C.U.* Snake wriggling along on the water-surface, *away from camera.*		7
26	*M.S.* Boy in pirogue, *facing camera.* He looks around, listens and touches the little salt-bag at his waist.	Music stops. *Commentator:* He'd never dream of being without this little bag of salt at his waist,	13
27	*C.U.* Bubbles coming up, disturbing the water-surface.		5
28	*As in 26.* Boy looks inside his shirt.	and the little something he carries inside his shirt.	37
29	The boy smiles and starts paddling *towards camera.*	*Music starts with a new theme: the 'boy's theme.'*	33
30	*C.S.* Racoon on a tree.	*Music louder.*	

The sequence is the slow beginning of a tale, a lyrical introduction to the beauties of the bayou-country and the mysteries of the swamp which lie ahead. Robert Flaherty's approach is a poetic, lingering one, admiring one object, then looking around and beyond it. Our surroundings are undisturbed by the hum-drum of civilisation and the editing is kept in harmony with these surroundings, free from the agitation of quickly changing scenes or intercuts.

Look for instance as a specific example at scene 8. For seventy feet, in one continuous shot, we glide through the swamp-water, discover the boy and follow him from far. Had this long scene been intercut with other detailed scenery, however beautiful, the feeling of complete tranquillity, the mystery and poetic atmosphere inherent in the image itself, would have been destroyed.

The introduction sets the pattern at the start with images of details. A leaf, strange and beautiful in form, a bird we do not see in our everyday life, the shadows of feathery branches, the silhouette of an alligator, a dewdrop glistening in the sunshine – together they form a pictorial narrative and indicate a strange and mysterious country. Only *after* we have seen these details is it revealed that we are in a forest, itself mysterious, for it is in the midst of a swamp. The huge oak trees have beards of silvery spanish moss hanging low. And then, almost unnoticed at first, we discover afar a human form, a little boy paddling his canoe through the silent waters.

This boy comes to us imbued with the mystery of the birds or the lotus-flower. We do not find it strange that his name is Alexander–Napoleon–Ulysses–Latour, for it is in keeping with grandiose and imposing surroundings. When we bend low with him, to pass underneath the spanish moss – as if parting a Japanese curtain – we penetrate farther into a fairyland and we accept readily that he believes in mermaids and carries charms to defend himself against werewolves and other unseen enemies of his imaginary world.

This ready conception and complete absorption of atmosphere is the result of the juxtaposition of shots. Had we, for instance, opened the sequence with the long continuous scene of the bearded forest (as an *orientation* scene of the locale in which the tale was set) we would have no preparation to understand and appreciate its charms and mysteries. The scene in that case would have represented nothing but a forest with a boy paddling through it. Had the details followed this scene they would have been mere images along the boy's course through the forest. In the continuity which we follow in the film we are emotionally prepared to appreciate the qualities of the forest. The preceding details, their mysterious quality and beauty, have awakened our curiosity and induce us to follow the boy eagerly and participate in his discoveries.

The choice of these scenes and their continuity was not decided upon *a priori*. Within the scope of the concept of the sequence their selection and continuity was determined by several factors:

1. *the subject-matter of each scene*;
2. *the spatial movement* of each image, which is not a dominant but operates alongside other factors. It is secondary in importance but cannot be ignored;
3. *the tonal value*. By this I mean the colour of a scene, its nuances within the range of black and white. In combination with other factors this colour can set or sustain an atmosphere. (For instance: a brilliant shot can represent simply the middle of the day, or it could represent a happy day. Brilliant combined with silvery reflections can create a magical atmosphere. Grey could be simply approaching night or a cloudy day with approaching rain. Grey could also be used emotionally to warn of impending disaster);

4. *the emotional content* which is the important and dominant factor.

It is important to remember that all of these factors have to be seen, judged and used *in conjunction* with each other, for it is the *collective* estimate of all these elements, of all these appeals which eventually will result in a successful juxtaposition of scenes.

To show the relative importance of each factor and the complexity of reasoning between each scene, let us analyse for example the first two scenes of the introduction. Paying attention for the moment *only* to *spatial movement*:

After a very slow fade in (eight feet) during which the camera panned upward slowly, the scene opens up on an enormous lotus leaf undulating lazily. Behind the leaf there is an almost imperceptible motion in the water caused by little bugs skimming the surface. In scene 2 we see an alligator swim slowly, making lazy ripples in the water-surface.

Analysing *only the movements* in both scenes we find that the upward slow pan of the camera in the first scene coincides with the slow movement of the undulating leaf, which in turn is in accordance with the lazy movements of the alligator in shot 2. An almost imperceptible sense of *direction* is created because in the first shot the leaf itself cups slightly towards the right and also bends over in the same direction, which is also the direction in which the alligator is swimming. The slight rippling in the water in shot 1 is continued in shot 2.

Bringing the *mechanical* continuity so much to the foreground without mentioning the other factors gives it a significance out of all proportion. Actually these movements may be hardly noticeable in the film; nevertheless they are part of the general appeal of the continuity of these two shots and they are part of the atmosphere and emotional content.

Examining the *tonal value*, we find that both shots have that silhouette-like quality, brilliant white in the reflected clouds, deep black in the reflected mud-patches. In one scene we have the black reflection of the lotus leaf, in the next the black form of the alligator. Both scenes indicate a brilliant, sunny day in beautiful surroundings. By itself this would mean nothing were it not so intimately connected with the other factors.

The *emotional content* in turn is a composite impression created through the subject-matter, the photographic quality and composition within the frame, the slow and lazy movements, the brilliant sunlight, the reflections and silhouette-like atmosphere. Each shot *by itself* records no more than a fixed event, fact or movement, and has a limited association. It is only when read in their present juxtaposition that these single associations, now combined, form a new concept. All these factors create a feeling of unreality. These two shots together indicate the indolence of the sub-tropics with the aura of mystery and magic which will be developed in the following scenes.

Let us go back a little to the breakdown of factors which led to the continuity of the first two scenes. Before any assembly is done, these two scenes might find themselves at widely separated places within the reels the editor is working with. The final continuity is the result of a long period of shifting scenes, now in one combination, then in another, until first some, then more, impose their own combination upon you. When in their right combination the scenes start speaking. The closer one comes to the final correct continuity the more the editor is able to read his scenes. Once the final continuity is reached one can read or analyse step by step all the factors which caused two or more images to demand to be in a certain continuity. The other way around seems to me to be impossible – unless everything, from the very first conception of the idea, is calculated beforehand (van Dongen, 1953).

This account is useful because it provides indications of the conventions used to guide spectators through a 'poetic-realist' film like *Louisiana Story*. Perhaps most important is the insistence on naturalness. However fantastic the qualities of the material, the spectator must be led to view it as natural, and the technical possibilities of the editing process are deployed to that end. It thus seems correct to say that in so far as editing is seen as a realistic device, it involves film and spectator alike in a process of naturalisation. This naturalisation is also, on the technical level, seen as the 'correct' way of putting the film together. It is also interesting to see that van Dongen draws most of her ideas about the role of editing from Eisenstein. On one level this might seem to be contradictory, since many of Eisenstein's ideas have been anathema to explicitly realist film-makers since about 1940. Van Dongen's borrowings from Eisenstein in fact reflect the view, widespread until at least 1950, that the 'recording' functions of film are menial and uninspiring although inevitable, and that it was only through the specific addition of editing that film could become artistic. Her text shows that such a position can easily be made compatible with the realist, documentary, or poetic outlooks.

Naturalisation does not exclude the telling of stories. Grierson again:

Question of theory and practice apart, Flaherty illustrates better than anyone the first principles of documentary. (1) It must master its material on the spot, and come in intimacy to ordering it. Flaherty digs himself in for a year, or two maybe. He lives with his people till the story is told 'out of himself'. (2) It must follow him in his distinction between description and drama. I think we shall find that there are other forms of drama or, more accurately, other forms of film, than the one he chooses; but it is important to make the primary distinction between a method which describes only the surface value of a subject, and the method which more explosively reveals the reality of it. You photograph the natural life, but you also, by your juxtaposition of detail, create an interpretation of it.

This final creative intention established, several methods are possible. You may, like Flaherty, go for a story form, passing in the ancient manner from the individual to the environment, to the environment transcended or not transcended, to the consequent honours of heroism. Or you may not be so interested in the individual. You may think that the individual life is no longer capable of cross-sectioning reality. You may believe that its particular belly-aches are of no consequence in a world which complex and impersonal forces command, and conclude that the individual as a self-sufficient dramatic figure is outmoded. When Flaherty tells you that it is a devilish noble thing to fight for food in a wilderness, you may, with some justice, observe that you are more concerned with the problem of people fighting for food in the midst of plenty. When he draws your attention to the fact that Nanook's spear is grave in its upheld angle, and finely rigid in its down-pointing bravery, you may, with some justice, observe that no spear, held however bravely by the individual, will master the crazy walrus of international finance. Indeed you may feel that in individualism is a yahoo tradition largely responsible for our present anarchy, and deny at once both the hero of decent heroics (Flaherty) and the hero of indecent ones (studio). In this case, you will feel that you want your drama in terms of some cross-section of reality which will reveal the essentially co-operative or mass nature of society: leaving the individual to find his honours in the swoop of creative social forces. In other words, you are liable to abandon the story form, and seek, like the modern exponent of poetry and painting and prose, a matter and method more satisfactory to the mind and spirit of the time (Grierson, 1932).

Description, for Grierson, means something like naturalism, a kind of wallowing in the surface of appearances. This is to be rejected because it is likely to lead only to aestheticism. Meaning, on the other hand, comes with the shaping of a narrative. But Grierson finds Flaherty's narratives too traditional, in that they are concerned with the problems of individuals. He wants a social aesthetic, one which represents the problems of masses of people in general.

Siegfried Kracauer attempts a description of the way Flaherty's narratives work:

The term 'slight narrative' originates with Rotha,[6] who says of Flaherty that 'he prefers the inclusion of a slight narrative, not fictional incident or interpolated "cameos," but the daily routine of his native people.' Rotha's observation amplifies part of a summary key statement by Flaherty himself: 'A story must come out of the life of a people, not from the actions of individuals.' Out of the life of a primitive people, Flaherty should have added, in order to present to the full the formula underlying his major films. This formula was of a piece with his passions and visions. Besides enabling him to satisfy his explorer instincts, it was rooted in his Rousseauan conviction that primitive cultures are the last vestiges of unspoiled human nature and in his sustained desire to show 'the former majesty and the character of these people, while it is still possible.'

Flaherty has been called a romantic and indicted for escapist leanings, because of his withdrawal from our modern world, with its pressing needs. To be sure, he *was* the rhapsodist of backward areas in a sense, but this does not impinge on the integrity of his films. Their inherent romanticism notwithstanding, they are cinematic documents of the highest order. Hence the general significance of Flaherty's formula. Now what matters here is exclusively his conception of a cinematic story, as defined in his programmatic statement quoted just above. This statement carries four important implications.

First, in immediately raising the issue of the story, Flaherty seems to take it for granted that a story is desirable for documentary. His own work bears witness to this belief; there is practically no Flaherty film that would lack structured sequences in the nature of an empathic narrative. Moreover, his films show an increasing tendency toward distinct story patterns. While *Nanook* still confines itself to a thoroughly coherent and understanding representation of the Eskimo way of life, *Louisiana Story* narrates the encounter between a Cajun boy and an oil derrick in terms which almost transcend Flaherty's program; one further step in this direction and the documentary would turn into an outright story film.

Second, a story must come out of the life of a people, says Flaherty, whereby it is understood that he means primitive people. Now primitive life unfolds in a natural setting and plays up bodily movements as well as events close to nature; in other words, one of its relevant features is its affinity for photography. Accordingly, if this part of Flaherty's statement is extended, it can be applied to stories which cover human reality as it manifests itself significantly in the physical world. So the narrative may not only grow out of primitive people but take its cue from crowds, street scenes, and what not.

Third, the story must not come from the actions of individuals. That this was tremendously important to Flaherty is corroborated by a biographical fact. Even though he was known to be 'one of the greatest yarn-spinners of our times,' he never displayed his brilliant gifts as a story-teller on the screen. His refusal to yield to this temptation, if temptation it was, is completely incomprehensible unless one assumes that he believes individual actions to be inconsistent with the spirit of his medium. Generally speaking, he shunned the full-fledged intrigue which traditionally features the individual. As a film-maker he certainly felt the need for a story, but he seems to have been afraid lest fully developed, rounded-out stories, which often have very pronounced patterns of meanings, prevent the camera from having its say. This helps explain why he preferred the 'slight narrative,' which sticks to the typical.

Fourth, the deliberate use of the verb 'come out' in Flaherty's statement testifies to his insistence on eliciting the story from the raw material of life rather than subjecting the raw material to its pre-established demands. 'There is a kernel of greatness in all peoples,' says he, 'and it is up to the film maker to . . . find the one incident or even the one movement that makes it clear.' His idea of 'discovering the *essential human story from within*' led him to evolve it during an incubation period in which he assimilated the life of the people he wanted to picture. And he was so averse to letting story requirements interfere with the experiences thus gathered and with his concurrent camera explorations that, in shooting the story, he used a working outline which could always be changed as he proceeded. It is as if the medium itself invited this kind of approach: in any case, Flaherty is not the only one to rely on improvisation in immediate contact with the material. When shooting *The Birth of a Nation*,[7] D. W. Griffith 'improvised freely as he went along'; by the way, Lewis Jacobs who mentions this adds that Griffith's confidence in his intuition also accounts for many an absurdity in his films. Similarly, the Rossellini of

[*Rome*] *Open City, Paisà* and *Germany Year Zero* develops his scenes on locale, with only a rudimentary story serving him as a guide. Nor does Fellini want to be incommoded by a well-written story: 'If I know everything from the start, I would no longer be interested in doing it. So that when I begin a picture, I am not yet sure of the location or the actors. Because for me, to do a picture is like leaving for a trip. And the most interesting part of a trip is what you discover on the way.' And did not Eisenstein undergo a change of mind when he saw the Odessa steps?[8]

If put into words, Flaherty's 'slight narrative' would be something like an interpretative account bordering on poetry. The unavoidable consequence of his solution is that it does not involve the audience as intensely as might a more outspoken story film. To the extent that his films evade the individual, the individual may not feel urged to surrender to them (Kracauer, 1960).

We have to balance Kracauer's belief that Flaherty is not interested in stories, and particularly not in individual stories, with the contrary assertion from Grierson and the clear evidence from van Dongen that the beginning of *Louisiana Story* is constructed, precisely, as the beginning of a story. Kracauer's account is not very helpful in that it draws principally on the overt subject-matter of Flaherty's films and very little on their stylistic procedures, ending with one of the many imprecise references to 'poetry' which we noted at the beginning of this section. Little progress has in fact been made with description or analysis of film narratives, though the growth of formal work inspired by film semiotics since the mid-1960s opens possibilities in this direction, and a different version of the same interest may be discerned in critics like Perkins (pp. 69–79). We should also note Kracauer's suggestion that the involvement of the individual spectator is more likely to be aroused by a film-narrative about an individual – or, to use the emotional language in which this topic is often evoked – he may 'surrender' to it.

As part of a ferocious, and practically unsuccessful if theoretically interesting, attempt to synthesise his own position with elements drawn from Flaherty and the Russian cinema of the 1920s, Grierson returns to the issue of Flaherty's procedures:

It is, I know only too well, difficult to be sure of one's attitudes in a decade like this. Can we heroicize our men when we know them to be exploited? Can we romanticize our industrial scene when we know that our men work brutally and starve ignobly in it? Can we praise it — and in art there must be praise — when the most blatant fact of our time is the bankruptcy of our national management? Our confidence is sapped, our beliefs are troubled, our eye for beauty is most plainly disturbed: and the more so in cinema than in any other art. For we have to build on the actual. Our capital comes from those whose only interest is in the actual. The medium itself insists on the actual. There we must build or be damned.

Flaherty's most considerable contribution to the problem is, as always, his insistence on the beauty of the natural. It is not everything, for it does not in the last resort isolate and define the purposes which must, consciously or unconsciously, inform our craftsmanship. But it does ensure that the raw material from which we work is the raw material most proper to the screen. The camera-eye is in effect a magical instrument. It can see a thousand things in a thousand places at different times, and the cunning cutter can string them together for a review of the world. Or he can piece them together — a more difficult task — for a review of a subject or situation more intricate and more intimate than any mortal eye can hope to match. But its magic is even more than this. It lies also in the manner of its observation, in the strange innocence with which, in a mind-tangled world, it sees things for what they are. This is not simply to say that the camera, on its single observations, is free from the trammels of the subjective, for it is patent that it will not follow the director in his enthusiasms any more than it will follow him in the wide-angled vision of his eyes. The magical fact of the camera is that it picks out what the director does not see at all, that it gives emphasis where he did not think emphasis existed.

The camera is in a measure both the discoverer of an unknown world and the re-discoverer of a lost one. There are, as everyone knows, strange moments of beauty that leap out of most ordinary news reels. It may be some accidental pose of character or some spontaneous gesture which radiates simply because it is spontaneous. It may be some high angle of a ship, or a crane, or a chimney stack, or a statue, adding some element of the heroic by a new-found emphasis. It may be some mere fore-shortening of a bollard and a rope that ties a ship to a quay in spirit as well as in fact. It may be the flap of a hatch cover which translates a gale. It may be the bright revelation of rhythms that time has worn smooth: the hand movement of a potter, the wrist movement of a native priest, or the muscle play of a dancer or a boxer or a runner. All of them seem to achieve a special virtue in the oblong of the screen.

So much Flaherty has taught us all. If we add to it such instruction as we have taken from Griffith and the Russians, of how to mass movement and create suspense, of how to keep an eye open for attendant circumstance and subconscious effect, we have in sum a most formidable equipment as craftsmen. But the major problem remains, the problem I have mentioned, the problem the critics do not worry their heads over, though creators must: what final honours and final dishonours we shall reveal in this English life of ours: what heroism we shall set against what villainy. The field of cinema is not only a field for creators but also for prophets.

The method followed by Flaherty in his own film-making might give us a most valuable lead. He took a year to make his study of the Eskimos and this after ten years' exploration in the Eskimo country of Labrador and Baffin Land. He took two years to make his study of Samoan life, and only now, after three more years in the South Seas, feels he could do justice to it. He soaked himself in his material, lived with it to the point of intimacy and beyond that to the point of belief, before he gave it form. This is a long method, and may be an expensive one: and it is altogether alien in a cinema world which insists on forcing a pre-conceived shape (one of half a dozen rubber-stamped dramatic shapes) on all material together. Its chief claim to our regard, however, is that it is necessary, and particularly necessary in England. We know our England glibly as an industrial country, as a beautiful country of this epic quality and that; we know it by rote as a maker of Empire and as a manipulator of world-wide services. But we do not know it in our everyday observation as such. Our literature is divorced from the actual: it is written as often as not in the south of France. Our culture is divorced from the actual: it is practised almost exclusively in the rarefied atmosphere of country colleges and country retreats. Our gentlemen explore the native haunts and investigate the native customs of Tanganyika and Timbuctoo, but do not travel dangerously into the jungles of Middlesbrough and the Clyde. Their hunger for English reality is satisfied briefly and sentimentally over a country hedge.

We might make an English cinema, as we might make English art again, if we could only send our creators back to fact. Not only to the old fact of the countryside which our poets have already honoured, but to the new fact of industry and commerce and plenty and poverty which no poet has honoured at all. Every week I hear men ask for films of industry. They want it praised and proclaimed to the world, and I would like to see their money used and their purposes fulfilled. But what advice can I give them? We can produce them the usual slick rubbish, some slicker, some less slick; but who of us knows an industry well enough to bring it alive for what it is? And what statescraft is willing to send a creator into an industry, so to know it: for a year, for two years perhaps, for the length of a hundred thousand feet of film and possibly more. Our businessmen expect a work of art to schedule, as the housewife expects her daily groceries. They expect it of a new medium. They expect it from raw material which they in their own hearts despise.

Flaherty, as an individual artist, cannot answer the whole problem. He knows his primitives and will do a job for them out of the strength of his affection. He could do a job for English craftsmanship and for the tradition of quality in English work, and for the native solidity in English institutions, and English criticism and character; but he is of a persuasion that does not easily come to grips with the more modern factors of civilization. In his heart he prefers a sailing barge to a snub-nosed funnel-after, and a scythe to a mechanical reaper. He will say that there is well-being associated with the first and none with the second, and in a manner he is right: right in his emphasis on well-being. But how otherwise than by coming to industry, even as it is, and forcing beauty from it, and bringing people to see beauty in it, can one, in turn, inspire man to create and find well-being? For this surely is the secret of our particular well-being, that men must accept the environment in which they live, with its smoke and its steel and its mechanical aids, even with its rain. It may not be so easily pleasant as the halcyon environment of Tahiti, but this is beside the point.

I think in this other matter one may turn to the Russians for guidance rather than to Flaherty. Their problem, of course, is different from ours. The industrial backwardness of the country, the illiteracy of their people, and the special factors of Russian psychology make for a rhetoric in their cinema which we cannot blindly imitate. Apart from this national difference, which is in effect their *style*, there is an ardour of experiment in their treatment of industrial and social material. They have built up rhythms for their machinery; they have made their work exciting and noble. They have made society on the move the subject-matter of art. Their sense of rhythm is not necessarily our sense of rhythm. Their sense of nobility and sense of social direction need not be identical with ours. The essential point, however, is that they have built up this rhythm and nobility and purpose of theirs by facing up to the new material. They have done it out of the necessity of their social situation. No one will say that our own necessity is less than theirs (Grierson, 1931).

Notes

1 *Man of Aran* (GB, 1933)
2 *Seifriz on Protoplasm* (USA, 1955), by William Seifriz and J. M. B. Churchill, Jr.
3 Films directed by Flaherty referred to in this extract: *Moana* (USA, 1924); *Nanook of the North* (USA, 1922).
4 *Louisiana Story* (USA, 1948).
5 Technical abbreviations used in this description of the sequence: L.S. = long shot; M.L.S. = medium long shot; M.S. = medium or mid shot; M.C.S. = medium close shot; C.S. = close shot; C.U. = close-up. The use of technical terminology tends to be variable, particularly in this area; Geduld and Gottesman's *Illustrated Glossary of Film Terms*, New York, 1973, is a useful introduction.
6 Paul Rotha (1907–   ), British film-maker, producer and critic; books include *The Film till Now*, Cape, 1930 (most recent revision 1967) and *Documentary Diary*, Secker & Warburg, 1973.
7 *The Birth of a Nation* (USA, 1915).
8 The 'Odessa Steps' sequence forms the climactic episode of Eisenstein's *Battleship Potemkin* (USSR, 1925).

Part III
Forms and ideologies

PARTLY AS a footnote to Grierson's reference to Griffith, we begin this part with two paragraphs from the French critic Léon Moussinac:

As we know, the Americans have done much to distentangle the cinema from one part of our preconceptions. Far from confusing it with theatre, they have applied, if not expressed, the primary laws specific to the cinema. They have understood perfectly the power of the moving image. They considered it as for the first time, in itself, and developed it with a ruthless logic which borrowed nothing from the past. In so doing they were greatly helped by their new, young civilisation, unencumbered by any long-standing cultural and artistic traditions. . . .
It was a pleasure to find in Griffith a genius concerned with profound emotions who uses all the resources of his inimitable technique to endow images with a precise truth and to elaborate a subject (I am of course disregarding his moral intentions here).[1] Griffith's work finds its justifications almost exclusively on the screen itself: thus it gives us a foretaste of everything to come (Moussinac, 1925).

In thus evoking the 'power of the image' Moussinac introduces another emphasis which has been important in the discussion of film realism, but in a number of different ways, all of which are contained as potentials within the way he introduces it. First, he links this power with the notion of cinematic specificity (cf. discussion p. 54). Second, the power is often directly linked with the cinema's supposed suitability for representing aspects of contemporary life. Third, the power has often also been seen as carrying a political weight, oppressive or liberating according to the perspective adopted. The fact that the image is 'moving' and 'truthful' is thought to give it extra power in all three of these areas.

Somewhat patronisingly, Grierson also salutes Hollywood:

Hollywood has always had the good sense to loose an occasional salute to the common life. Behind its luxuries there has always been a suggestion of origin in Kanka Kee or Kalamazoo. Behind the gowns and gauderies there has been a frank allowance that the lady inside them started under honest parents as a shop girl. Tales of the Frontier and the Railroads and the Gangs and the War have remained still more faithful to the notion that rank was but the guinea stamp and a man was a man for a' that.

The manhood may have been romanticized, but behind it, dimly, has been the presupposition that common things have virtues and that straight-up braveries are the essence of nobility. It is this presupposition which has made me prefer American films to English ones. I imagine most people are with me.

Say what you will of the Americans: they do not take their subjects and settings from one silly stratum of near-society. They use the stuff in front of their noses, even if they colour it with the baby pinks and baby blues of happy endings and luxury finales. Not one of us but knows their soda fountains better than our own cafés, their cops better than our police, their department stores better than our shops, their newspapers and business offices better than Fleet Street and the City.

There is a limit, of course: the limit reflected in the baby blues and baby pinks: the showman's fear of introducing the sordid. Hollywood has made a dream world even of its realities. I know there may be a case for filling the world's head with dreams, but one finds it a relief when a story of commoners stays rooted to the solid earth. We want it romanticized just the same, but we want our romance with the sweat and the smells thrown in. It is a better romance (Grierson, 1932).

Both Grierson and Moussinac make it clear that while the sentimental or romantic aspects of Hollywood films were to be rejected, the Hollywood cinema *en bloc* could validly be seen as realistic. Subsequent criticism has tended to fluctuate between denying this position and accepting it but characterising realisms of the Hollywood type as essentially repressive. We shall return to this question further on.

While he favours borrowing elements of their styles from the Russians (see p. 106), Grierson is also unhappy about some of them. Here are his brief dismissals of Pudovkin, Eisenstein and Vertov:

It may be – and what I understand of aesthetic bids me believe – that in making art in our new world we are called upon to build in new forms altogether. Fantasy will not do, nor the dribblings of personal sentiment or personal story. The building of our new forms has been going on, of course, for a long time in poetry and the novel and architecture, and even within such limitations of medium as one finds in painting and sculpture. We have all been abstracting our arts away from the personal, trying to articulate this wider world of duties and loyalties in which education and invention and democracy have made us citizens.

It would, I know, be easy to find a description of the problem as far back as Socrates. Was there not something to the effect that everything I have comes from the state, that in the state is my only self worth worrying about, and that my all must be found for the state? I forget the lines, but where the state is so much vaster and more complex than the one-horse town of Athens, and the work of learning how to govern it decently is so important and so pressing, there is an urgency in the problem of articulating it to ourselves which is without parallel in the history of citizenship. What sentiments will we have in this new world to warm and direct our will in it? How shall we crystallize them and teach them if we are to stave off chaos?

Do not believe it if people tell you we have only to go to the Russians for our guide. The Russians are naturally on the same job as ourselves, and more deliberately, and with less patience of the reactionary and sentimental Poets-in-Blazers who take the honours of art in our own country. But, looking at the core of the problem, what in fact have they given us? Pudovkin is only D. W. Griffith in Revolutionary garb, with the sensation of a Revolutionary victory by arms to balance the Ride of the Klansmen and the other fake climaxes of Griffith cinema. Who in the name of sense can believe in revolution as a true climax? As a first act climax perhaps, but not as a fifth. By these terms Pudovkin is, *qua* artist, no revolutionary at all. The pastures of his art are old pastures, eaten to the roots.

Eisenstein is something different, if on the whole not quite so successful. He plays the mass and thinks without a doubt in the mass, but again the fake climax of Revolution in *Potemkin*. And when he had a chance to make a climax of peace-in-the-mass instead of

war-in-the-mass, he failed. *The General Line* is no less in its fundamentals a failure than Creighton's *One Family*.[2] This is a hard saying
with so many brilliant criticisms about on the subject, but I shall stand
by it; and the Russians, I know, will take my point. Eisenstein does not
get inside his Russian peasants nor, with true affection, inside the
problem of co-operating them. He is looking at their peace drama
from the outside, being clever about it, even brilliant about it, but from
the outside. The struggle of their communal farms strikes no fire in
him [. . . .]

   With Dziga Vertov's *Man With the Movie Camera* we are at last
initiated into the philosophy of the Kino Eye. Some of us have been
hearing a great deal about the Kino Eye and it has worried us considerably. Only the younger high-brows seemed to know anything
about it. They have dashed back from their continental rambles with
hair more rumpled, neck more open, and tie more non-existent for
gazing on it. But on the whole articulation has failed them, and it has
been difficult to gather from their wild young words what particular
mesmeric virtue this Kino Eye possessed.

   Now that Vertov has turned up in the original, it is easier to see why
intelligent students of cinema were betrayed into their extremity. The
Vertov method of film-making is based on a supremely sound idea,
and one which must be a preliminary to any movie method at all. He
has observed that there are things of the every-day which achieve a
new value, leap to a more vigorous life, the moment they get into a
movie camera or an intimately cut sequence. It is at that point we all
begin; and, backing our eye with the world, we try to pick the leapers.
The secret may be in an angle, or an arrangement of light, or an
arrangement of movement, but there is hardly one of us but gets more
out of the camera than we ever thought of putting into it. In that sense
there is a Kino Eye. In that sense, too, the Kino Eye is more likely to
discover things in the wide-world-of-all-possible-arrangements
which exists outside the studios.

   Vertov, however, has pushed the argument to a point at which it
becomes ridiculous. The camera observes in its own bright way and he
is prepared to give it his head. The man is with the camera, not the
camera with the man. Organization of things observed, brain control,
imagination or fancy control of things observed: these other rather
necessary activities in the making of art are forgotten. *The Man With
the Movie Camera* is in consequence not a film at all: it is a snapshot
album. There is no story, no dramatic structure, and no special
revelations of the Moscow it has chosen for a subject. It just dithers
about on the surface of life picking up shots here, there and everywhere, slinging them together as the Dadaists used to sling together

their verses, with an emphasis on the particular which is out of all relation to a rational existence. Many of the shots are fine and vital; some of the camera tricks, if not very new, are at least interesting; but exhibitionism or, if you prefer it, virtuosity in a craftsman does not qualify him as a creator.

The Man With the Movie Camera will, however, bring a great deal of instruction to film students. The camera is a bright little blackbird, and there are rabbits to be taken out of the hat (or bin) of montage which are infinitely magical, but . . . articulacy is a virtue which will continue to have its say-so. Here by the *reductio ad absurdum* is proof for the schoolboys.

I have just been watching an Atlantic liner putting to sea, from – I am happy to say – the liner's point of view. Shots have been cropping up for an hour that I would describe as sheer cinema. The patterns of men rolling up the cargo net, the curve of the rope shot in parabola to the tug, the sudden gliding movement-astern of the tug, the white plume on the *Mauretania* high up in the dry dock, the massed energy of the black smoke pouring in rolls from the funnel and set against the rhythmic curve of the ship against the sky – they have all, possibly, a visual virtue in themselves. But the dramatic truth, and therefore, finally, the cinematic truth too, is that the ship is putting to sea. She is in process and continuity of something or other. Say only that she is setting out to cross an ocean and has the guts for it; or say, by the Eastern European emigrants in the steerage, that a bunch of people are going with hope to a new world; say what you like, according to your sense of ultimate importances, the necessity is that you say something. The Kino Eye in that sense is only the waiter who serves the hash. No especial virtue in the waiting compensates for a lunatic cook (Grierson, 1930–1).

Between 1923 and 1928 the Russian Left Front of the Arts, a loose association of artists and critics from the Futurist, Constructivist and Formalist movements, published two successive avant-garde journals, *Lef* and *Novy Lef*. Broadly speaking, the journals took up positions against realism and the imitation or copying of life, which meant that they were against most known forms of literature and art, and in favour of the development of art-forms which would emphasise the nature of the artistic material itself. This overt construction of new artistic forms would, it was hoped, parallel the construction of new forms of life under socialism. Just as the success of socialism would depend on the material forces of technology, so the success of socialist art would depend on the material character of its own new constructions. There was a corresponding emphasis on the usefulness of such art-productions: use and activity were in, contemplation and reflection out.

Eisenstein and Vertov were both associated (though not identified) with the journals, which devoted several articles and debates to film questions. These debates are often confused, with their participants in the difficult position of rejecting both realism and the use of art as an instrument of cognition, yet simultaneously calling for a cinema of fact which could be socially and politically useful. The futurist poet and playwright S. M. Tretyakov discusses the distinction then current between 'play' and 'unplayed' films:

Nowhere is Lef working more intensively than in the cinema. Yet lately we have been criticised for not practising what we preach: it's been said that Lef theory can sometimes be diametrically opposed to the work it is doing in the production sphere. This is the first question we need to confront.

We need to confine our work in terms of what we reject, what we consider arbitrary and what we believe needs to be argued in words and action. Lef does have a general line, but the weight of work at the level of production has meant that it has been only partially articulated – it needs to be made explicit.

The second question concerns the basic problem of contemporary cinema – the 'play' film/'unplayed' film controversy. This requires a theoretical analysis to clarify distinctions and oppositions. Perhaps the actual 'play' film/'unplayed' film opposition is itself an unfortunate formulation of the problem.

There have been attempts to establish the degree of 'play' involved at the various stages of film production. The element of 'play' is the random personal factor which may be introduced by the director, the scenario writer, or the actor, and it is this element which determines the degree of 'play' in a given film sequence. . . .

It has never been my view that Lef should be concerned with the documentary exclusively – this would be rather one-sided. I have always felt that there is every justification for the fact that the Lef cover bears two names: Eisenstein and Vertov. These two men are working with precisely the same apparatus, but with two different methods. With Eisenstein the agitational aspect predominates and the film material is subordinated to this function. With Vertov it is the informational aspect which predominates with the stress on the material itself.

But can Vertov's work be called pure documentary? Pure documentary is the editing of facts simply in terms of their actuality and social significance. When a fact becomes a brick in a construction of a different kind – the pure documentary concept disappears; everything depends on the montage.

Whether or not a film is a 'play' film or an 'unplayed' film to my mind is a question of the degree of deformation of the material out of which the film is composed: the random personal factor in any given film. 'Interpretation' is from the start a one-sided exploitation of the material. I would for instance call the film *The Great Road*[3] a 'play' film, but a film 'played' by a single character, Esther Ilishna Shub. The personal factor in her case is artistic, her selection of material purely aesthetic, directed towards achieving a certain emotional charge in the auditorium through the arrangement of montage attractions. But Shub is here dealing with material of a certain cultural level which has been minimally deformed.

The reaction of a viewer who said with feeling after watching Shub's *Fall of the Romanov Dynasty*: 'It's a pity there are those gaps, they should have been scripted in', was not such a stupid one. This man valued not the authenticity of the material, but the effect the film had on him on the strength of which he asked for the blanks to be filled in by inauthentic material. . . . I think that in order to distinguish between the 'play' film and the 'unplayed' film (the terminology is arbitrary) one must have in mind the scale of deformation in the elements from which the film is composed. By deformation I mean the arbitrary distortion and displacement of 'raw' elements.

Such deformation operates first of all on the level of the material (from the moment the question 'What is to be filmed?' is asked and a selection made of the material required from the total mass of material available). Second, the deformation of material occurs with the selection of camera position, the arrangement of lighting, and third, at the stage of montage, through the director.

Measured against such a deformation scale, the material falls into three categories: *in flagrante*, scripted, and '*played*'. The first category covers material caught red-handed, Vertov's 'life caught unawares'. Here deformation is minimal, but it nevertheless has its own scale since it is possible, for instance, to film a subject without his being aware of being filmed. . . . I have for example discussed with Shub the possibility of walling cameras up in the street to film passersby. . . . This would produce shots of the typical in which the personal element in choice of camera position has been eliminated.

When a cameraman films, he inevitably introduces something individual into his work. This is not problematic if he proceeds from certain premises: natural lighting, calculated sharpness in focus, a preliminary working out of relationships between groups, etc. But ought we to take a stand against randomness in the cameraman's selection of camera position? Why does a cameraman need to dance around his subject? The usual explanation is that in this way the subject is shown from all sides. But there is surely a distinction between the position necessary for the fullest representation of the object, and an arbitrary aesthetic 'contemplation' of the object from all sides.

The material '*in flagrante*' of the first category is therefore the most objective. The next degree along the deformation scale represents the slightly more impure '*in flagrante*' material which results when the presence of a camera affects the behaviour of the subject being filmed. He sees the handle turning and his movements become artificial, he begins to give a distorted version of himself, to present himself as an icon rather than as you want to see him.

The third degree along the scale in this category is the filming of life '*in flagrante*', but using artificial lighting; for instance the filming of a peasant family in natural conditions, in a dark hut, when the natural lighting is changed by the positioning of lights in various corners of the room.

The second category, which I have labelled 'scripted' material, I will illustrate with the following example. I film a woodcutter at work; I bring him to a tree selected by me, and ask him to chop it down while I film. His work is being done to order, but I have set in motion his professional habits and therefore the deformation involved is minimal. This is in fact a description of the way work with the actor-model operates; he is selected as material which corresponds in its concrete qualities, habits and reflex actions to the image required on the screen. This is how Eisenstein works – he chooses people with the appropriate faces, habits and movements. There is of course an undoubted orientation towards play in this structure but to a far lesser degree than with the professional actor. The 'free' personal element introduced by the actor is here replaced by the authentic action of a correctly selected reflex. . . .

The task of a director of the 'unplayed' film is to get as close as possible to the 'raw', to material 'as it is'. For us in Lef it is important to delimit the practical possibilities in relation to the dictates of social command and thus to establish the limit towards which our concrete daily work must be directed. This is why, in setting up our maximum-programme we demand: give us 'Kino-eye' and 'life caught un-awares'.

But insofar as there is a need for emotional stimulus, we work with the montage of attractions method, and insofar as we must be free to affect the viewer, we will also need to concern ourself with material of another kind. We may perhaps also need to defend scripted material, that is, to work with the methods of Eisenstein.

And now for a word or two about depersonalised material.

The documentary needs clear indication that the image on the screen represents a particular man at a particular moment in a particular place, doing something specific. The loss of this 'specificity' of the image generalises the object and the viewer observes it as a depersonalised, 'type' representation.

Example: barge haulers towing a barge, the usual colour combinations are: barge haulers, ropes and barge, grey. The cameraman, waits for a ray of light, then shoots an effective shot but does not convey that this represents barge haulers taken at a moment of visually effective lighting. The viewer therefore receives an impression of barge haulers which is exceptional, not typical.

Finally, film direction. There is on the one hand the director-cameraman who looks for the typical shot and natural lighting, without forcing the material. And then there is the 'play' director who sees himself as the sole master and interpreter of the material. He usually justifies his random free personal interpretation of material on the basis of intuitions: the director who is at once a specialist and a publicist is rare. Most often the director will tell you: 'That's how it seemed to me, that's what I felt'. He has a visual taste approach to the evaluation of a film which is personal to him.

And so it seems to me that the apparently sharp demarcation line between the 'play' film and the 'unplayed' film is in fact extremely relative.

The question of 'play' film as against 'unplayed' film is the question of respect for fact as against fiction, for contemporaneity as against the past (Tretyakov, 1927).

The idea of the 'social command' which Tretyakov invokes originated in the Futurist notion that individual artists have direct, unconscious access to the will of the social collective, and thus express it directly and intuitively in their work. This idea did not find favour with the main stream of Russian critical opinion, but it is evidently indispensable to the *Lef* position. Perhaps Tretyakov's most important point is the statement that since deformation is inevitable in the process of film-making, an 'unplayed' film is strictly speaking an impossibility. Despite this recognition, their belief in the social command and the force of their rejection of illusionism led the *Lef* contributors to favour the 'unplayed' end of the spectrum. The formalist theoretician Viktor Shklovsky suggests a focus on 'the material' as a correct way of solving the play/unplayed problem:

The point is that there are some extremely useless clever people about and some extremely useful mistakes. Talking to the documentary film-makers, I find it is relatively easy to break them down, but the mistakes they are making are extremely useful in terms of both art and cinema: they are the mistakes that lead to innovation.

The distinction between 'play' and 'unplayed' film is an elementary one of course, but there is nothing to be gained from hammering something we haven't understood: the material itself is always intelligent, if we haven't been able to analyse certain distinctions within it, the fault is with our analysis and not with the material.

It's been suggested here that Kuleshov and Eisenstein are the 'play' film, while Shub and Vertov are the 'unplayed'. But they all sat in the same company, Shub learnt her montage on the 'play' film, while the play film director studied montage on the documentary.

It's a very old problem: Goethe once said – 'You sit right opposite a tree, draw it as carefully as you can, and what becomes of that tree on paper?'

It's the same with the camera. Certain problems are not easy to solve by the laws of physics: whether to have a fixed camera position, or whether the cameraman should move round a 'play' actor or the actor around the 'unplayed' cameraman. The problem is raised from the very beginning, by the way a shot is set up, which already involves an element of 'play'. . . .

The best moments in Shub's film are the sequences which show Dybenko[4] – he has no idea how to face a camera and wavers between smiles and looking heroic. And this piece of 'play' with the cameraman constitutes a moment of genius in this excellent film.

I've watched VIPs being filmed and they could be signed up in the artists' union right away. The camera no sooner starts to roll than they're there in the frame, in position, and launched into conversation with each other.

Obviously the 'play'/'unplayed' division itself is at fault because it generates a general law. . . .

The play side of art shouldn't be exaggerated. The phenomenon of 'play' is inherent in art, but art itself periodically reorientates itself towards the material.

And in this respect the erring documentary film-makers were correct and are correct now in that they rightly bring forward the material. The consequence is that the material takes priority. For today.

For this reason I consider that for all the complexity and controversial nature of the 'play'/'unplay' question, the problem is not one of who is doing the seeing or revealing, or how he sees or reveals, but how to assess the degree of usefulness and depth achieved.

Lef is faced with a task that is more extensive than the problem of the 'play' film as against the 'unplayed' film, and that is the question of the priority of the material. . . .

Let's take the formula for the composition of a work: some people have the very strange idea that the starting point is a narrative structure which is then filled out by material. The Lef idea is that a man begins by studying the material, only then does the question of how that material is to be formulated arise.

There are moreover both narrative and non-narrative representations of reality; non-narrative cinema is nevertheless thematic. . . .

What practical suggestions do I have? Firstly – instead of the division into film documentary and 'play' film, a division between narrative and non-narrative cinema (Shklovsky, 1928).

In the *Novy Lef* perspective, the work of neither the 'unplayed' Vertov nor the 'play' Eisenstein was entirely satisfactory. Osip Brik attempts to reconcile formalism with the 'social demand'. Art was to work through the formal play of its own devices, but this play was to be considered in the light of its potential social utility: 'not an aesthetic end in itself, but a laboratory for the best possible expression of the facts of the present day.' Here Brik criticises Vertov's film *The Eleventh*[5] and Eisenstein's *October:*

The Eleventh

Dziga Vertov's film *The Eleventh* is an important frontline event in the struggle for the 'unplayed' film: its pluses and minuses are of equal significance and interest.

The film consists of a montage of 'unplayed' film material shot in the Ukraine. Purely in terms of camerawork. Kaufman's filming[6] is brilliant, but on the level of montage the film lacks unity. Why?

Primarily because Vertov has ignored the need for an exact clearly-constructed thematic scenario. Vertov's thoughtless rejection of the necessity for a scenario in the 'unplayed' film is a serious mistake. A scenario is even more important for the 'unplayed' film than for the 'play' film where the term is understood not simply as a narrative-structured exposition of events, but rather as the motivation of the film material. The need for such motivation is even greater in the 'unplayed' film than in the 'play' film. To imagine that documentary shots joined without any inner thematic link can produce a film is worse than thoughtless.

Vertov tries to make the film titles do the work of a scenario but this attempt to use written language as a means of providing the cinematic image with a semantic structure can lead nowhere. A semantic structure cannot be imposed on the film from outside, it exists within the frame and no written additions can compensate for its absence. The reverse is also true, when a determined semantic structure is contained within the frame, it should not be exchanged for written titles.

Vertov has chosen particular film shots from a complete film sequence and joined them to other frames from a different sequence, linking the material under a general title which he intends will merge the different systems of meaning to produce a new system. What happens in fact is that these two sections are drawn back into their basic film parts and the title hovers over them without uniting them in any sense.

The Eleventh contains a long sequence on work in coal mines which has its own semantic structure, and another sequence showing work in a metallurgical plant which also has its own, distinct, semantic structure.

Vertov has joined a few metres from each sequence, intercutting the title 'Forward to Socialism'. The audience, watching the coal mining shots registers the system of meaning of this complete sequence, sees the metallurgical shots and registers this sequence, and no association with the new theme 'Forward to Socialism' is provoked. For this to be achieved new film material is essential. . . .

This fact needs to be firmly established – the further development of the 'unplayed' film is being impeded at the moment by its workers' indifference to the scenario and the need for a preliminary thematic structuring of the overall plan. This is why the 'unplayed' film at present has a tendency to dissolve into separate film parts inadequately held together by heroic inscriptions.

It is curious that Shub's *Fall of the Romanov Dynasty*, put together out of old film strips, makes a far more total impression, thanks to careful structuring on the levels of themes and montage.

The absence of the thematic plan must inevitably affect the cameraman. For all the brilliance of Kaufman's filming, his shots never go beyond the visual illustration, they are filmed purely for their visual interest and could almost be included in any film. The reportage/publicism element is completely lacking and what emerges is essentially beautiful 'natural' shots, 'unplayed' images for a 'play' film.

This is because Kaufman did not know what theme he was filming for, from what semantic position those shots were to be taken. He filmed things as they seemed most interesting to him as a cameraman; his taste and skill are undeniable, but his material is filmed from an aesthetic, not a documentary, position.

October

Sergei Eisenstein has slipped into a difficult and absurd situation. He has suddenly found himself proclaimed a world-class director, a genius, he has been heaped with political and artistic decorations, all of which has effectively bound his creative initiative hand and foot.

In normal circumstances he could have carried on his artistic experiments and researches into new methods of film-making calmly and without any strain: his films would then have been of great methodological and aesthetic interest. But piece-meal experiments are too trivial a concern for a world-class director: by virtue of his status he is obliged to resolve world-scale problems and produce world-class films. It comes as no surprise therefore that Eisenstein has announced that he intends to film Marx's *Capital* – no lesser theme would do.

As a result there have been painful and hopeless efforts to jump higher than his own height of which a graphic example is his latest film, *October*.

It would, of course, be difficult for any young director not to take advantage of all those material and organisational opportunities that flow from the title of genius, and Eisenstein has not withstood the temptations.

He has decided that he is his own genius-head, he has made a decisive break with his comrades in production, moved out of production discipline and begun to work in a way that leans heavily and directly on his world renown.

Eisenstein was asked to make a jubilee film for the tenth anniversary of October, a task which from the Lef point of view could only be fulfilled through a documentary montage of existing film material. This is in fact what Shub has done in her films, *The Great Road* and *The Fall of the Romanov Dynasty*. Our position was that the October Revolution was such a major historical fact that any 'play' with this fact was unacceptable. We argued that the slightest deviation from historical truth in the representation of the events of October could not fail to disturb anyone with the slightest cultural sensitivity.

We felt therefore that the task that Eisenstein had been set – to give not the film-truth (*kinopravda*), of the October events, but a film-epic, a film-fantasy – was doomed in advance. But Eisenstein, who in some areas has moved towards the Lef position, did not share the Lef viewpoint in this instance: he believed that it was possible to find a method of representing October, not as documentary montage, but through an artistic 'play' film. Eisenstein of course rejected the idea of straightforward historical reconstruction from the start. The failure of *Moscow in October* – a film based purely on the reconstruction of events – showed him to be right in this regard. What he needed was an artistic method of the representation of October events.

From the Lef standpoint such a method does not exist and indeed cannot exist. If Eisenstein had not been loaded down by the weighty title of genius, he could have experimented freely and his experiments might have brilliantly demonstrated the impossibility of the task set him. Now however, alongside pure experiment, he was obliged to create a complete jubilee film, and therefore to combine experiments with form and trite conventions in a way that sits curiously in one and the same work. The result is an unremarkable film.

While rejecting straightforward reconstruction, Eisenstein was obliged one way or another to deal with Lenin, the central figure of the October Revolution, in his jubilee film. To do so he resorted to the most absurd and cheapest of devices: he found a man who resembled Lenin to play the role of Lenin. The result was an absurd falsification which could only carry conviction for someone devoid of any respect or feeling for historical truth.

Eisenstein's film work on the heroic parts of his film [is] analogous to the operations of our cliché painters, like Brodsky or Pchelin, and these sequences have neither cultural nor artistic interest.

Only in episodes fairly distantly related to the development of the October Revolution is his work as a director apparent and it is to these episodes that any discussion of the film has to be limited.

The Women's Battalion. This theme is given much greater prominence in the film *October* than the women's battalion had in the actual historical events. The explanation for this is that women in military uniform represent right material for theatrical exploitation.

However, in structuring this theme Eisenstein has committed a crude political mistake. Carried away by his satirical portrayal of the woman soldier, he creates, instead of a satire on the women who defended the Provisional Government, a general satire on women who take up arms for any cause at all.

The theme of women involving themselves in affairs that don't concern them draws further strength in Eisenstein's work from juxtapositions in a metaphorical relation of the woman soldier and images like Rodin's The Kiss and a mother and child.

The error is committed because Eisenstein exaggerates the satirical treatment of the women without constructing a parallel satire on the power which they were defending and therefore no sense of the political absurdity of this defence is conveyed.

People and things. Eisenstein's search for cinematic metaphors gives rise to a whole series of episodes which intercut the lines of objects and people (Kerensky and the peacock, Kerensky and the statue of Napoleon, the Mensheviks and the high society dinner plate) and in all these constructions, Eisenstein commits the same error.

The objects are not given any preliminary non-metaphorical significance. It is never made apparent that these objects were all to be found in the Winter Palace, that the plate, for instance, was left in the Smolny by the Institute originally housed there. There is therefore no context for their sudden and inexplicable emergence in a metaphorical relation.

While the verbal metaphor allows us to say 'as cowardly as a hare' because the hare in question is not a real hare, but a sum of signs, in film we cannot follow a picture of the cowardly man by a picture of a hare and consider that we have thereby constructed a metaphor, because in a film, the given hare is a real hare and not just a sum of signs. In film therefore a metaphor cannot be constructed on the basis of objects which do not have their own real destiny in terms of the film in which they appear. Such a metaphor would not be cinematic, but literary. This is clear in the sequence which shows a chandelier shuddering under the impact of October gunfire. Since we have not seen this chandelier before and have no sense of its pre-revolutionary history, we canot be moved by its trembling and the whole image simply calls up incongruous questions. . . .

The unthought out linkage of objects and people leads Eisenstein to build relations between them which have no metaphorical significance at all but are based purely on the principle of visual paradox; thus we have tiny people alongside huge marble feet, and the overlap from earlier metaphorical structures leads the viewer to look for metaphorical significance where none proves to exist.

The opening of the bridge. As a film director Eisenstein could obviously not resist filming the raising of the bridges in Petrograd, but this in itself was not enough. He extended the episode with piquant details, women's hair slipping over the opening, a horse dangling over the Neva. It goes without saying these *guignol* details have no relation to any of the film's themes – the given sequences are offered in isolation, like some spicy side dish, and are quite out of place.

Falsification of history. Every departure from historical fact is permissible only where it has been developed to the level of [the] grotesque and the extent of its correspondence to any reality is no longer relevant. . . .

When departure from historical fact does not approach the grotesque, but remains somewhat halfway, then the result is the most commonplace historical lie. There are many such instances in *October*.

1. The murder of a bolshevik by women in the July Days: there was a similar incident which involved the murder of a bolshevik selling *Pravda* by junkers. In an attempt to heighten the incident, Eisenstein brings in women and parasols – the result is unconvincing and in the spirit of trite stories about the Paris Commune. The parasols prove to have no symbolic value, they function as a shabby prop and distort the reality of the event.

2. The sailors' smashing of the wine cellars: everyone knows that one of the darker episodes of *October* was the battle over the wine cellars immediately after the overthrow and that the sailors not only did not smash the wine cellars, but looted themselves and refused to shoot at those who came after the wine. If Eisenstein had found some symbolic expression for this affair, say, demonstrating some kind of eventual resolution between proletarian consciousness and the incident, the sequence might have had some justification. But when a real sailor energetically smashes real bottles, what results is not a symbol, not a poster, but a lie. Eisenstein's view as it has been expressed in his most recent articles and lectures is that the artist-director should not be the slave of his material, that artistic vision or, to use Eisenstein's terminology, the 'slogan' must be the basis of cinematography. The 'slogan' determines not only the selection of material, but its form. The Lef position is that the basis of cinematic art is the material. To Eisenstein this seems too narrow, too prone to nail the flight of artistic imagination to the realm of the real.

Eisenstein does not see cinema as a means of representing reality, he lays claim to philosophical cinema-tracts. We would suggest that this is a mistake, that this direction can lead no further than ideographic symbolism. And *October* is the best proof of this.

From our point of view, Eisenstein's main contribution lies in his smashing the canons of the 'play' film, and carrying to the absurd the principle of creative transformation of material. This work was done in literature by the symbolists in their time, by the abstract artists in painting, and is historically necessary.

Our only regret is that Eisenstein, in the capacity of a world-class director, feels obliged to construct 80 per cent of his work on the basis of worn out conventions which consequently considerably lower the value of the experimental work he is trying to carry on in his films (Brik, 1928).

Brik's call for the 'clearly-constructed thematic scenario', using film material to construct the relationships between different sequences, suggests the point at which the Lef writers think the social command can intervene, in combination with a disciplined form of montage, to create politically acceptable forms of avant-garde cinema. As we have seen (pp. 27–8) Vertov defended himself against the charge of not organising his scenario, but subsequent critics have tended to agree with Brik rather than with Vertov. It is interesting that Brik should criticise Eisenstein for not establishing a coherent representational framework for his use of the Tsar's possessions in *October*. This demand for a 'preliminary non-metaphorical significance', and the attacks on the Women's Battalion and wine-cellar episodes for being untrue to known historical events, suggest a closer relationship to more traditional realist positions than other parts of Brik's argument. The attempt at ideographic symbolism which Brik rejects and which Shklovsky in the extract that follows seems to half-accept (while drawing attention to the risk of its degenerating into static metaphor) was indeed at the heart of Eisenstein's efforts in *October*:

Sergei Mikhailovich Eisenstein's talk of the need for a special department in cinema is unnecessary – his film is understandable in a general, not in a special way, and it doesn't call for panic.

Sergei Mikhailovich has raised the question of the reasons for failure, but first we must define what constitutes failure. We all know, many things were received as failures when they first appeared and only later re-assessed as innovations in form.

Sergei Mikhailovich has doubts about his own film in this respect and I too feel there are elements of straightforward failure in the film.

In terms of artistic devices, the film divides into two parts, Lef and academy[7] sections; and while the former is interestingly made, the latter is not.

The academy section of Eisenstein's film is distinguished mainly by its scale and the vast numbers of light units employed. Just by the way, isn't it time an end was put to the filming of wet things? The October Revolution did not take place in a constant downpour and was it worth drenching the Dvortsovaya Square and the Alexandrovsky Column? Thanks to the shower and the thousands of lights, the images look as if they've been smeared with machine oil, but there are some remarkable achievements in these sequences.

One of the branches of cinema is at the moment treading a line somewhere between vulgarity and innovation.

The essential task at the moment is to create the unambiguous cinematic image and reveal the language of film. In other words, to achieve precision in the action of cinematic expression on viewer, to create the language of the film shot and the syntax of montage.

Eisenstein has achieved this in his film. He sets up lines of objects and, for instance, moves from god to god coming in the end to the phallic negroid god and from this through the notion of 'statue' to Napoleon and Kerensky, with a consequent reduction. In this instance the objects resemble each other through only one of their aspects, their divinity, and are distinct from one another through their reverberations on the level of meaning. These reverberations create the sense of differentia essential to an art product. Through the creation of this transitional series, Eisenstein is able to lead the viewer where he wants him. The sequence is linked to the well-known ascent of the (Winter Palace) staircase by Kerensky. The ascent itself is represented realistically, while at the same time the film titles list Kerensky's ranks and titles.

The overstatement of the staircase and the basic simplicity of the ascent, carried out at the same regular pace, and the very disparity between the notions 'ascent' and 'staircase' together constitute a clearly comprehensible formal device. It represents an important innovation, but one which may contain within it certain flaws, that is, it may be imperfectly understood by the author himself.

A degenerate version of this innovation would take the form of an elementary cinematic metaphor with too close a correspondence between its parts; for instance a flowing stream and a moving stream of people, or the heart of some person as a forgetmenot. It is important in this context to bear in mind that the so-called image functions through its non-coincident components – its aureoles.

In any case, Eisenstein has forged a long way ahead in this direction. But a new formal means when it is created is always received as comic, by virtue of its novelty. That was how the cubists were received, and the impressionists, that's how Tolstoy reacted to the decadents, Aristophanes to Euripides.

A new form is therefore most suited to material where the comic sense is appropriate. This is how Eisenstein has used his innovation. His new formal device, which will no doubt become general cinematic usage, is only employed by him in the structuring of negative features, to show Kerensky, the Winter Palace, the advance of Kornilov, etc.

To extend the device to the pathetic parts of the film would be a mistake, the new device is not yet appropriate to the treatment of heroism.

The film's failures can be explained by the fact that there is a dislocation between the level of innovation and the material – and therefore the official part of the film is forced rather than creative, instead of being well-constructed it is merely grandiose. The thematic points of the film, its knots of meaning, do not coincide with the most powerful moments of the film.

. . . but art needs advances rather than victories. Just as the 1905 revolution cannot be evaluated simply as a failure, so we can only talk of Eisenstein's failures from a specific standpoint (Shklovsky, 1928).

In discussing Bazin (p. 54) we introduced the notion of cinematic specificity and its various aliases. One of the most brilliant early articulations of this notion is provided by another Russian formalist, the critic, novelist and screen-writer Yury Tynyanov. In the text that follows, 'Fundamentals of the Cinema', Tynyanov is firstly concerned to rebut realism by arguing that what is specific to cinema is not its ability to reproduce visible people and things, but rather the meanings produced by what, stylistically, cinema is able to do with those reproductions. Meaning is produced by style and by construction. The material bases of style and construction are primarily technical; for Tynyanov they are montage/editing, lighting, and the choice of camera-angle. One important limitation on the text is Tynyanov's rejection of sound – prior to its actual development – on the ground that it would cause stylistic chaos. But this opinion was common among people who had theorised film partly on the basis of its silence, and should not distract us from paying attention to Tynyanov's other points:

1

The invention of the cinematograph was welcomed with as much joy as the invention of the phonograph. It was a joy that recalled the emotions of the caveman who for the first time drew a leopard's head on the blade of his weapon and at the same time learnt to pierce his nose with a stick. The hullabaloo in the press was like the chorus of savages which sang a hymn of praise in honour of those earliest inventions.

The caveman was probably very soon convinced that a stick planted through the nose was goodness only knows what sort of invention. In any case it took him much longer to reach that point than it did the European to become infatuated with the phonograph. The problem is clearly not that the cinematograph is a technique, but that it is an art.

I have heard people deplore the fact that the cinema lacked depth and colour. I am convinced that the first inventor to draw a leopard's head was visited by a critic who referred to the drawing's lack of resemblance, and then by a second inventor who advised him to stick real leopard fur onto the drawing and to gouge a real eye. But since fur does not adhere very well to stone, writing was born of a casually drawn leopard's head; the casualness and the lack of precision in the drawing was no obstacle, on the contrary it helped to transmute it into a sign. Secondary inventors are usually unlucky. So much so, that the vistas offered by the Kinetophone,[8] stereoscopic film and film in colour, hold scarcely any appeal for us. This is because a real leopard would have been a definite failure and equally because art has nothing to do with real leopards. Art, like language, tends to abstract its methods. And all are not necessarily valid.

When the caveman drew the head of the big cat on the blade of his weapon, he was not content to simply *reproduce* it; it also communicated to him a magical courage. His totem was with him, on his weapon; his totem buried itself in the chest of the enemy. In other words, the drawing had a twofold function: material reproduction and magic. This invention had an accidental consequence. The leopard's head came to decorate all the spears of the tribe, becoming in some way the distinctive sign of their weapons as opposed to those of the enemy, and so first a mnemonic sign, then an ideogram, a letter. What had happened? A fixation of one of the results and at the same time a commutation of functions.

So the transition from technical to artistic means was accomplished. In the same way live photography, whose essential goal was to resemble the nature represented, became cinematic art. At the same time, the function of all its processes was changed. From being processes in themselves, they were now scored by the blade of art. In the course of this transition, the 'poverty' of the cinema, its lack of relief and colour, became *positive*, genuine artistic processes, just as the imperfection and primitivism of the totem drawing were positive processes on the way to becoming writing.

2

The Kinetophone and stereoscopic cinema are inventions which belong to the first stage of cinematography and assume the function of material reproduction. They still concern 'photographs as such'. They do not begin from the image-fragment as a sign with a given signification in terms of the overall dynamics of the images, but from the image as such.

Quite probably, viewers will experience a sense of greater similarity when stereoscopic cinema shows them building walls in relief and human faces in relief, but so many different planes alternating in the course of the editing with other planes, faces in relief linked onto other faces in relief would produce an incredible chaos, made up of credible individual things.

Quite probably, nature and man in their normal colours would closely resemble the original, but an enormous face seen in close-up and in natural colour would be a monstrous and pointless excess, in the same way as a coloured statue with swivel-eyes, mounted on ball bearings. And what is more, colouring annuls a major stylistic process, namely, the alternation of different lighting on a monochrome material.

The most perfect Kinetophone would need to achieve the most hellishly precise editing so that the actors' faces produced the sounds they needed, the actors that is (not the cinema), completely independently of the laws governing the way that cinematic material unfolds. The result in that case would not only be a chaos of unwanted sounds and speech, but even the normal alternation of images would lose its credibility.

To put the worthy inventor in his place, we have only to think of the lap-dissolve process,[9] used when the character speaking is remembering another dialogue. The so-called 'poverty' of the cinema is in fact embedded in the principle of construction. And really, it is high time to stop paying the cinema the backhanded compliment of calling it the

'Great Silent Art'. It never worries us that photographs of various heroines are not tacked onto verses that sing their praises and no one would dream of calling poetry 'Great' because it is 'Blind'. Every art uses one element of the perceptual world, as a resonant element of construction, presenting the others under its sign and in the form of imagined elements.

Concrete, pictorial representations, therefore, are not excluded from the domain of poetry, but there they assume a particular quality and application. In an eighteenth-century descriptive poem, the objects are not all named, but 'described' by means of metaphors, thanks to links and associations borrowed from different series. So, in order to convey 'tea pouring from a teapot', the author may say, 'a burning, fragrant steam gushed from the gleaming copper'. The concrete, pictorial representation is not given, it serves to motivate the link between numerous verbal series whose dynamic is founded on the enigma formulated. It goes without saying, this chain does not give concrete, authentic representations, but verbal representations in which the major role goes, not to the objects themselves, but to the semantic colouring of the words and their interplay. If we inserted real objects into this verbal series we would obtain nothing more than a chaos of things which bore no resemblance to anything. In the same way, the cinema in its turn uses words, either to motivate the linking of images, or as an element which acts, solely in relation to the image, in the role of contrast or illustration. To fill the cinema with words would achieve a chaos of words and nothing more.

For cinema as an art, what matters is no longer inventions as such, but technical means which perfect the basic elements of cinema, and are selected accordingly to their correspondance with its principal processes. The interaction of technique and art is the opposite of what it was to begin with: art itself gives the *impulse* towards the technical processes. It is art which selects them in the course of its progression, modifying their application and function, and finally rejecting them. The driving force is not therefore from technique to art.

Cinematic art already has its material. That material is capable of being diversified and perfected and nothing more.

3

The 'poverty' of the cinema, its lack of relief and colour, is really the essence of cinematic construction. It does not call up new processes to compensate, but on the contrary creates them and is therefore the basis of their growth. The cinema's lack of relief (which does not mean lack of perspective), that so-called technical 'deficiency', has its repercussions in cinematic art in the positive, constructive principles of *simultaneity* between several series of visual representations, the basis on which gesture and movement acquire a completely new interpretation.

Let us look at the well known lap-dissolve process. Fingers hold a sheet of paper on which sloping characters are visible. The letters fade, the edges of the paper blur, and a new image is outlined through the sheet, the silhouette of moving figures which gradually concretise and finally completely eliminate the image of the paper covered with writing. Clearly, the linkage of these images is only possible if they are flat. Were the images in relief, their interpretation and their simultaneity would not convince. This composition, which is not only the reproduction of movement, but is constructed on the principles of movement, is possible only because it is based on the utilisation of that simultaneity. Dance can be shown in an image, not only as a 'dance', but also as a 'dancing' image by means of a 'camera movement' or a 'movement of the image'. In such an image everything oscillates, the series of characters dance one after another. A particular spatial simultaneity is rendered. The law of non-penetration of bodies is conquered by the cinema's two dimensions, its lack of relief and its abstract nature.

However, simultaneity and spatial unity are not important in themselves, but as the semantic signs of the image. As one image succeeds another, it bears the semantic sign of the preceding image and is coloured by it on the level of meaning for the whole of its duration. The image, shaped and constructed according to the principles of movement, shifts away from the material reproduction of movement towards its semantic representation. (Which is how Andrei Bely[10] occasionally constructs his sentences – what is important is not the direct meaning, but the phraseological design.)

The absence of colour in the cinema allows it to present a *semantic*, non-material juxtaposition of dimensions, a monstrous clash of perspectives. Chekhov in one of his stories has a small boy drawing an enormous man and a tiny house and what is involved is clearly an artistic process. Dimension, detached from its basis of material reproduction, becomes thereby one of the semantic signs of art. An image in which everything is enlarged succeeds an image where the perspective is reduced. An image filmed from above showing a small character follows an image of another man filmed from below. (See, for example, Akaki Akakeyevich and the enormous face in the sequence from *The Overcoat*[11] in which Akaki Akakeyevich is reprimanded. Natural colour would have effaced the major emphasis: the semantic value of dimension. Had it been given in natural colour the close-up, which detaches the object from spatial and temporal correlation, would have lost its *meaning*.)

Finally, the cinema's muteness, or more exactly the impossibility on the level of construction of loading images with words and noises reveals the nature of that construction. The cinema has its particular 'hero' (its specific element) and its particular linking processes.

4

The divergences which emerge in relation to this 'hero' are characteristic of the very nature of cinema. In its material the cinema is close to the plastic, spatial arts, that is, to painting; and in the way it unfolds, it is close to the 'temporal' arts of literature and music.

This has given rise to some pompous metaphorical definitions: 'Cinema is painting in motion' (Louis Delluc), or 'Cinema is the music of light' (Abel Gance).[12] These are not all that far from the definition already mentioned that seeks to elevate the cinema into 'the Great Silent Art'. It is as sterile to define the cinema in terms of neighbouring arts as it is to define those arts in terms of the cinema; painting becomes 'static cinema', music a 'cinema of sounds', literature a 'cinema of words'. This is particularly dangerous in the case of a new art. Defining a new phenomenon in terms of old shows proof of a reactionary addiction to the past.

The fact is that art does not need to be defined, it needs to be studied. And it is perfectly understandable that in the beginning the 'visible man' and 'visible thing', in other words the object of material reproduction, should have been called the 'hero' of the cinema (Béla Bálazs).[13] The arts distinguish themselves from each other not only and not so much by their objects as by the way in which those objects are treated. If it were otherwise, simple conversation and speech would be verbal art. For ordinary speech has the same 'hero' as poetry, namely the word, which is why the 'word' in general does not exist. In poetry the word plays an absolutely different role from the one it plays in conversation. In prose, from genre to genre, it plays a different role from the one it plays in verse.

And it is a mistake to choose 'visible man' and 'visible thing' as the hero of cinematic art. Not because the realisation of a cinema without an object is possible, but because the choice of such a 'hero' fails to stress the specific function of the material; and only this function can transform the material element into art.

In cinema, the visible world is not given as such but in its semantic correlation. Were this not so, the cinema would be no more than a live (or non-live) photography. The visible man and visible thing only become an element of cinematic art when they are presented as a semantic sign.

From the first thesis follows the idea of cinematic style, from the second, that of cinematic construction. The semantic correlation of the visible world is achieved through its stylistic transformation. The correlation between characters and things in the image, of characters to each other, of the whole and the part, everything that is conventionally called the 'composition of the image', the angle of vision, the perspective within which things are captured, and finally the lighting, have a colossal importance. By virtue of its technical lack of relief and its monochrome nature, cinema transcends lack of relief. Compared with the fantastic freedom the cinema has in the arrangement of perspective and point of view, the theatre, which possesses all three dimensions and therefore relief, is condemned (precisely because of that property) to a single point of view, to non-relief, as an element of the art.

The angle of vision transforms the visible world stylistically. For instance, a factory chimney, shot slightly inclined from the *horizontal*, or someone crossing a bridge, filmed from below; in cinematic art these represent the same transformation of the thing as the whole battery of stylistic processes which endow the object with novelty in verbal art.

Of course, not all angles and types of lighting are equally powerful stylistic processes. Strong stylistic processes are not applicable in all cases. Nevertheless the artistic difference between cinema and theatre persists.

5

The problem of unity of place does not exist for the cinema, only the problem of unity of angle of vision and light is important. The 'studio' for cinema represents hundreds of angles, a medley of different kinds of lighting, and undoubtedly hundreds of different correlations between man and thing, between things, and hundreds of different 'places'. In the theatre, five sets are simply five 'places' seen from the same angle. And complicated theatrical stages where the perspective is skilfully calculated are false to the cinema. Nor is the striving after photogenicness justified. Objects are not photogenic in themselves, it is the angle and the lighting which make them photogenic. The idea of 'photogenicness'[14] has generally to give way to that of 'cinegenicness'.

This is valid for all the stylistic processes of the cinema. Legs walking shown instead of the men doing the walking focus the attention on the associative detail, just as the synecdoche does in poetry. In both fields the important fact is that in place of the thing onto which attention is directed, *another* thing associated with it is given (in cinema the associating link will be movement or pause). This sort of replacement of a thing by a detail changes our attention. Different objects (as a whole and as detail) are given under the same sign and the change seems to break down the visible thing – which is, in fact, a series of things with a single semantic sign, in fact, the *semantic object* of cinema.

Obviously then, in such a stylistic (possibly even semantic) transformation, it is not the 'visible man' nor the 'visible thing' which constitutes the 'hero' of cinema, but a 'new' man and 'new' thing – men and things transformed on the level of art, cinematic 'man' and 'thing'. Visible correlations between visible people are severed and replaced by the correlation of 'people' within cinema at every instant, unconsciously and almost naïvely. When Mary Pickford takes on the role of a small girl she surrounds herself with exceptional actors and carries it off, probably without even thinking that she would not manage it in the theatre. (Here we are dealing not with a stylistic transformation, but only with the technical utilisation of a law of art.)

6

What are the foundations of this *new* man and *new* thing? Why does cinematic style transform them?

Because every stylistic means is at the same time a semantic factor, on condition that the style is organised, the angles and the lighting not random, but constitutive of a system. There are literary works in which the simplest events and relationships are presented with stylistic means of such a nature that they take on the aspect of enigmas. The reader begins to confuse the notion of the relation between great and small, usual and strange. In his hesitation he follows where the author leads and confuses the 'perspective' of things, and the 'lighting' (as for example in Joseph Conrad's novel *The Shadow Line*, where a simple event, a young naval officer becoming the captain of a ship, takes on grandiose proportions). The important element in this instance is the particular semantic structure of things, the special way the reader is introduced into the action. The same possibilities are there in cinematic style, and essentially, things present themselves in the same way. Confusion of visual 'perspective' is at the same time a confusion of the *correlation* between objects and men, a semantic restructuring of the world. A succession of numerous different lightings (or the adherence to a single style) restructures the *milieu*, in exactly the same way as the angle of vision does for relations between men and things.

Again, the visible object is replaced by the artistic object.

In film, metaphors have the same significance. One and the same act is carried out by other agents; for example, when doves kiss instead of people. The visible object is broken down, different characters and things are presented under the same semantic sign, at the same time, the act itself is broken down and its semantic colouring shifted onto the second parallel (the doves).

These simple examples are sufficient to convince one that film transforms naturalist and 'visible' *movement*. It may either be broken down, or it may be shifted onto another object. Movement exists either as *motivation of the angle of vision*, from the point of view of a man walking, or as one of his characteristics (gesture), or again as *changes in the correlation* between men and things. The degree to which particular men or objects draw near or move away from men (or objects), i.e. movement in the cinema, does not exist in itself but as a particular semantic sign. This is why, outside the semantic function, movement within the image is not absolutely essential. The semantic function can be fulfilled through montage or through the alternation of images which can themselves be static. (Movement within the image as an element of film is generally excessive – comings and goings at any price are tiring.) And while 'movement' may not be 'visible' in cinema, film nevertheless operates through 'its own time'. When the film-maker wants to stress the duration of a situation, he *repeats* the image. The image, in a variety of forms or in the same form, is interrupted a minimum number of times. Its duration is therefore a long way from normal duration, from the 'visible' notion of duration. This new duration is totally relative; if the repeated image inter-cuts a great number of images, it will be long, although the 'visible duration' of the repeated image may be insignificant. Hence the conventional significance of *irising in* and *fading out* as signs of a precise spatial and temporal delimitation.

The specific character of 'time' is revealed in a process like the close-up, which abstracts the object, detail, or face from spatial correlations and at the same time from the temporary structure. *The Devil's Wheel*[15] contains a scene showing looters fleeing from a ransacked house. The film-makers had to show the bandits and filmed them as a group in long shot. The result was incoherent – why were they dawdling? Had they been shown in close-up, they could have taken all the time they wanted since the close-up would have abstracted them, snatched them out of the temporal structure.

The duration of the image is thus achieved by means of its repetition; that is, through a correlation between images. Temporal abstraction results from an absence of correlation between objects (or groups of objects) themselves within the image.

All this underlines the fact that 'cinematic time' is not a real duration but a conventional one, based on the correlation of images or the correlation of visual elements within an image.

7

The specific nature of an art always has repercussions in the evolution of its artistic processes. This tells us a great deal. In its primitive aspect, the motivation of the angle of vision was the point of view of the spectator or of a character. Similarly, the detail given in close-up was motivated by the way it was perceived by the character.

The unusual point of view, motivated by the angle of vision of the character, then lost that motivation and was presented as such. It thus became the point of view of the spectator, a stylistic process of the cinema.

The look of the person in the image fell on an object or on some detail, which was then offered in close-up. If this motivation is destroyed, the close-up will become an autonomous process, serving to highlight and emphasise the thing, understood as a semantic sign, and outside temporal and spatial relations. Usually, the close-up plays the role of 'epithet' or 'verb' (a face with the expression intensified by being in close-up), but other applications are also possible where the extra-temporal, extra-spatial nature of the close-up is used as a stylistic process for figures of comparison, metaphors, etc.

If an image featuring a man in a field in close-up is followed by another close-up showing a pig in the same field, the laws governing the *semantic correlation* of images and the *extra-temporal, extra-spatial value* of the close-up will overcome a motivation which might be as strongly naturalist as man and pig walking in the same field, at the same time and in the same place. The alternation of images produces not a logical, temporal and spatial sequence from man to pig, but a figure of semantic comparison: man-pig.

The importance of the evolution of cinematic processes lies in such advances by its autonomous semantic laws and in the rejection of 'naturalist' motivation.

That evolution has affected processes as solidly motivated as, for example, the 'lap-dissolve'. This process is firmly and unilaterally motivated by 'evocation', 'vision', 'narration'. Nevertheless the 'quick-lap-dissolve' – used when an image of a 'memory' still retains the face of the one evoking the memory – destroys the by now extraneous literary motivation of 'memory' as an alternative moment in time, and shifts the centre of gravity onto the *simultaneity* of the images. Here 'memory' or 'narration' do not exist in the literary sense. Instead there is a 'memory' within which the face of the one remembering continues to be seen at the same time. In its purely cinematic signification, this process is close to others: the 'lap-dissolve' of a face onto a landscape or scene of dimensions disproportionate in relation to the face. In its external, literary motivation, this process is diametrically opposed to the 'memory' or 'narration', but the cinematic meanings are very close.

This is how the evolution of cinematic processes has to be understood. The processes detach themselves from 'external' motivations and acquire a meaning very much 'their own'. In other words, they detach themselves from a single, extrinsic meaning and acquire 'their own' numerous intrinsic meanings. It is this multiplicity and polysemy on the level of meanings which gives a particular process the possibility of anchoring itself and transforms it into an element 'proper' to an art, in this case into the 'word' of cinema.

We may note with surprise that neither language nor literature contain a word corresponding to the cinematic 'lap-dissolve'. In every given case and every given application it can be *described* in words without our managing to find an equivalent word or notion in language.

The close-up, which sometimes presents a particular detail from the point of view of a character or viewer, and sometimes gives the results of this isolation of a detail – i.e. extra-temporality and extra-spatiality – can be used as a semantic sign in some way.

8

The cinema arose out of photography.

The umbilical cord was cut from the moment when the cinema achieved awareness of itself as an art. For photography has properties which are *unconscious* and in a sense illegitimate aesthetic qualities. Photography puts the accent on resemblance, a troublesome factor since we tend to deplore the fact that photographs are 'too like' the original. And for this reason photography surreptitiously deforms the material. Such deformation is tolerated solely on condition that resemblance is preserved. Although photography deforms the face, through the pose, the lighting, etc., we accept all that, on condition that the portrait has resemblance. From the point of view of the essential goal of photography which is resemblance, deformation is a 'fault'; its aesthetic function is in some sense a bastard child.

As the cinema has a different goal, the 'fault' of photography becomes its asset, its aesthetic quality. This is where the radical difference between the photograph and cinema has to be seen to lie.

The photograph has other 'faults' which are transformed into 'qualities' in the cinema.

In reality, all photography deforms the material. One only has to look at photographic 'views'. Perhaps my assertion will seem subjective, but I never manage to identify the similarity of views to the original, except by picking landmarks, or more exactly, differentiating details – a tree, a bench, a sign. Not because 'it's nothing like it', but because the view is *isolated*. What, in nature, only exists in association with other things and is not delimited, the photograph isolates into an autonomous entity. A bridge, a quay, one or more trees, etc., do not exist as entities when one contemplates them in reality. They are always linked to the surroundings. Their recording is momentary and transitory. Once achieved, it exaggerates individual features of the view a thousand times and this is what provokes the effect of 'non-resemblance'.

This is equally valid for the 'long shot' where the choice of angle of vision, however elementary, and the choice of setting, however extensive, lead to identical results.

The isolation of the material onto the photograph and the resultant tightening of correlations between all the objects or elements of an object in the photograph, is what determines the unity of each photograph. As a result of this internal unity, the correlation between objects, or within an object between elements, changes its distribution. The objects are deformed.

But this 'defect' is the photograph, its unconscious, 'un-canonised' qualities, to adopt the formula of Viktor Shklovsky, are canonised in the cinema and transformed into primary qualities and fundamental supports.

The photograph offers a *single* situation. In the cinema, this becomes a unit or measure.

The image represents the same unit as the photograph and as the complete line of verse. By this law, all the words which compose a line enter into a particular correlation and closer interaction with each other. Thus the meaning of the word in verse is different in comparison not only to all forms of practical language, but also compared to prose. This is why all the auxiliary, secondary words which are not very important in ordinary language, are exceptionally evident and important in poetry.

The same is true of the image. Its unity changes the distribution of the semantic value of all the objects shown, and each object enters into correlation with other images and with the image as a whole.

Taking this fact into account we have to advance another thesis. What are the conditions under which all the 'heroes' of the image (men and things) enter into relations with each other, or more exactly, are there not conditions which hamper these relations? Yes, there are.

The 'heroes' of the image, like the words (and sounds) in verse, have to be differentiated, *different*; only then do they exert a reciprocal action and mutually colour each other in taking on meaning. This is the basis of the *choice* of men and things, and of the angle of vision, understood as a stylistic process of delimitation, in other words of *differentiation*. That 'choice' is born of naturalist resemblance, the correspondence between the cinematic man and thing and the man and thing of the outside world, what in practice is called the 'choice of type'. But in cinema as in all art, what is introduced for very precise reasons begins to play a role which sheds its connections with those reasons. 'Choice' serves above all to *differentiate the actors* within the film. It is not just external, it is also intrinsic to the film.

From the necessity to differentiate the 'heroes' of the image also flows the significance of *movement* in the image. Smoke from the ship's funnel and clouds floating across the sky are useful not just as themselves; they are also useful in the same way as a passerby wandering by chance into a deserted street, or like mimicry and gesture in relation to men and objects; that is, as differential signs.

9

This apparently elementary fact determines the whole system of mime and gesture in film and resolutely marks it off from the system of mime and gesture in prosaic language. In the latter case, mime and gesture realise or 'manifest' verbal intonation in the motor and visual domain, where they appear to complete the word.

This is the role of mime and gesture in the spoken theatre. In pantomime they 'substitute' for the speech suppressed. Pantomime is an art founded on suppression, a sort of game of 'loser wins', consisting precisely in compensating for the missing element by introducing others. In the art of the word itself, there are cases where 'complementary' mime and gesture are an embarrassment. Heinrich Heine[16] asserts that mime and gesture were inimical to the verbal witticism. 'Its (Heine is referring to the speaker's face) muscles are ever in strange nervous movement, and he who observes them sees the orator's thoughts, before they are spoken. This spoils his witty outbursts.'[17]

This would indicate that the realisation of verbal intonation through mime and gesture works against (in this instance) the verbal structure and violates the internal relations. Heine placed an un-expected witticism at the end of a poem and would never allow a lively piece of mime or even the beginnings of a gesture to signal the joke before it had been formulated. The verbal gesture of the speaker does not simply accompany speech, it signals and announces it.

This is why theatrical mime is so alien to the cinema. While it cannot accompany the non-existent word, it signals and *suggests* it. The words suggested by gestures turn the cinema into an inadequate Kinetophone.

In the image, mime and gesture are primarily *a system of relations between the 'heroes' of the image.*

10

But mimicry in film can also be independent, the clouds may not roll. Relativity and differentiation may be located in another domain; they may be transferred from the *image* onto the sequence of images, or onto the *editing*. And static images which succeed one another in a particular way allow movement within the image to be reduced to a minimum.

Montage is not a linking of images, but their differentiated *succession*, and this is precisely why images which have in common a point of correlation are able to succeed one another. The correlation may be connected not just to the fable (fabula), but also, and in a much broader way, to the style. In our own cinematic practice, the only kind of montage is the kind which relates to the fable. Moreover, angles and lighting are arranged in a random way. This is a mistake.

We have established that style is a matter of semantics. Which is why the absence of stylistic organisation, the random composition of angles and lighting, is like throwing intonation into verse pell-mell. Lighting and angles, by virtue of their semantic nature, are of course contrasted and differentiated and for this reason their sequence is, like the order of succession connected with the fable, also a kind of montage of the images (rendering them correlative and sequential).

In cinema, images do not 'unfold' in a sequential order, nor is their development progressive. They *alternate*. That is the principle of montage. They alternate in the same way that one metrical unit replaces another on a precise frontier in verse. The cinema makes 'jumps' from image to image as poetry does from line to line.

Strange though it may seem, if we are to establish an analogy between cinema and the verbal arts, the only legitimate one would be not between cinema and prose but between cinema and poetry.

One of the major consequences of the 'jumping' nature of film is the differentiation of images and their existence as units. *Images as units are equal in value.* When a long image is succeeded by a very short one, the brevity of the image does not deprive it of its independence and correlation with the rest.

Strictly speaking, the importance of an image is related to the degree to which it is *'representative'*. In the case of the memories rising up in the 'lap-dissolve', not all the images that make up the scene the character is remembering are given but only a detail, a single image. In the same way, the image generally does not exhaust a situation given by the fable but is only 'representative' of it within the correlation of images. In practice, in the framework of the new montage, this presents the possibility of cutting images to a minimum and using, for its 'representative' quality, an image which comes from a totally different situation in the fable.

One of the differences between 'old' and 'new' cinema is connected with the notion of montage. In the old cinema, montage was a means of soldering and joining, of explaining the situations of a fable while keeping the means itself hidden and imperceptible. In the new cinema, montage has become a basic factor, one of the instances perceived, a perceptible rhythm.

It was the same in poetry. The agreeable monotony and non-perceptibiliy of frozen prosodic systems gave way in free verse to a sharp perception of rhythm.

In Mayakovsky's early verses[18] a line composed of a single word followed a long line. The same weight of energy falling on a long line then fell on the short one (lines, like rhythmical series, are equal in value), and for this reason energy was emitted in impulses. The same is true for perceptible montage; the energy which accents a long fragment then falls on a short. The short fragment composed of one 'representative' image is of equal value to the long fragment. Like a line of verse composed of one or two words, the short image highlights its own specific signification, its proper value.

In this way the process of montage highlights the culminatory points of the film. In non-perceptible montage the weight of time which accents the culminatory point is greater. When montage becomes the perceptible rhythm of the film, *it is precisely brevity which highlights the culminatory point.*

This would not be so if the fragment as a unit were not a correlative measure. Our appreciation of a film proceeds by involuntary jumps from one unit to the next. Productions by eclectic directors cause the viewer physiological irritation because they apply, in part, the principle of old montage as montage-joining where the exhaustive 'scene' (the situation on the level of the fable) serves as the unique measure, and, in part, the principle of new montage where montage becomes a perceptible element of construction. Our energies are assigned a certain goal and a certain activity; then suddenly this is changed. The initial impulse dissipates and since we were given one direction at the beginning of the film, we do not look for a new one. Such is the force of measure in cinema; its role is close to that of measure or metre in verse.

This said, what does cinematic rhythm, a term often used and misused, consist of?

Rhythm is the interaction of stylistic and metrical moments in the unfolding or dynamics of the film. Angles and lighting are important not only in the succession of image-fragments where they act as indicative signs to the sequence. They are also important in the highlighting of culminatory fragments. This has to be borne in mind in the utilisation of special angles and lighting. These should not be random, not 'beautiful' and 'good' in themselves, but 'good' in the particular case, in terms of their interaction with the metrical progression or 'measure' of the film. The angle and lighting which highlight a metrically accented fragment play a totally different role from the angle and lighting which highlight a fragment weakly accented on the metrical level.

The analogy between cinema and verse is not absolute. Cinema is in itself, like poetry, a specific art. But people of the eighteenth century would not have understood our cinema, any more than they would have understood the poetry of today. 'Our age has offended you, your verse is an offence.'

The 'jumping' nature of cinema, the role of the image-unit, the semantic transformation of everyday objects (words in verse, things in the cinema), are what relate film and verse to each other.

11

This explains why the film-novel is such an original genre, every bit as much as the novel in verse. Pushkin said: 'I am not writing a novel, but a novel in verse. There's the devil of a difference.'

What is the 'devil of a difference' that divides the film-novel and the novel as a written genre?

It lies not just in the material but in the fact that, in the cinema, style and the laws of construction transform all the elements which might be called common and similarly adapted to all species and genres of art.

It is in these terms that the question of fable (*fabula*) and subject (*syuzhet*)[19] are posed by cinema. To resolve the problem of fable and subject, attention has always to be given to the material and style specific to the art in question.

Viktor Shklovsky, founder of the new theory of the subject, offers two approaches to the question: 1) subject as development; 2) the links between the processes of subject composition and style. The former, which shifts the examination of plot from the level of static motifs (and their historical existence), towards the way in which these motifs appear and disappear within the total construction, has already borne fruit and taken firm root. The second has not yet taken root and has apparently been forgotten.

It is the second approach I wish to discuss here.

Since the question of fable and subject in the cinema has not been greatly explored and since it calls for extensive preliminary study, I shall elaborate it in the more thoroughly explored context of literature, in order simply to pose the question of fable and subject for cinema. I believe this approach will not be without its uses.

Generally, what is called fable is a static schema of relations of the type: 'She was worthy of love and he loved her. He, however, was not lovable, and she did not love him' (Heine[20]).

The schema of relations (the 'fable') in Pushkin's *The Fountain of Bakhchisarai*[21] would be more or less as follows: 'Girei loves Maria, Maria does not love him. Zarema loves Girei, he does not love her.' It is perfectly clear that the schema does not explain anything, either in *The Fountain of Bakhchisarai*, or in the Heine epigraph, and that it is equally applicable to thousands of other things, from the epigraph to Pushkin's poem. Let us take another current notion of the fable, as the schema of the action. The fable would then emerge in roughly this minimal form: 'Girei despises Zarema because of Maria. Zarema kills Maria.' But what do we do about the fact that the dénouement is absolutely not there in Pushkin? Pushkin only permits us to guess at the dénouement which is deliberately veiled. It would be impudent to suggest that Pushkin had rejected our schema of the fable because he too was not really concerned about it. This amounts to more or less the same thing as scanning some consciously irregular line of Pushkin's verse:

Mŏi dýadă sámych chéstnўkh právĭl
Kŏgdá ně v śhutkŭ zăněmóg . . .[22]

and deciding that with the word '*zăněmóg*' the poet had deliberately rejected the iamb. Surely it would be more advisable to reject the schema rather than to decide that the work constitutes its 'rejection'? It is in reality more correct to adopt, not the 'foot' or schema, but the tonic outline (i.e. the pattern of tonic accents) as the metre of poem. On this basis 'rhythm' becomes the poem's overall dynamic which draws its configuration from the interaction of metric (tonic pattern), discursive links (syntax) and sound links ('repetitions').

The question of the fable and the subject works in much the same fashion. Either we try to create schemas which fail to integrate into the work, or we have to define the fable as the semantic (i.e. meaning-linked) pattern of the action. The subject would then be defined as the dynamic of the work which takes its form from the interaction of all the connecting links of the material (including the fable as the action linkage), arising from style, from the fable, etc. The lyric poem also has a subject, but the fable in this context is of quite a different order and its role in the development of a subject is entirely different. The notion of the subject does not overlap the notion of the fable. The subject can be de-centred in relation to the fable. In the relationship between subject and fable which concerns us here, several types are possible:

1. The subject may be essentially supported by the fable and on the semantics of the action.

Here the distribution of the fable-lines acquires a particular importance in terms of which line blocks another and it is this which advances the subject. A curious example is the type where the plot develops along a false fable-line. Ambrose Bierce's short story, *An Occurrence at Owl Creek Bridge*,[23] is one of these. A man is hanged, the rope breaks and he falls into the river. The plot then develops along a false fable-line: he swims to safety, runs home and there he finally dies. In the last lines of the story, the reader discovers that the escape is a vision the man had just before dying. The same is true of Leo Perutz's *Der Sprung ins Unbekannte* (*Leap into the Unknown*).[24]

It is interesting to note that in one of the novels most rich in action, Victor Hugo's *Les Misérables*, the 'blockage' is achieved equally as much by the superabundance of secondary fable-lines as by *the introduction of historical, scientific, descriptive material as such*. The latter is characteristic of the development of the subject and not of the fable. The novel, in its capacity as a major form, demands this development of subject outside the fable. Subject development which conforms to the fable characterises adventure narratives. (Incidentally, the 'major form' in literature is not a question of the number of pages anymore than it is a question of footage in film.) The idea of a 'major form' is based on energy; what needs to be considered is the amount of effort consecrated to the construction by the reader (or viewer). Pushkin created a major verse form on the principle of digression. In actual dimensions, *The Prisoner of the Caucasus* is no greater than certain of Zhukovsky's *Epistles*.[25] The former is nevertheless a major form because digression into a material far removed from the fable expands the 'space' of the poem to a remarkable degree. The number of verse lines in Zhukovsky's *Epistle to Voyekov* and *The Prisoner of the Caucasus* is more or less the same, but the digressions of Pushkin's poems mean that the reader is obliged to expend quite a different amount of effort in each case. (I offer this example because in his poem, Pushkin uses the material of Zhukovsky's *Epistle*, but turns it into a *digression* in relation to the fable.)

Such blockages in out-of-the-way material are characteristic of a major form.

Similarly in the cinema: the 'major genres' distinguish themselves from the 'chamber' genres, not only by the number of fable-lines involved, but also by the quantity of blockage material in general.

2. The subject develops to one side of the fable.

In this case, the fable proposes a 'riddle' through which riddle and dénouement then simply motivate the development of the plot, and the dénouement may not be given. Here the plot is shifted onto the assembling and soldering of the various parts of the discursive material – exterior to the fable. The fable is not given and it is the 'search for the fable' in its capacity of equivalent and substitute which serves as a spring-board and leads the game home. Such for example are numerous works by Pilniak, Leonhard Frank and others.[26] In 'hunting the fable' the reader manufactures the web of connections and achieves the assemblage of parts linked to each other on the level of style (or through the most general motivation, for example unity of time or place).

Obviously, in this last type it is *style*, the stylistic relations between the interlinked fragments, which assumes the function of motor-principle on the level of plot.

12

The way the process of plot construction is linked to style may also be demonstrated in works in which the plot is not de-centred in relation to the fable.

Let us take as an example Gogol's short story *Nos* (*The Nose*).[27] The framework and semantic system of the fable in this work are such that they bring to mind a madhouse. It is enough to follow the schema of a single fable-line, the Nose-line, to see this: Major Kovalyov's amputated nose walks around the Nevsky Prospect as 'The Nose'; 'The Nose', which attempts to flee to Riga in a post-chaise, is seized by a local policeman and delivered wrapped in a rag to the original owner. Altogether, how was it possible for such a fable-line to take shape within a plot? How was simple nonsense turned into artistic 'Nonsense'? What becomes apparent is that here, the overall semantic system plays a role. The system of connotation in *The Nose* is so arranged that it makes the fable possible.

Let us take the first appearance of the amputated nose:

'. . . saw something gleaming white . . . "solid," he said to himself . . . "what could it be?"'

'. . . a nose, a nose indeed . . . and a familiar one at that.'

'. . . "I shall put it in a corner, after I've wrapped it in a rag; let it lie there for a while and later I'll take it away."'

'. . . "Do you think I'd let a cut-off nose lie about in my room? . . . Away! Take it away! Out of my sight with it!"'

'. . . After all, bread is something baked and a nose is something altogether different.'

A stylistic analysis going into the particulars of the reader's first encounter with the amputated nose would lead too far, but from the passages quoted it is clear that the amputated nose is transformed into something ambiguous: *shto-to* (something); *plotnoye* (solid) [gender neuter]; *evo* (him); *on* (he: a very frequent pronoun whose objective, real characteristics at times fade out); *pozvolit nosu* (permit the nose) [personification], etc. And each of these threads permeating the semantic mood builds up the fable-line of the cut-off nose stylistically, in such a way that the reader, already prepared and already involved in that semantic mood, can read without surprise such strange sentences as: 'The Nose looked at the Major and slightly knitted his brows.'

A particular fable thus becomes a component part of the subject by means of the style generated by the semantic mood of the work.

It could be objected that *The Nose* is an unusual work. To me it simply provides a position from which to show that, in Andrei Bely's *Petersburg* and *Moskovskiy Chudak* (*The Moscow Eccentric*)[28] and many other works, objects assume precisely the same stance (one only has to take one look at the 'well-worn' nature of the fable in both these nevertheless highly remarkable novels to become aware of this).

But we may not assume that in works where the style is 'restrained' or 'colourless', etc., style has no function. Every work, whatever its nature, forms of itself a semantic system and however 'restrained' the style may be, it nevertheless exists as a means of building up that semantic system; a direct connection exists between the semantic system and the subject, regardless of whether the subject develops with the help of the fable or externally to it.

In different works the systems are of course different in each case. But within verbal art, there is a genre in which the fundamental connection btween the semantic system and the style is especially evident. This is the semantic system which produces verse.

In poetry, whether in the eighteenth-century heroic epic or in

Pushkin's *poema*, that connection is manifestly clear. Therefore a discussion of the metrical system in poetry constantly turns out to be a discussion of the semantic system. And ultimately, through such discussions, the question of the treatment of the plot in poetry pre-judges the question of the inter-relation between subject and fable.

Indeed for this reason the problem of genre is bound up with the question of the relation between subject and fable. Not only is this relation different in different novels, novellas, epic and lyrical poems, it also differs from novel to novella, from epic to lyric.

13

In this section I wish simply to *pose* the following problems: 1. The link between subject and style in the cinema; 2. how cinematic genres are determined by the relation of subject to fable.

To pose these two problems I have once again taken my 'impetus' from literature. The 'leap' into cinema necessitates extended studies. We have seen that in literature it is not possible to speak of fable and subject 'generally', and that subject is closely linked to a given semantic system which is in turn determined by style.

The subject function assumed by the semantic and stylistic means in *Battleship Potemkin* strikes one immediately and yet it has not been the object of a study. Studies yet to be done will cast a light on this question and not just in such manifestly clear examples. Pointing to the 'restraint' or 'naturalism' of the style in the case of some film or some director is not the same as sweeping away the role of style. Quite simply, there are a variety of styles and they have various roles, according to their relationship to the development of the subject.

Future studies of subject in cinema will be located in the study of cinematic style and in the specificities of the material.

The method film criticism adopts for the discussion of film, a method by now well established and respectable, shows how naïve we are on this level: the script is discussed (on the basis of the finished film) and then the writer turns to discussing the director. But it is a mistake to talk about the script on the basis of the finished film. Almost always, the script presents the fable 'generally', with certain elements which approach the 'jumping' nature of film. How the fable will develop, what the plot will be, these are things which the scriptwriter has no idea of, anymore than does the film director before the projection of the rushes. At that point the particularities of some given style or material may allow the fable as presented by the script to develop as a whole; that is, the script-fable may enter the film 'entire'. But those particularities may also not allow this, and in the course of work on the film, the fable is imperceptibly changed in its detail, the development directing the plot.

Discussion over a 'cast-iron' script can only occur where standardised directors' and actors' styles prevail; that is, where the script already departs slightly from a recognised cinematic style.

The absence of studies on the level of theory gives rise to even more substantial faults on the level of practice.

This is true of the problem of genres in the cinema.

Genres stemming from literature (and the theatre) are often transported into the cinema wholesale and ready-made. The results are sometimes unexpected.

For example, the documentary historical chronicle. Transported entirely from written art into cinema, it produces a film which is first and foremost *a gallery of animated portraits*. In literature, the essential element (authenticity) is self-generating by virtue of the presence of historical names, dates, etc. While in cinema, where the standpoint is a documentary one, it is authenticity itself which is the major problem. The viewers begin by asking 'is that what it was like?'

When we read a novel about Alexander I,[29] whatever his acts in the course of the narrative, they remain the acts of Alexander I. If they do not have similarity, it will be because the work 'is not a faithful portrayal', but Alexander I remains the premise. In the cinema, the naïve viewer will say: 'That actor looks just like (or not at all like) Alexander I.' And he will be right, and in all innocence, even while paying the compliment, he will be destroying the very premise of the genre — authenticity.

The problem of genre is thus closely linked to the problem of specific material and style.

The cinema has existed substantially within genres which are alien to it: the 'novel', the 'comedy', etc.

In this respect, the primitive 'slapstick comedy' was more honest and its manner of posing the problem of cinematic genre more valid than the compromise which is the film-novel.

In 'comedy' the development of the plot occurred externally to the fable; or more exactly, in terms of the fable-line of early cinema, the plot unfolded on accidental (from the point of view of the fable, but in fact specific) material. The basis of the problem is precisely there: not in the external, secondary signs of the genres of neighbouring arts, but in *the relation between the fable and the specific cinematic subject*.

Maximum accent on the subject equals minimum accent on the fable and vice versa.

'Slapstick' recalled not comedy so much as humorous verse, since the plot developed in a manner shorn of all semantic and stylistic processes.

Timidity alone prevents us from bringing out in current film genres not just the film-poem, but the lyric film-poem. Timidity alone restrains us from announcing a historical documentary as 'a gallery of animated portraits' from such and such a period on film posters.

The problem of the relation between subject and style in cinema and their role in the determination of film genres demands, as I have said, extensive studies. I have confined myself to posing the problem (Tynyanov, 1927).

So much has been written arguing or assuming the basic similarity of film with the still-photographic image that Tynyanov's insistence on their differences is useful. His attribution of the 'leaping' character of film images (which he sees as making film akin to poetry in that they both have dynamic sources in metre and rhythm) to the alternating characteristics of montage/editing has to be related to the general emphasis on montage common to the Russian Constructivist-Formalists in particular and established film-theorists in general. It has become clear since the 1920s that films can have strong poetic, rhythmical and dynamic aspects without their styles being based on any principle of alternation in the editing.

More interesting (especially considering their date) are Tynyanov's introduction of the notion of genre, and his speculation on the links between style, theme and subject. If the stress on montage and some of the terminology place Tynyanov close to the 'factographers' of *Novy Lef*, the emphasis on style and meaning establish a relation with the *mise-en-scène* criticism of the 1950s and 1960s. Tynyanov is interested in narrative structures which express their themes directly and also in those which act as a 'puzzle' or problem alongside the thematic material of the film. From either angle the articulation of the narrative-structure will be an essential part of the film's process.

Much of the Russian material of the 1920s is concerned to try and establish a basic working-system for film in its own right: a working-system that draws heavily on the technical and material characteristics of the medium. What is less clear in these texts is the varying weight of their appeals to notions of ideology. Ideology is itself a basically problematic concept. In the context in which we are looking at it here, it has a range of possible meanings, encompassing at least the three following areas: a) the relationship of film to society in general or a set of social structures; b) the way(s) in which spectators view and comprehend cinematic products – here ideology is sometimes seen as meaning roughly 'experience', implying a largely un-reasoned, 'natural' process which operates against knowledge or science, both of which depend on the distanced elaboration of concepts; c) the production of a clear political content, either directly in the films or indirectly through a procedure of foregrounding (i.e. 'exaggerating' through technique) certain chosen elements. Here the very process of exaggeration is thought to produce awareness of the 'gaps' in 'natural' experience; it is then hoped that political consciousness will spring through the gaps and give birth either to knowledge or at least to a 'better' ideology.

More recent marxist and marxist-influenced theory attempts to develop combinations of these three notions of ideology. Where traditional ('vulgar') marxism tended to see the presence of a story as a necessary condition for the artwork to provide a real (i.e. potentially critical) account of the real world and its social structures, constraints and ideologies, some modern marxists see the narrative structure – or at any rate, narrative structures deriving from the nineteenth-century novel – as a constitutive element of falsehood, working in such a way as to bind the spectator into a false (though 'natural') conception of 'the real'. Narrative is an element that militates against knowledge (the true consciousness?) because it attempts to conceal itself, to imply that this is how the world is. Colin MacCabe on what he calls 'The Classic Realist Text':

One of the difficulties of any discussion about realism is the lack of any really effective vocabulary with which to discuss the topic. Most discussions turn on the problems of the production of discourse which will fully adequate the real. This notion of adequacy is accepted both by the realists and indeed by the anti-realists whose main argument is that no discourse can ever be adequate to the multifarious nature of the real. This notion of the real is, however, I wish to suggest, a notion which is tied to a particular type of literary production – the nineteenth century realist novel. The dominance of this novel form is such that people still tend to confuse the general question of realism with the particular forms of the nineteenth century realist novel. In order to make the discussion clearer I want therefore to attempt to define the structure which typifies the nineteenth century realist novel and to show how that structure can also be used to describe a great number of films. The detour through literature is necessary because, in many ways, the structure is much more obvious there and also because of the historical dominance of the classic realist novel over much film production. What to a large extent will be lacking in this article is the specific nature of the film form but this does not seem to me to invalidate the setting up of certain essential categories from which further discussion must progress. The structure I will attempt to disengage I shall call the classic realist text and I shall apply it to novels and films.

A classic realist text may be defined as one in which there is a hierarchy amongst the discourses which compose the text and this hierarchy is defined in terms of an empirical notion of truth. Perhaps the easiest way to understand this is through a reflection on the use of inverted commas within the classic realist novel. While those sections in the text which are contained in inverted commas may cause a certain difficulty for the reader – a certain confusion vis-à-vis what really is the case – this difficulty is abolished by the unspoken (or more accurately the unwritten) prose that surrounds them. In the classical realist novel the narrative prose functions as a metalanguage that can state all the truths in the object language – those words held in inverted commas – and can also explain the relation of this object language to the real. The metalanguage can thereby explain the relation of this object language to the world and the strange methods by which the object languages attempt to express truths which are straightforwardly conveyed in the metalanguage. What I have called an unwritten prose (or a metalanguage) is exactly that language, which while placing other languages between inverted commas and regarding them as certain material expressions which express certain meanings, regards those same meanings as finding transparent expression within the metalanguage itself. Transparent in the sense that the metalanguage is not regarded as material; it is dematerialised to achieve perfect representation – to let the identity of things shine through the window of words. For insofar as the metalanguage is treated itself as material – it, too, can be reinterpreted; new meanings can be found for it in a further metalanguage. The problem is the problem that has troubled western thought since the pre-Socratics[30] recognised the separation between what was said and the act of saying. This separation must be thought both as time and space – as the space, which in the distance from page to eye or mouth to ear allows the possibility of misunderstanding – as the time taken to traverse the page or listen to an utterance which ensures the deferred interpretation of words which are always only defined by what follows. The problem is that in the moment that we say a sentence the meaning (what is said) seems fixed and evident but what is said does not exist solely for the moment and is open to further interpretations. Even in this formulation of the problem I have presupposed an original moment when there is strict contemporaneity between the saying and what is said, but the difficulty is more radical for there is no such original moment. The separation is always already there as we cannot locate the presence of what is said – distributed as it is through space – nor the present of what is said – distributed as it is through time.

This separation bears witness to the real as articulated. The thing represented does not appear in a moment of pure identity as it tears itself out of the world and presents itself, but rather is caught in an articulation in which each object is defined in a set of differences and oppositions.

It is this separation that the unwritten text attempts to *anneal*, to make whole, through denying its own status as writing – as marks of material difference distributed through time and space. Whereas other discourses within the text are considered as material which are open to re-interpretation, the narrative discourse simply allows reality to appear and denies its own status as articulation. This relationship between discourses can be clearly seen in the work of such a writer as George Eliot. In the scene in *Middlemarch*[31] where Mr Brooke goes to visit the Dagleys' farm we read two different languages. One is the educated, well-meaning, but not very intelligent discourse of Mr Brooke and the other is the uneducated, violent and very nearly unintelligible discourse of the drunken Dagley. But the whole dialogue is surrounded by a metalanguage, which being unspoken is also unwritten, and which places these discourses in inverted commas and can thus discuss these discourses' relation to truth – a truth which is illuminatingly revealed in the metalanguage. The metalanguage reduces the object language into a simple division between form and content and extracts the meaningful content from the useless form. One can see this process at work in the following passage which ends the scene:

He [Mr Brooke] had never been insulted on his own land before, and had been inclined to regard himself as a general favourite (we are all apt to do so, when we think of our own amiability more than what other people are likely to want of us). When he had quarrelled with Caleb Garth twelve years before he had thought that the tenants would be pleased with the landlord's taking everything into his own hands.

Some who follow the narrative of this experience may wonder at the midnight darkness of Mr Dagley; but nothing was easier in those times than for a hereditary farmer of his grade to be ignorant, in spite somehow of having a rector in the twin parish who was a gentleman to the backbone, a curate nearer at hand who preached more learnedly than the rector, a landlord who had gone into everything, especially fine art and social improvement and all the lights of Middlemarch only three miles off.[32]

This passage provides the necessary interpretations for the discourses that we have read earlier in the chapter. Both the discourses of Dagley and Mr Brooke are revealed as springing from two types of ignorance which the metalanguage can expose and reveal. So we have Mr Brooke's attitude to what his tenants thought of him contrasted with the reality which is available through the narrative prose. No discourse is allowed to speak for itself but rather it must be placed in a context which will reduce it to a simple explicable content. And in the claim that the narrative prose has direct access to a final reality we can find the claim of the classic realist novel to present us with the truths of human nature. The ability to reveal the truth about Mr Brooke is the ability that guarantees the generalisations of human nature.

Thus then a first definition of the classic realist text – but does this definition carry over into films where it is certainly less evident where to locate the dominant discourse? It seems to me that it does and in the following fashion. The narrative prose achieves its position of dominance because it is in the position of knowledge and this function of knowledge is taken up in the cinema by the narration of events. Through the knowledge we gain from the narrative we can split the discourses of the various characters from their situation and compare what is said in these discourses with what has been revealed to us through narration. The camera shows us what happens – it tells the truth against which we can measure the discourses. A good example of this classical realist structure is to be found in Pakula's film *Klute*.[33] This film is of particular interest because it was widely praised for its realism on its release. Perhaps even more significantly it tended to be praised for its realistic presentation of the leading woman, Bree (played by Jane Fonda).

In *Klute* the relationship of dominance between discourses is peculiarly accentuated by the fact that the film is interspersed with fragments of Bree talking to her psychiatrist. This subjective discourse can be exactly measured against the reality provided by the unfolding of the story. Thus all her talk of independence is portrayed as finally an illusion as we discover, to no great surprise but to our immense relief, what she really wants is to settle down in the mid-West with John Klute (the detective played by Donald Sutherland) and have a family. The final sequence of the film is particularly telling in this respect. While Klute and Bree pack their bags to leave, the soundtrack records Bree at her last meeting with her psychiatrist. Her own estimation of the situation is that it most probably won't work but the reality of the image ensures us that this is the way it will really be. Indeed Bree's monologue is even more interesting – for in relation to the reality of the image it marks a definite advance on her previous statements. She has gained insight through the plot development and like many good heroines of classic realist texts her discourse is more nearly adequate to the truth at the end of the film than at the beginning. But if a progression towards knowledge is what marks Bree, it is possession of knowledge which marks the narrative, the reader of the film and John Klute himself. For Klute is privileged by the narrative as the one character whose discourse is also a discourse of knowledge. Not only is Klute a detective and thus can solve the problem of his friend's disappearance – he is also a man, and a man who because he has not come into contact with the city has not had his virility undermined. And it is as a full-blooded man that he can know not only the truth of the mystery of the murders but also the truth of the woman Bree. Far from being a film which goes any way to portraying a woman liberated from male definition (a common critical response), *Klute* exactly guarantees that the real essence of woman can only be discovered and defined by a man.

The analysis sketched here is obviously very schematic but what, hopefully, it does show is that the structure of the classic realist text can be found in film as well. That narrative of events – the knowledge which the film provides of how things really are – is the metalanguage in which we can talk of the various characters in the film. What would still remain to be done in the elaboration of the structure of the classic realist text in cinema is a more detailed account of the actual mechanisms by which the narrative is privileged (and the way in which one or more of the characters within the narrative can be equally privileged) and also a history of the development of this dominant narrative. On the synchronic level it would be necessary to attempt an analysis of the relationship between the various types of shot and their combination into sequences – are there for example certain types of shot which are coded as subjective and therefore subordinate to others which are guaranteed as objective? In addition how does music work as the guarantee or otherwise of truth? On the diachronic level it would be necessary to study how this form was produced – what relationship obtains between the classic realist text and technical advances such as the development of the talkie? What ideological factors were at work in the production and dominance of the classic realist text?

To return, however, to the narrative discourse. It is necessary to attempt to understand the type of relations that this dominant discourse produces. The narrative discourse cannot be mistaken in its identifications because the narrative discourse is not present as discourse – as articulation. The unquestioned nature of the narrative discourse entails that the only problem that reality poses is to go and look and see what *Things* there *are*. The relationship between the reading subject and the real is placed as one of pure specularity. The real is not articulated – it is. These features imply two essential features of the classic realist text:

1 The classic realist text cannot deal with the real as contradictory.
2 In a reciprocal movement the classic realist text ensures the position of the subject in a relation of dominant specularity.

The Classic Realist Text as Progressive art

. . . It may be objected that the account that I have given of the classic literary text is deficient in the following extremely important fashion. It ignores what is the usual criterion for realism, that is to say subject matter. The category of the classic realist text lumps together in book and film *The Grapes of Wrath* and *The Sound of Music, L'Assommoir* and *Toad of Toad Hall*.[34] In order to find a criterion with which to make distinctions within the area of the classic realist text it is necessary to reflect on contradiction. I have stated that the classic realist text cannot deal with the real in its contradiction because of the unquestioned status of the representation at the level of the dominant discourse. In order to understand how contradiction can be dealt with it is necessary to investigate the workings of an operation that is often opposed to representation, namely montage.

In his essay on 'Word and Image' in *The Film Sense*, Eisenstein defines montage. Amongst numerous examples of montage he quotes the following from Ambrose Bierce's *Fantastic Fables*:[35]

A Woman in widow's weeds was weeping upon a grave.
'Console yourself, madam,' said a Sympathetic Stranger.
'Heaven's mercies are infinite. There is another man somewhere,
beside your husband, with whom you can still be happy.'
'There was,' she sobbed – 'there was, but this is his grave.'[36]

Eisenstein explains the effect of this fable in terms of an interaction
between the visual representations in this story. The woman is a
representation and so is the mourning dress – they are, in Eisenstein's
terms, objectively representable – but the juxtaposition of these
representations gives rise to a new image that is not representable –
namely that the woman is a widow. It is the expectation created by
the juxtaposition which is undercut by the final line uttered by the
woman. For the moment we shall only notice the following point:
1. that Eisenstein, concerned very largely with a simple definition of
representation, fails to recognise that widow is just as objective a
representation as woman or mourning dress and
2. that montage involves both an interaction between representations and a shock.
Eisenstein continues his explanation by expanding his distinction
between representation (the raw material of the montage) and image
(that which is produced by the montage itself).

Take a white circular disc of average size and smooth surface, its
circumference divided into sixty equal parts. At every fifth division
is set a figure in the order of succession of 1 to 12. At the centre of
the disc are fixed two metal rods, moving freely on their fixed
ends, pointed at their free ends, one being equal to the radius of the
disc, the other rather shorter. Let the longer pointed rod have its
free end resting on the figure 12 and the shorter in succession
pointing towards the figures 1, 2, 3 and so on up to 12. This will
comprise a series of geometrical representations of successive
relations to the two metal rods to one another expressed in the
dimensions of 30, 60, 90 degrees, and so on up to 360 degrees.
If, however, this disc is provided with a mechanism that imparts
steady movement to the metal rods, the geometrical figure formed
on the surface acquires a special meaning: it is now not simply a
representation, it is an *image* of time.[37]

The confusion that led Eisenstein to count woman and mourning
dress as representable but widow as non-representable can be seen at
work again in this passage. Eisenstein thinks of the world as being
composed of basic objects available to sight which are then linked
together in various ways by the perceiving subject with the aid of his

past experiences. That this is his position is made abundantly clear in the passage which follows the passage I have just quoted. He takes the example of Vronsky looking at his watch, after Anna Karenina has told him that she is pregnant,[38] and being so shocked that he sees the position of the hands but not the time. Thus the position of the hands is the primitive object in the world and the time is what the human subject creates through his linking of the object with other items of his experience. Montage is thus, for Eisenstein, in this passage (which must not be confused with Eisenstein's cinematic practice), the manipulation of definite representations to produce images in the mind of the spectator. But now it can be seen that this definition of montage does not contradict representation at all. If we understand by representation the rendering of identities in the world then Eisenstein's account of montage is not opposed to representation but is simply a secondary process which comes after representation. Eisenstein would have montage linking onto representation but not in any sense challenging it. The representation starts from an identity in the world which it re-presents, the montage starts from representations, identities, and combines them to form an image.

Eisenstein's acceptance of representation can be seen in those passages where representation is contrasted with montage. For Eisenstein the opposite to montage is 'Affidavit-exposition' which he defines as *'in film terms, representations shot from a single set-up'*.[39] Thus montage is the showing of the same representation from different points of view. And it is from this point that we can begin to challenge Eisenstein's conception of montage. A point of view suggests two things. Firstly a view − something that is seen − and secondly a location from which the view may be had, the sight may be seen. Thus the suggestion is that there are different locations from which we can see. But in all cases the sight remains the same − the activity of representation is not the determining factor in the sight seen but simply the place from where it is seen. The inevitable result of this is that there is something the same which we all see but which appears differently because of our position. But if there is identity; if there is something over and above the views which can be received at different points then this identity must be discernible from some other 'point of view'. And this neutral point of view is exactly the 'representations shot from a single set-up'.

What is at work in Eisenstein's argument is the idea that there is some fixed reality which is available to us from an objective point of view (the single set-up). Montage is simply putting these fixed elements together in such a way that the subject brings forth other elements in his experience − but without any change in the identities, the elements that are being rendered. It is essential to realise that this account leaves both subject and object unchallenged and that montage becomes a kind of super-representation which is more effective at demonstrating the real qualities of the object through the links it can form within the subject. Thus Eisenstein would analyse the Bierce story as the representation of a given set of elements which are first organised in one way then in another. There are, however, no such set of fixed elements in the Bierce story. It is not that there is a set of elements which the reader composes 'in his mind' but rather that these elements are already determined by the method of representation. What Eisenstein ignores is that the method of representation (the language: verbal or cinematic) determines in its structural activity (the oppositions which can be articulated) both the places where the object 'appears' and the 'point' from which the object is seen. It is this point which is exactly the place allotted to the reading subject.

A careful analysis of the Bierce story may enable us to discover how montage operates and why that operation is difficult to grasp. We can read three different discourses at work in the Bierce story (a discourse being defined as a set of significant oppositions). The narrative discourse, the discourse of the Sympathetic Stranger and the discourse of the Woman. The question is whether as Eisenstein holds, that the narrative discourse represents simply a woman and a mourning dress. But 'woman' is not some simple identity as Eisenstein would have us believe. Whereas the Sympathetic Stranger identifies woman in terms of religion and state – thus our relationships are determined in heaven and are institutionalised by the state on earth – the Woman determines her own identity as 'woman' in terms of desire and transgression – relationships are formed through the transgressing of the state's institutions and this transgression is linked with a certain sexuality; for relationships between a man and a woman outside the bond of holy matrimony are explicitly sexual. We can now understand that the montage works through a contest between the identities offered by the different discourses. In the Bierce story, the woman's statement jars with what has gone before so that we re-read it – the identifications that we made (that were made for us) are undermined by new ones. What is thrown into doubt is exactly the identity (the nature) of woman and this doubt is achieved through the 'shock' of the woman's statement as the identity already proferred is subverted. It is also clear from this analysis that there is no neutral place from which we can see the view and where all the points are located. There is no possible language of 'affidavit-exposition' that would show the scene 'as it really is'. For how we see the scene will be determined by the way in which we identify 'woman' – and this determination is a feature of the available discourses; the discourses in which 'woman' can figure.

We are still, however, left with the problem of how we can mistake this effect of montage, as I have suggested Eisenstein has done, and the answer to this question can be found in the apparent similarity of the discourses in the Bierce story. For the three discourses are so similar that we can be persuaded to read them as one. All that is missing from the first and second is provided by the third. The third discourse can be read as 'closing' the text. For with the information thus given to us we can read the previous discourses in a 'final' – that is to say *once and for all* – manner. We can fill in the gaps in the first two discourses – see the real identities which are mistaken. But this is to ignore the fact that what is at question in the story are different discourses. Different discourses can be defined as discourses in which different oppositions are possible. Although at one level – the level of the legal relationship to the body and the grave – both discourses coincide (she *is* or *is not* the wife), at another level there are a set of oppositions of an emotional nature (she *does* or *does not* mourn some man) which the stranger cannot articulate outside the oppositions determined by the legal relationship. Bierce's story, through the coincidences between the discourses on one level, suggests to Eisenstein a set of identities in the world. But the identities rest in the discourses. Thus opposed to Eisenstein's concept of montage resting on the juxtapositions of identities already rendered, we could talk of montage as the effect generated by a conflict of discourse in which the oppositions available in the juxtaposed discourses are contradictory and in conflict.

All this by way of explaining that the classic realist text (a heavily 'closed' discourse) cannot deal with the real in its contradictions and that in the same movement it fixes the subject in a point of view from which everything becomes obvious. There is, however, a level of contradiction into which the classic realist text can enter. This is the contradiction between the dominant discourse of the text and the dominant ideological discourses of the time. Thus a classic realist text in which a strike is represented as a just struggle in which oppressed workers attempt to gain some of their rightful wealth would be in contradiction with certain contemporary ideological discourses and as such might be classified as progressive. It is here that subject matter enters into the argument and where we can find the justification for Marx and Engels's praise of Balzac and Lenin's texts on the revolutionary force of Tolstoy's texts which ushered the Russian peasant onto the stage of history. Within contemporary films one could think of the films of Costa-Gavras or such television documentaries as *Cathy Come Home*.[40] What is, however, still impossible for the classic realist text is to offer any perspectives for struggle due to its inability to investigate contradiction. It is thus not surprising that these films tend either to be linked to a social-democratic conception of progress – if we reveal injustices then they will go away – or certain *ouvrieriste* tendencies which tend to see the working class, outside any dialectical movement, as the simple possessors of truth. It is at this point that Brecht's demand that literary and artistic productions be regarded as social events gains its force. The contradictions between the dominant discourse in a classic realist text and the dominant ideological discourses at work in a society are what provide the criteria for discriminating within the classic realist text. And these criteria will often resolve themselves into questions of subject-matter. That this tends to leave open any question about the eternal values of art is not something that should worry us. As Brecht remarks: 'To be frank, I do not set such an excessively high value on the concept of endurance. How can we foresee whether future generations will wish to preserve the memory of these figures [*figures created by Balzac or Tolstoy*]? (Balzac and Tolstoy will scarcely be in a position to oblige them to do so, however ingenious the methods with which they set their plots in motion.) I suspect it will depend on whether it will be a socially relevant statement if someone says: "That" (and "that" will refer to a contemporary) "is a Père Goriot character". Perhaps such characters will not survive? Perhaps they precisely arose in a cramping web of relations of a type which will no longer exist [. . .]' (MacCabe, 1974).

The most interesting parts of this text concern the ideas drawn from linguistics: the insistence that all languages are material, and the rejection of realism's claim that its own metalanguage is transparent. Also derived from linguistics is the idea that language is 'an articulation in which each object is defined in a set of differences and oppositions'. But the text stands or falls by its idea that it is the narrative (prose in the novel, organisation in film) which is 'in a position of knowledge' and 'tells the truth'. In one sense this position re-states Bazin ('the camera shows us what happens'), while shifting the emphasis from the technical impression of reality to narrative organisation. But it could certainly be argued that there are very many films in which neither narrative nor visual appearances provide such a transparency, and that even in the ones where they do, such transparency is given as a convention, a device which the spectators are invited to be aware of. Thus there has to be a real doubt whether the category of classic realist text' is a meaningful one, and whether there is much to be gained from relating films to nineteenth-century novels.

Another problem arises from the imprecise use of the term 'discourse'. Traditionally, it has a range of meanings in the area of speech, conversation, talk, reasoning. MacCabe uses it to define both the overall action of a text (book or film) and specific elements within such texts. Without wishing to deny that particular characters in 'realist' films or novels may well embody or vocalise particular positions which the organiser of the narrative wishes the reader to take seriously, it seems difficult to take Bree in *Klute* or the woman in Bierce's story as productions of 'the discourse of the Woman'. And while any narrative structure must have 'closures' – must orient its readers/spectators in specific directions – it does not necessarily follow that these choices enclose the spectator in one allotted space or 'point from which the object is seen'. MacCabe comments that Eisenstein's montage is 'a kind of super-representation', which is quite correct on one level (see pp. 18–22), but ignores Eisenstein's effort to 'change ... the elements that are being represented' in the process of montage itself.

MacCabe's endorsement of Brecht's 'demand that literary and artistic productions be regarded as social events' seems rather naïve. As we have seen, since the earliest theory film productions have been regarded as social events. The problem is rather that as yet there are no very convincing models for understanding films as both artistic productions and social events. Marxist and non-marxist critics alike have tended to assume fairly simple relationships between films, their production contexts and their audiences. MacCabe attempts to elaborate a complicated relationship, but the elaboration rests in the last analysis on a familiar simple relationship: the film tells the spectator what he should be thinking.

Brecht wrote very little about cinema, and his involvement in it was marginal. He seems often to have taken the traditional marxist view that it is a drug, a permanent seduction of the working class away from their own true interests. On the other hand, the following short extracts from *The Threepenny Opera*

Trial propose some more interesting ideas. In this section of his report on the trial, Brecht is criticising 'a certain number of *representations* characteristic of the present state of bourgeois ideology'. The representations, which he sees as having the force of being typical, are listed in italics and inverted commas at the head of each paragraph:

'Film needs art'

'The sound film would gain infinitely from being enlivened by the genuinely poetic script' (*Kölnische Zeitung*).[41]

'I find this attitude on the part of producers and their following totally unproductive. As far as I'm concerned, they need to know nothing about art, but they ought to be capable of assessing its economic worth and proceeding purely in terms of expediency, just as a progressive manufacturer does when he assigns certain kinds of work to real artists' (*Frankfurter Zeitung*).

The demand that a film ought to be artistic has not met with opposition from any quarter. It features equally forcefully in the columns of the press and the administration of the film industry. Since films are saleable only as luxury goods, they have from the outset shared the same market as art and the generally accepted notion that luxury products need refining, which is the job of art, itself the most refined of all luxury goods, has ensured that artists are regularly engaged to work in the cinema.

No attempt will be made here to pose that familiar and subtle distinction between true and false art in order to prove that film has instinctively grabbed hold of the false (to be saleable, art has first to be on sale). Their definition as luxury goods has already conferred inverted commas on both kinds of art. In any case 'art' has forcefully carried the day as far as the apparatus of cinema is concerned. Almost everything we see on the screen today is 'art'. It has to be 'art'. It is as 'art', albeit under a rather different and nowadays slightly obsolete form, that the novel, the drama, travel journals and works of criticism have already been imposed, i.e. put on the market. The cinematic form has opened up greater possibilities of dissemination (as well as of huge returns on capital), and to the charms of the past it has added those of modern technology. Only thus can the film director assert his 'art', with encouraging pressure from the sales department, in the face of the new equipment; what he thus asserts is what he manages to do himself, in the way of what he, as average viewer, understands as art. He doesn't know what art should do. He probably thinks it concerns generating universal emotions, assembling impressions and all that sort of thing. He works with about as much intelligence in the field of art as would an oyster, and likewise in the field of technology. Since he is unable to understand anything about the equipment, he violates it with his 'art'. In order to grasp reality with the new equipment, he would need to be an artist, or at least a connoisseur of reality, but never a 'connoisseur of art', and thus he uses it, since it's much easier to produce 'art', the familiar, the well tried, the good sellers. He gains a reputation as a tasteful arranger; that is, 'he understands something about art' — as if it were possible to understand something about art without understanding something about reality. So reality is constituted by the equipment as well as, at the same time, by the content. Such a situation deprives the new equipment of some of the opportunities that were once open to it. This is to leave completely aside the question of whether or not its principal task was to produce the social phenomenon called art, though it could more easily have tackled the production of that art as well had it been able to disregard in the first place the demand to produce something like the old 'art'. Had cinema been applied to sciences, such as medicine, biology, statistics, etc., to record visible behaviour or to show simultaneous processes, it might have learnt more easily than it will now to record people's reciprocal behaviour. This is difficult enough and will not be achieved unless the cinema is assigned an absolutely firm and positive function among the concerns of society as a whole. What complicates the situation still more is that, now more than ever, the simple 'reproduction of reality' says very little about that reality. A photograph of the Krupp factories or of the AEG[42] reveals practically nothing about those institutions. Actual reality has slid into the functional. The commercialisation of human relations, at the factory, for example, means that those relations can no longer be expressed. It is thus in effect necessary to 'construct something', something 'artificial', 'set up'. Art is therefore as necessary as ever, but the old notion of art as based on experience has broken down. For whoever presents only that part of reality which is capable of being lived is not restoring reality. The possibility of living it as a total experience is long past. Those who present us with the obscure associations and the anonymous feelings which they produce are no longer presenting reality as it is. It is no longer possible to tell the fruit from its flavour. When we say this we are talking about an art which has a completely different function in social life, namely that of presenting reality. We do so solely in order to liberate 'art' as it exists here and now, from such demands as do not derive from its function.

It is therefore incorrect to say that the cinema needs art, without establishing a new conception of art. . . .

'A film is a commodity'

'. . . this does not allow us to assert that there are no grounds for treating the film-maker less well or otherwise than the author of a play. The former is the manufacturer of a mass commodity which has to be disseminated world-wide. Because of this and the attendant commercial risk, he is weighed down by a heavier economic burden. A different value has also to be placed on the financial expenditure involved . . . but in other respects too, the business practice of a film manufacturer whose production is totally geared to the manufacture of a commodity which must be sold, is different. With his money at stake, he is much more dependent on the times, the tastes of the public, the topicality of the subject and world competition, than a theatre director working in his own town' (Supreme Court judgment).

'All those who have professional or business relations with the cinema should be clear that they are addressing themselves to an industry, to people who stake all their money on one card, and who must then either clean up in thousands of cinemas or else simply lose their money' (*Kinematograph*).

There is general agreement that a film, even the most artistic, is a commodity. But some people believe this does not in any way detract from the film which is only incidentally a commodity, the commercial form being only the one under which it trades and which must in no way brand it once and for all. Indeed the whole art is precisely to free film from such a fall from grace. Those who think like this have no idea of the transmuting power of commerce. The fact that under capitalism the world is transformed into a production *in the form of exploitation and corruption* is less important than the fact of this *transformation* itself. Others say that film is differentiated from and may be more than a work of art in that it is a commodity: in other words, that its essence is constituted by its commercial character. This fact is deplored almost without exception. Apparently, no one is capable of imagining that being put into trade in such a way might be beneficial to the work of art. The fact that an object is saleable, however, is glossed over by invoking 'heroic realism' (seeing things as they are) – something that no businessman would do. There remain works of art of other types which are not commodities, or are only so in small part, so that they are hardly ruffled, so to speak, by the commercial character. But only those whose eyes are closed to the monstrous power of that revolutionary process which sweeps all the objects of this world, without any exception or hesitation, into commercial circulation, could believe that works of art of whatever type could escape. For the deeper meaning of this process lies in that fact that nothing is left unrelated to something else, everything is interlinked, just as all men (in the form of commodities) are delivered up to all men; this is the process of communication pure and simple.

We are therefore dealing with two erroneous ideas:

1. The commercial ('bad') nature of the film is transcended by art.
2. The artistic nature of other types of art is not disturbed by this ('bad') process which affects the cinema.

'The cinema serves leisure'

'Producers cannot do otherwise. A film represents such a great financial undertaking, and constitutes such a sum total of risk, capital investment and work, that it should not have to be endangered by the whims of the *prima donna*, by ignorance of the demands of the cinema, or, as in the Brecht case, by political tendentiousness no less' (Dr Frankfurter, Counsel for the film company, in *Frankfurter Zeitung*).

As long as the social function of cinema is not examined critically, all film criticism will be nothing more than a critique of symptoms and will itself be of a purely symptomatic nature. It exhausts itself on questions of taste and thus remains totally imprisoned within class-based prejudices. It does not recognise taste as a commodity or weapon of a particular class but sets it up as an absolute (something everyone can buy and is thus within everyone's reach, but not everyone can afford it). Thus *within* a particular class (in this instance one with purchasing power) taste may be a productive force in that it creates something like a 'life-style'. (Immediately after the bourgeois revolution of 1918, tendencies in this direction were evident in cinema. Large strata of white-collar workers who saw in inflation a chance to rise into the ruling classes, learnt from Bruno Kastner[43] and the like a remarkable stylised demeanour, which could at that time be observed in any café.) But it is precisely this sharp opposition between work and leisure so characteristic of the capitalist mode of production which divides all intellectual activities into those serving work and those serving leisure and which organises the latter into a system for reproduction of the strength to work. Entertainment must not contain anything that work contains. In the interests of production, entertainment dwells on matters unrelated to production. A homogeneous life-style cannot, of course, be created thus. This failing cannot be attributed to art being swept into the production cycle, but on the contrary to the fact that this has happened only in such an incomplete way and that it has had to create an island of 'non-production'. Once in front of the screen, the man who has bought a ticket is transformed into a loafer, an exploiter, and, given that the object of exploitation is located within himself, it could be said that he is a victim of 'imploitation'.

'Humanity must play a role in cinema'

'The human aspect must be deepened' (Film director).

'It doesn't matter what the story is about, it may even be thoroughly foolish so long as, as is almost always the case these days, the foolishness or sentimentality of the framework of the plot is embedded in dramatic-mimetic details which are true to life and close to reality, through which the human aspect triumphs in a hundred single instances over the crude unlikelihood of the whole structure' (Thomas Mann).

This notion corresponds to the notion that all films should be petty-bourgeois. The general acceptability of this apparently reasonable notion (reasonable in that who would want to make any other kind of film, or if one such were made, want to watch it?) is generated by the relentless demands for 'depth' made by the 'art'-obsessed metaphysicians of the press. It is also they who wish to see the 'fateful' stressed in human relations. Once an exalted conception, fate has long since become no more than a banal commonplace by means of which people's accommodation to their conditions of existence has brought about that longed for 'transfiguration' and 'interiorisation'. The notion of fate has also become a neat notion of the class struggle in which one class 'inflicts' the fate of another. The demands of our metaphysicians are as usual never too hard to satisfy. One can easily imagine all they reject presented to them in such a way that they welcome it rapturously. If for them certain love stories were elevated or reduced to *Romeo and Juliet*, and thrillers to *Macbeth*, that is, famous plays which must contain nothing else (which must show no other kind of human conduct, or explain the course of the world by any other driving force) they would certainly immediately cry that it is the 'how' and not the 'what' that makes these stories petty-bourgeois. Their beloved 'human' aspect, the 'humanity' (particularly when qualified by the word 'eternal' and intended as something like indanthrene) of

Othello ('my wife belongs to me!'), of Hamlet ('better to sleep on it one more time'), of Macbeth ('I was meant for better things') and so on, all this seems, on the mass-scale today, simply petty-bourgeois and nothing more. If one demands to have the human aspect one can have it only in this form, the demand itself being petty-bourgeois. The grandeur of those passions, the extent to which they were non-petty-bourgeois, was once determined by the role they played in society, i.e. by their revolutionary role. Even the effect *Battleship Potemkin* produces on these people is derived from the revulsion they would feel if their wives were to serve them up rotten meat ('That's going a bit too far!'). And Chaplin too is well aware of the need to be 'human', i.e. petty-bourgeois, if he wants to try something different. This is why he occasionally modified his style without too many scruples (cf. the famous close-up of the dog's expression which ends *City Lights*).[44]

What cinema really needs is external action, not introspective psychology. And in this sense, capitalism, by instigating, organising and automatising certain needs on the mass-scale, acts in a way that is straightforwardly revolutionary. By concentrating on 'external' action alone and reducing everything to processes, no longer recognising the hero as the mediator, or man as the measure of all things, it demolishes the introspective psychology of the bourgeois novel and so lays waste whole stretches of ideology. This external standpoint is appropriate to the cinema and makes it important. Film can freely adopt the principles of a non-Aristotelian dramaturgy (i.e. one that does not rest on empathy and *mimesis*.) Thus, for example the Russian film *The Road to Life* reveals these non-Aristotelian methods simply by the thematic of the film (the education of abandoned children by specifically socialist methods) leading the viewer to make causal connections between the attitude of the teacher and that of the pupils. The decisive (educational) scenes ensure that the investigation of causes is the principal object of interest for the viewer so that he 'instinctively' rejects any of the reasons for homelessness which the old dramaturgy based on empathy would provide (domestic unhappiness, then spiritual suffering, rather than world or civil war). Even the use of work as a pedagogical method fills the viewer with scepticism, for the simple reason that the film does not show that in the Soviet Union, in complete opposition to what happens in other countries, work indeed determines morality. As soon as man emerges as an object, causal relations become decisive. The great American comedies also present man as an object and could well have an audience of noisy reflexologists. Behaviourism is a psychology which stems from the need of commercial production to acquire means of influencing the buyer. Thus, it is an active psychology, totally progressive and revolutionary. It has limits, which correspond with its capitalist function (reflexes are biological, only in certain Chaplin films do they begin to become social). Here too the only way lies over the corpse of capitalism, but again this is a good way.

'A film must be the work of a collective'

'I imagine it would be of great importance for those concerned, artists as well as producers, to engage in discussions on the question of the formation of a collective and its methods of work' (*Reichsfilmblatt*).

This is a progressive idea. Indeed, the cinema should not produce anything that a collective cannot produce. This limitation alone would in itself be a very fertile rule, since it would at least eliminate 'art'. A collective, quite unlike an individual, cannot work without precise guidelines, and a cosy chat is not what is meant by a firm line. For instance, if the collective had specifically didactic intentions, it would immediately constitute an organic body. It is not because of some universally applicable law, but because of the nature of capitalism that everything 'unique' and 'particular' can be created only by individuals and that collectives generate only standardised mass-produced goods. What sort of collective do we have in the cinema today? A collective composed of the financier, the salesmen (who know about audiences), the director, technicians and writers. The director is necessary because the backer does not want to have anything to do with art; the salesman because the director has to be corrupted; the technician, not because the equipment is complicated – it is incredibly primitive – but because the director does not have even the most primitive idea of technical matters; and, finally, the writer, beause the public is too lazy to write for itself. In such circumstances, who could fail to want the individual's contribution to production to be unrecognisable? At no point during work on *The Threepenny Opera*, including work done for the trial, did those concerned have the same conception of the content, the aim of the film, the audience, the equipment and so on. In fact a collective can only create works which transform the 'public' into collectives as well (Brecht, 1931).

Brecht's general aesthetic positions are both realist – in that he believes in a real world and in a necessity for art to give an account of it – and anti-realist – in that he demands that the principal action should take place inside the spectator's head as well as on the stage. The account of the world is a process of criticism in which the spectator is invited to take some part. But it is hard to reconcile the vision of the film-spectator as 'lazy and exploitive' with the subsequent discovery that the cinema's taste for 'external action' as opposed to introspective psychologism disposes the same spectator towards social action. Brecht's rejection of 'art' and his acceptance of film as merchandise are tonic, and the point that film-work is collective is a simple but important one, often omitted from critical discussion, but Brecht did not have enough interest in film to think his ideas through very far.

The aftermath of the events of May 1968 in France produced an upsurge of interest in marxist accounts of film. This interest took many forms; the one that most directly concerns discussions of film and realism derives principally from the marxist distinction between Ideology (lived experience and its reflections, e.g. philosophy, systems of belief, art) and Science (the production of self-conscious theory out of ideology). The distinction was given new force in the late 1960s and early 1970s by the writings of the French marxist philosopher Louis Althusser. Althusser's ideas had some influence on discussion of film, as the following text by Jean-Paul Fargier of the magazine *Cinéthique* demonstrates. Fargier attempts to chart the relationship between film and politics, and to place film firmly in the area of ideology:

When bourgeois idealists baldly assert that the cinema has 'nothing to do with' politics, we immediately feel tempted to assert the exact opposite: that the cinema is always political, because in the class struggle nothing is irrelevant, nothing can be put in PARENTHESES. With this head-on clash of views, one being the exact *reverse* of the other, a theoretically ill-defined subject, the cinema, enters a theoretically well-defined practice, politics. Such a *situation* cannot be anything but ideological. The bald statement from which it proceeds cannot be integrated into a theory of the cinema until we recognise that it carries any number of imprecisions which have to be clarified, and that it implies an unsolved problem, which has to be correctly formulated before it can be answered. This problem is: there is a RELATION between politics and the cinema, but what is it? Put another way: does the cinema belong to the political sphere of influence, or some other? If the former, what is its particular function? if the latter: what are and what could be, its links with the political sphere of influence?

We must make clear from the very beginning, what our ultimate aim is in doing this work. We want to establish a few of the theoretical elements necessary for a cinema practice that will effectively serve the proletarian cause. We are attempting to discover in what areas (instances) and along what lines the cinema can be integrated into revolutionary practice. Our project is not empty speculation; it is directly linked to a precise political project. It is absolutely necessary, because 'there is no revolutionary practice without revolutionary theory.'

At every step in the progress of our theoretical work we shall continuously be defining the ideology we reject. So, in working towards an answer to the questions we asked in the first paragraph, we shall first compare the ideological NOTION with the theoretical CONCEPT of the cinema, and then proceed to discuss their 'relations' in terms of the METAPHORS, parenthesis (standing for the idealist function), and indirect route (standing for the theoretical function).

correct use of the parenthesis

Let us look for a moment at a metaphor which accurately crystallises one aspect of the problem: the parenthesis. A metaphor is always a symptom of a certain ideological system, and we have to find out which one 'parenthesis' is symptomatic of, even if only to appreciate fully its negative effects. For we are only introducing the *notion of parenthesis* here in order to negate it by a materialist discourse, and try to find out in the process what are the idealist positions on art.

It is, in fact, to an idealist notion of the written sentence that the idea in question relates. The expression 'to put something in parentheses' indicates a hierarchic system of signs: those in parentheses being less important than the others, if not completely unimportant. But important in relation to what? In relation to the only thing that really counts in idealist rhetoric: the meaning. This is understood as having an existence prior to the sentence, which only renders it, expresses it, with a greater or lesser degree of exactness. It is understood that anything in parentheses renders the meaning inexactly, if at all. Such an idea is mystifying. It conceals the material nature of the written word, the fact that a sentence is a collection of signs which *produce* a meaning by being put in certain relationships to each other, and among which those in parentheses have a specific, non-hierarchic role to play. There is a materialist way of treating signs within a sentence which destroys the idealist notion of 'parenthesis' (see the use which Philippe Sollers[45] makes of it in *Nombres*).

To introduce, metaphorically, the notion of parenthesis into the ideological discourse on the relationship between cinema and politics is an excellent way for us, from our materialist standpoint, to reveal the mystifications involved in such a discourse. It amalgamates two mistakes, a linguistic and a political one. It is a secret doorway into the enemy's wider ideological strategy: the way in which they set up the distinctions: non-signifying/signifying, secondary/principal, which are always resolved by the complete *neutralisation* of the first term, with the result that one element (the cinema, for example), on the pretext that it belongs to a certain sphere of influence (the arts, [where it is] admittedly the late-comer, but better late than never) is refused any role in another (politics of course). The manoeuvre is simple: all that has to be done is to reduce the field of politics to that of political 'life' (elections, governments) and that of the cinema to cinematographic *entertainment*. But if you introduce the concept of class struggle in place of the notion of 'politics' and the metaphorical 'parenthesis' in place of the empty 'nothing to do with' you have a Marxist reflex which explodes the bald statements of bourgeois idealism.

But if this metaphor is effective in showing up the twofold error of idealism, it is useless, even dangerous, to think that by simply negating, or rather, inverting it, you will get the correct materialist formulation of the relationship between cinema and politics. For by inverting the metaphor all you do is place the cinema unequivocally *inside* the political sphere of influence, just as the signs contained within parentheses are also contained within the sentence: signs, equal to all the other signs. Whichever way we turn we find ourselves very quickly in an idealist dead end, unless we are prepared to go into some detailed definitions of what constitutes politics and cinema. First, what does the word *cinema* correspond to?

the word, the mask: the cinema

The *word* cinema, as the ruling class insists it be used, relates to an abstraction. In the light of the preceding discussion its ideological content is easy to discern.

The cinema *in itself* does not exist. When we say 'cinema' we are almost certainly, *because of the pressures of the system*, thinking of the CINEMA AS ENTERTAINMENT. But entertainment films are by no means the sum total of cinema (though they are the most important category, and the most advanced technically). There are also scientific films (medical, ethnological, chemical, political), pornographic films (with their own clandestine 16 and 8 mm circuits), militant films (also clandestine, for Politics, like Sex, is one of the major outcasts of capitalist society), military films (*they* have society's official blessing – the fourth festival of military films has just been held at Versailles), and finally, advertising films (a very prosperous category this, and expanding rapidly). So, there are many and varied branches of the cinema, but the dominant usage has granted one of them a partial monopoly of the name.

Entertainment value thus becomes the *general criterion* for judging all the other categories, and it is true that they invite this fate by imitating entertainment films. 'It's good (not good) cinema': that is how people judge, for example, a scientific film, meaning 'It is (is not) entertainment'. In this way the cinema as entertainment becomes a mask which hides any other cinematic practice, a way of rejecting anything other than itself including the 'political' cinema, if such a thing exists. The first conclusion to be drawn from this is how important the cinema must be among the arsenal of means employed by the bourgeoisie to maintain its power and defend its interest, but also how forceful an effect any kind of cinema which rejected the entertainment criterion could have.

Our attempt at a theoretical definition of the cinema will be grounded in cutting ourselves free from the idealist conception outlined above. We shall not assess the cinema in terms of entertainment (or even, as some people have done, in terms of 'anti-entertainment'; a simple inversion of this nature remains ideological), but in MATERIALIST terms: what it is PHYSICALLY, in audio-visual terms, as a collection of sounds and images projected on a screen; and what it does SOCIALLY: its function in this or that branch of *social practice*.

The word 'cinema' should never be written without additional qualification, indicating the particular practice in which it is integrated (bearing in mind that this may or may not also be 'praxis' – tending to revolutionary change). The problem which concerns us (theoretical definition of the relationship between cinema and politics) can be put this way: is it theoretically justifiable to talk about 'political cinema'?

NB: We are continuing to use the word 'cinema' without qualification here, not because we are not aware of its different sub-divisions, but because we are discussing its material, physical form (its 'nature') existing prior to the subdivisions conferred on it by social practice, if such a distinction can be made. We shall discuss what specific role the cinema acquires by virtue of its material form (the perspective code which it reproduces) later in our argument.

political practice and theory

'By *practice* we mean, in general, any process *transforming* a given raw material into a given *product*, the transformation being effected by a given expenditure of labour using given means (of production).'

'This general definition of practice includes within itself the possibility of particularity. There are different practices which are really distinct from each other, although belonging organically to the same complex whole.' (Louis Althusser: 'On Dialectical Materialism' in *For Marx*.)[46]

This complex whole is social practice. It implies a structured totality comprising all the practices of a given society.

It can be divided into economic practice (which is the determining one in the last instance), political practice, ideological practice, and theoretical practice.

When we were listing, above, the various categories of cinema, we made no attempt to structure them. To proceed scientifically we have to do so. We must place the cinema SPECIFICALLY in one of the categories of social practice, and ascertain its links with others.

Politics is a *practice* which transforms its raw material (given social relations) into a given product (new social relations) by the systematic use of given means of production (the *class* struggle). In the case of a Marxist party, this practice is based on a *theory*: 'it is not spontaneous but organised on the basis of the scientific theory of historical materialism.' (Althusser: ibid.)

We can now pose the question as follows: Has cinematographic practice a place in political practice? At no moment in political practice does it have a specific role to play, so we have to conclude that IT IS NOT SPECIFICALLY POLITICAL. (To put it another way, it is neither a means, nor a product, nor a raw material of political practice.) When someone does affirm, despite the evidence, that the cinema belongs within the political sphere of influence, it means that he is either irresponsibly shutting his eyes to the specific nature of the class struggle, or deliberately trying to hold it back by putting it in the wrong context.

We can now see the beginnings of an answer to our problem emerging: the relation between cinema and politics is not that they are the same. The cinema is not *specifically* political. This does not mean that it and politics have no bearing on each other, or that there cannot be some political *films*. But then what is the relation, and what particular conditions qualify a film as political?

indirect influence: specificity

In *Cinéthique* no 4[47] we studied the relation between *cinema and economy*. To recapitulate on our findings:

We set ourselves the question: *what* produces a film, and came to the conclusion that a film is the product of several determining factors, of which economics is an important one (here as everywhere) but not the most important, which was ideology.

We then attempted to discover what the film produces, and chiefly if it figures in the manufacture of economic products. We decided that it did, but in a special way. It does not take part in the process of transforming raw material into products in such a directly instrumental way as machinery or human labour, but it does contribute to the process by indirect influence, propagating obscurantist ideology which inculcates in the exploited workers the idea that their situation as alienated producers is normal and natural.

These conclusions establish the RELATION BETWEEN CINEMA AND ECONOMY: *they converge at the juncture of economy and ideology.*

If we study the function referred to as 'indirect influence' above, it will cast light on the relation between cinema and politics, because it too occurs at a point of juncture, this time where ideology converges with politics. If we bring this conclusion, and the conclusion of the last paragraph together, we discover the cinema's specific place: WITHIN THE IDEOLOGICAL SPHERE OF INFLUENCE.

We can now set down the conditions under which cinema and political practice converge. A film can, at a given historical moment, hold back, mask, or reactivate the class struggle, by modifying the subjective factor in the struggle, i.e. the class consciousness of the proletariat, which is at present the principal aspect of the principal contradiction (bourgeoisie/proletariat). This is its specific relationship to the class struggle: it has 'something to do with' the minds of those who practice it (or don't practice it). 'Something'. But what?

ideological function of the cinema

'An ideology is a system (possessing its own logic and rigour) of representation (images, myths, ideas or concepts, as the case may be) existing and having a historical role within a given society.' (Louis Althusser: 'Marxism and Humanism' in *For Marx*.)

The cinema's particular ideological function is integrated within this general definition.

Its 'nature' (its material form) confers a twofold ideological function on the cinema, which has been reinforced by its history:
(a) It REPRODUCES, it reflects existing ideologies. It is therefore used (consciously or unconsciously, it makes little difference) as a vector in the process of circulating ideologies.
(b) It PRODUCES its own ideology: THE IMPRESSION OF REALITY. There is nothing on the screen, only reflections and shadows, and yet the first idea that the audience gets is that reality is there, as it really is. People used to say about statues and portraits, 'He looks as though he might open his mouth any minute and say something', or 'He looks as though he might burst into movement'. But the 'as though' gives the game away; despite the appearance, something was *lacking*, and everyone knew it. Whereas in the cinema, there is no 'as though'. People say 'The leaves are moving.' But there are no leaves. The first thing people do is deny the existence of the screen: it opens like a *window*, it is *'transparent'*. This illusion is the very substance of the specific ideology secreted by the cinema.

If one understands that ideology always presents itself in the form of a body of ideas and pictures of reality which people spontaneously accept as true, as *realistic*, it is easy to see why the cinema, by its specific nature, plays such a privileged role in the general ideological process. It REINFORCES the impression that what looks realistic must be real, and thus reinforces the ideology it reflects. It presents it as true, by virtue of its self-evident existence on the screen.

For this reason FUNCTION B IS INDISPENSABLE, in the cinema, to the exercise of function A. If the impression of reality ceases the ideologies reflected in it collapse, deprived of their support (only in the cinema of course, they continue to flourish in their native soil: society). When the mirror ceases to reflect, it is no longer a mirror. (But then, if the cinema loses its ideological existence, what kind of existence will it have to pass on to, in order to carry on functioning?)

TWO PRECISE PHENOMENA throw light on the relationship cinema/politics at the juncture ideology/politics.

The first is that of RECOGNITION. The audience recognise themselves in the representations on the screen: characters, ideas, myths, stories, structures, way of life. Here, much more than the concept of *identification* (which is too psychological), it is the concept of recognition which is at work. But because the dominant ideology in the cinema is that of the ruling class (as it is in the other media) it follows that most of the audience (which is known to be chiefly bourgeois and petit bourgeois) identify with and recognise themselves in what they see on the screen in one and the same function. It is indeed *their* world which *comes alive* in the darkened room. The reflection in the mirror is a 'faithful' one.

But to another section of the public, the mirror 'tells lies'. We have a class society dominated by the bourgeoisie, in which the cinema claims to be the same for everybody. However, a section of the cinema-going public consists of exploited workers, and in their case a second (but concomitant) ideological phenomenon occurs: MYSTIFICA-TION. They identify with what happens on the screen (mechanically) but they *cannot*, or ought not to be able to, recognise themselves in it. Working class people show they are aware of this when they describe anything ostentatiously phoney as '*du cinéma*'. Unconsciously, the exploited react against an entertainment based on an ideology which justifies the theft of their surplus value, and which presents the existing abnormal relations of production as natural and right.

We asked: how can the cinema serve the revolution? We should now re-formulate it thus: how can we destroy this mystification? how can we displace the mechanism of recognition?

the impossible reversal

Destroy, subvert, transgress. But, and this is an important point, we are not saying that all ideology ought to be abolished, or that all ideology is necessarily 'bad'. ('It presupposes an ideological viewpoint to conceive of societies existing without any ideology, and it is completely Utopian to think that ideology as a whole, and not just one or other of its forms, will ever completely disappear from the world, and be replaced by science.' – Althusser: *For Marx*.) What we want to do is to establish the conditions in which the cinema can serve the proletarian cause. In other words, what it is decisive to know is: can the film transmit a proletarian ideology? And can the cinema have any other than an ideological function: a theoretical one for example?

Before we attempt to formulate a theory, we must examine the concrete experience constituted by those films which do attempt to serve the proletarian cause. These are the *socialist films* of the people's democracies, the '*social*' *films* of the bourgeois democracies, and the *militant films* of both. Their historical functions are different: one section aim at destroying the bourgeoisie, the other at advancing the dictatorship of the proletariat. But all have the same leading idea, to REVERSE the existing situation.

In *The German Ideology*[48] Marx at one stage compared the action of the ideology to the action of the camera. He said that ideology showed us men and their relations upside down, 'as in a *camera obscura*', and it seems as though makers of socialist, social and militant films have adopted this as an all-purpose rule of thumb for making subversive pictures. 'The bourgeois cinema shows the bourgeois and their world view. All right then, we'll show workers and their world view' is what they seem to be saying. In other words, they are demanding a reversal of the situation, so that what was previously upside-down should now be right-way-up. But *what* are they actually proposing to reverse? We have to answer that question, or otherwise we shall be in a dead-end again. For if the cinema produces an indestructible illusion (idealist ideology) it is useless trying to reverse it. You cannot reverse an illusion, you can only destroy it.

Because their makers have never tackled the problem of the specific nature of the cinema all of these films, with a few exceptions (which we shall look at in detail), fall into the trap of *cinematic idealism*. How serious the results of this failure are depends on the historical situation: they are less grave in the socialist countries than they are under capitalism.

SOCIALIST FILMS

In a country where the proletariat is the ruling class, because it has taken possession of the means of production, ideological and economic, the specific ideological effect of the cinema (the impression of reality) works in its favour. It reinforces the credibility of representations of working class nobility, strength, and victory. These words sum up the *humanist* element of socialist realism. As 'the most important of all the arts' (Lenin) the cinema in a socialist society assumes first and foremost a *humanist* role: '. . . the avant-garde art *par excellence*, the art which is of a stature to translate the era of the victorious socialist revolution, the art which can most perfectly materialise the features of the new man of our times.' (EISENSTEIN: *Notes of a Film Director*.)

Far be it from us to deny the tactical importance of an idealist use of the cinema. Genuine humanism is an ideological necessity in a socialist society, and we shall attempt in a future issue of *Cinéthique* to study Socialist Realism from the point of view of its historical necessity, and not, as has been exclusively the case till now, from the point of view of its academic transgression of (bourgeois) aesthetics. But it is reasonable to ask whether the proletariat, at an advanced stage in its dictatorship, has much to gain from the image of itself reflected in such a fundamentally idealist method. Its assurance of its own victory, its strength, and its 'existence' might be better consolidated by liberating and developing the materialist truths of the cinema, which the bourgeoisie have of course never developed.

SOCIAL FILMS

Social films call for a much more severe treatment because they are produced in a historical context in which the proletariat is the exploited class. In other words, the impression of reality does not work in favour of its ideology. Someone who spends his whole career making films promoting the reverse of the ideology, may (with all the goodwill in the world) turn out in the end to have been an unconscious accomplice of the dominant ideology. The reason is that in a capitalist society, where the cinema is automatically aimed at the entire public, without distinction of class, these films can only reproduce (and so are produced by) the image of 'real life' acceptable to that section of bourgeois ideology known as 'the guilty conscience'. Any other image is not acceptable because the 'audience who count' (and obviously they count in other places as well as the cinema) would not recognise themselves in it. So the very thing these films cannot do is exactly the thing they ought to do in order to serve the proletarian cause—be *class* films. Film-makers cannot achieve the objective they set out to achieve, provoke recognition, stir up consciousness, because they have never considered the real economic and political context and its precise implications in the production and distribution of the object that is a film, and they have never thought about the specific ideological effects of the film camera.

MILITANT FILMS

Militant film-making is practised clandestinely and the products distributed selectively, which shows that it is conceived as an arm in the class struggle. In this it has a real advantage over social films. But the revolutionary zeal of those involved in it (to the point where zeal sometimes dissolves into wishful thinking) is hindered in achieving anything of importance by neglect of the specific ideological effect. Militant film-makers believe they are contributing to revolutionary action by reproducing it on the screen, but they forget that revolution can only be represented in the cinema as an *absence* and that all depictions of it do not compensate for the fact that it has not yet been achieved, even if the final effect of these films is to provoke a desire, to compensate, to take revenge.

the theoretical issue

All these attempts ultimately come up against a blank wall, some sooner than others, and we are forced to the conclusion that the 'nature' of the cinema and its history have integrated it into idealist ideology. The only way which can transgress and break out is via theoretical practice.

If the cinema is integrated into theoretical practice it can go beyond its idealist, ideological role. The break which exists in general between a theory and the ideology which preceded it is represented in the cinema by the break existing between the function of knowledge, and the function of recognition.

There are two roles which the cinema could play in the theoretical process. We shall detail later those few, exceptional films which have already assumed them, with varying degrees of success:
(a) It can REPRODUCE KNOWLEDGE produced by one or other of the sciences (historical materialism, medicine, physics, geography,

etc). It acts as a vector in the process of communicating knowledge. (b) It PRODUCES SPECIFIC KNOWLEDGE about itself. It can show the material facts of its physical and social existence. It can draw away the veil which normally covers a film's ideological, political and economic function, and by doing so denounce the ideology inherent in the cinema's 'impression of reality'. Through this action, it becomes theoretical.

From the foregoing it should be clear that function (b) is of prime importance. It conditions the exercise of function (a). A film has to work on the theoretical level before it can communicate knowledge.

We can therefore formulate the following decisive rule: IN THE CINEMA THE COMMUNICATION OF KNOWLEDGE IS AT-TENDANT UPON THE PRODUCTION OF KNOWLEDGE ABOUT THE CINEMA. If the two functions do not coincide the film relapses into ideology. Truths presented in it convince not because they are known theoretically, but because they are made credible by the film.

Of course there is not an equal quantity of both functions in every theoretical film (there is generally more communication of knowledge than there is production of specific knowledge about the cinema) but there is always a trace of specific knowledge.

As we said before, the films which work on a theoretical level are few and far between. The only socialist films among them are the works of Eisenstein and Vertov, and they could be said to be theoretical in part only, for in their case the theoretical break often takes place within the film. There are no social films which work on a theoretical level: all are idealist; certain militant films do effect the break, with varying degrees of decisiveness: *Un Film comme les autres, Flins, La hora de los hornos* [Hour of the Furnaces].[49] Some films will not go into either the socialist or the militant category, but still belong within the general description which we would apply to all the films we have mentioned, *materialist cinema: Octobre à Madrid, Méditerranée, le Joueur de quilles.* All these are films which we ought to study and keep on studying if we want to see the way ahead into a cinema which will really be of use to the proletariat in its struggle for power.

the indirect route, the different struggle

The cinema is not outside the class struggle, but it does not participate in it directly, in that it is not a specific means of political practice. However, it does have an influence on it, via the INDIRECT ROUTE of its particular field of operations: *the mortal struggle between materialism and idealism* which is directly linked to the class struggle. The struggle for the cinema is always different in kind; it is a *struggle at one remove*. A strike, for example, is a political weapon of the proletariat; a film about a strike is not (even if it is Eisenstein's). A film is only a weapon in its own area, which is not politics but the particular indirect route (ideology) connecting it to politics.

Further: a film about politics is more closely related to political practice than a film about love, but it still has to take that famous indirect route. It may be depicting political events (ideological function: communication of ideologies) or it may be the vehicle for a concrete analysis of a concrete situation (theoretical function: communication of knowledge); it always does it outside the field of political practice (the class struggle), in the field of ideological practice (the struggle between materialism and idealism) – at the cinema. This discussion only refers to cinema films, not to television or video-tape. The instantaneous image produced by the mobile television camera does enter directly into political practice (this is particularly evident at election-time). It has a similar effect to a tract or a speech. This poses some problems of definition.*

We must stress yet again that the cinema cannot and does not influence the balance of forces in the political sphere (i.e. between bourgeoisie and proletariat) but in the ideological sphere (between idealism and materialism). And even here the changes it can effect are dependent on the social and economic climate. But not entirely so – this is why effective action is possible in this field without a change in the balance of political power. So the cinema is *relatively* autonomous and *relatively* determining, and we should work in the knowledge that a change in political relationships will affect our work, and that the progress towards the seizure of power by the proletariat will be extended to what we do.

We know that all the different areas of influence in a given society are linked to each other, in their process of transformation, according to

* It would be interesting to analyse the way candidates for the French presidency used the medium during their electoral campaigns. The ones who claimed to represent historical dialectical materialism (Duclos, Krivine, Rocard) used it in just the same way as the bourgeois idealists, without having thought about, or taken any measures appropriate to the problems of its specific nature. Was it really of so little relevance?

systematic rules of determination and superdetermination. From this we can proceed with every confidence to say that the cinema is *not* irrelevant to the social whole. The route which links it with the whole is an indirect one, but on its own ground, it is decisive. For the proletariat must appropriate the means of production in the cinema. It will not be able to appropriate them completely unless it has first taken over the means of economic production and the state machine, but after that the takeover must be complete. It never has been, so far.

When we referred metaphorically to the cinema's 'indirect route' to political action, we felt the metaphor took account of its complex network of relationships, and implied both moments of juncture and moments of divergence. By analogy, one might say that the opposite and mistaken proceeding is to take a short cut by placing the cinema right *inside* politics, even while flying in the face of their different specific natures. One metaphor underlines the complete impossibility of confining the cinema's activity to the short straight road of reproducing political 'spectacles' or transmitting political analyses. It points out that the cinema can proceed along the new route of theoretical practice. (We shall have to define and try out the practicabilities of this new route, paying special attention to the problem of fiction.) The 'indirect route' also includes a place for historically superseded ideologies, which can form a *reservoir* of influence in the cinema (if they remain alive), or take the form of stocks of historically determined products which can nonetheless link with other situations, whether of the same historical moment or another (the 'timelessness' and 'universality' of art). Finally the metaphor of the indirect route, and the concept of the cinema's difference from politics have themselves originated from theoretical work (by Jacques Derrida).[50] Anyone practising materialist research into the cinema would profit from taking cognizance of this work at one stage or another.

definitions, openings

It is now possible to define the kind of film which is 'useful to the proletariat': a materialist film, a dialectical film, a film which is integrated into the history of the proletariat.

A MATERIALIST FILM is one which does not give illusory reflections of reality. In fact it 'reflects' nothing. It starts from its own material nature (flat screen, natural ideological bias, audience) and that of the world, and shows them both, all in one movement. This movement is the theoretical one. It provides scientific knowledge of the world and the cinema, and is the means whereby the cinema fights its part of the battle against idealism. But in order to win it has to be dialectical as well, otherwise it is only a beautiful but useless piece of machinery, which carries on functioning in a void without ever having been harnessed for the transformation of reality. A DIALECTICAL FILM is one made in the consciousness, which it is able to transmit to the audience, of the exact process whereby an item of knowledge or a depiction of reality is transformed by degrees into *screen material* to be then re-converted into knowledge and a view of reality in the audience's mind.

But, given that we accept that the film is not a magic object, functioning either by occult influence, divine grace, or talismanic virtue, we have to accept that the dialectical process must be backed up by work on the part of the audience, they must decipher the film, read the signs produced by its inner working.

It is only in this category (dialectical materialist cinema) that we can find any films at all which, *theoretically* speaking, could be qualified as political, with all the reservations that we indicated. These are the films which transmit knowledge produced by historical materialism, the theory which informs the political practice of Marxist parties. Theoretically speaking one cannot describe an idealist film about politics as political, because it moves entirely in the ideological sphere, politically and cinematically (turning everything into a spectacle). It is necessary to keep insisting on this point, because the INFLATION OF THE WORD POLITICAL is an ideological by-product which blurs the area of confrontation, which is always to the benefit of the ruling class, who do not need theoretical clarity to impose their ideas.

Finally, is it necessary to point out that a film which will be of use to the proletarian cause has to be produced in organic relationship with working class organisations, and that its date in the struggle ought to be *written* on it? (Fargier, 1969).

One useful aspect of Fargier's text is its attempt to specify a relationship between politics and films without collapsing one entirely into the other. The central argument, that the specific function of film is to purvey 'the impression of reality', is one we are already familiar with from Bazin and Grierson. Fargier spells out the position implicit in Brecht and MacCabe: the ideological effect of this 'impression' is to persuade the workers that what they see on the screen is 'natural' rather than the product of particular social practices. All film is thus by definition ideological, but some film can also be theoretical in so far as (following Althusser's definition of theory) it constructs its own object and transmits a consciousness of this process of construction to its audience. Historically, this idea, which is not particular to Fargier, has led to a spate of films part of whose projects has been to criticise or attempt to destroy the impression of reality. Sometimes these kinds of film have a distinct political content (as, for instance, in works by Jean-Luc Godard); others make essays in illusionism and anti-illusionism by focusing on basic technical properties of the medium. It has to be said that this kind of theoreticism, in which Theory, under its marxist name of Knowledge, perpetually leads the film-makers on but can never be attained by them, finds it difficult to cope with some of the visual aspects of cinema, asserting functions for them which seem far from proven (Fargier's notion that bourgeois ideology 'turns everything into a spectacle', MacCabe's 'relations of dominant specularity'). Nor is it able to analyse the possibility that the very complications of 'theoretical' film might lead not to anything that we might reasonably call 'Knowledge' but rather to a new and more sophisticated form of aesthetic fascination.

Notes

1 This is a reference to the sentimental and moralising tendencies manifest in Griffith's films, particularly after *Intolerance* (1916).
2 *One Family,* directed by Walter Creighton (GB, 1930). A whimsical, feature-length narrative about the collection of the ingredients for the King's Christmas dinner from all over the British Empire. The almost simultaneous failure of *One Family* and success of *Drifters,* a documentary about a Scottish fishing fleet (produced and directed by Grierson himself) helped confirm Grierson in his ideas about public-service documentary.
3 Films made by Esther Shub referred to in this extract: *The Fall of the Romanov Dynasty* (USSR, 1927), composed out of newsreel material of 1912–17 and the private collection of the imperial family; *The Great Road* (also known as *The Great Way,* USSR, 1927), from newsreels of 1917–27.
4 P. E. Dybenko (1889–1938), Soviet military leader and statesman, member of the Council of People's Commissars in 1917. From the prints currently available in Great Britain, it is impossible to be sure which Shub film Shklovsky is referring to, though other members of the Council of People's Commissars do make somewhat self-conscious appearances in *The Great Road.*
5 Films referred to in this extract: *The Eleventh* (USSR, 1928), directed by Dziga Vertov, celebrating the eleventh year of Soviet power; *October* (USSR, 1928), dir. S. M. Eisenstein, and *Moscow in October* (USSR, 1928), dir. Boris Barnet, both about the Bolshevik seizure of power.
6 Mikhail Kaufman (1897–   ), Vertov's brother and chief cameraman.
7 By 'academy', Shklovsky means 'official' or 'respectable'.
8 The Kinetophone was a 'sound' version of the Edison Company's Kinetoscope or peep-hole moving picture machine. A small phonograph was built into the Kinetoscope to provide a musical accompaniment. Only forty-five Kinetophones were produced between 1895 and 1899. Tynyanov is using the term loosely to mean 'sound film', though neither the Kinetoscope nor the Kinetophone can be considered, strictly speaking, as film equipment, since neither involved the element of projection.
9 Effect by which one shot appears to dissolve slowly into the next. More commonly referred to as a dissolve or (in Great Britain) as a mix. It has of course more uses than the one Tynyanov here ascribes to it.
10 Andrei Bely (1881–1934), Russian poet, novelist and theorist of symbolism.
11 *The Overcoat* (USSR, 1926), directed by Grigori Kozintsev and Leonid Trauberg, a film version – said to be influenced by German expressionism – of Gogol's story *The Overcoat,* of which Akaki Akakeyevich is the principal character.
12 Louis Delluc (1890–1924), French film-maker, critic and theorist, was, with Léon Moussinac, one of the earliest practitioners of independent

film criticism as distinct from film publicity. Abel Gance (1889–   ), French film director and experimentalist, best known for *La Roue* (The wheel, France, 1922), which is a thorough exploration of rapid cutting and montage techniques, and *Napoléon* (France, 1927), which used a triple screen and several other technical innovations.

13 Béla Bálazs (1884–1949), Hungarian writer and film theorist, best known for his book *Theory of the Film*, Dennis Dobson, 1952. He believed that the cinema needed an aesthetic of its own, and that the techniques of close-up and montage could 'create the world afresh'. Most of his writing on cinema was done in the 1920s.

14 The term 'photogenic' has been in use in the conventionally accepted sense since the nineteenth century. In the context of film, however, it was given a more specialised meaning by Delluc's book *Photogénie* (1920).

15 *The Devil's Wheel* (USSR, 1926), directed by Kozintsev and Trauberg.

16 Heinrich Heine (1797–1856), German romantic poet and liberal journalist.

17 This sentence is loosely quoted in the Russian original, and so much out of context that it is not clear that the miming and 'witty outbursts' in question relate to a political speech. The passage is taken from Heine's description of the then (1828) opposition leader Henry Brougham's appearance in Parliament (from *Englische Fragmente*, chapter 8, 'Die Oppositionsparteien'; English translation by Charles G. Leland, *Pictures of Travel*, Philadelphia, 1856, p. 42).

18 Vladimir Mayakovsky (1893–1930), Futurist poet who also wrote some plays and film scripts. Editor of *Lef* and *Novy Lef*.

19 The Russian words *'fabula'* and *'syuzhet'* are very difficult to translate into English, particularly in the specialised senses in which some of the Formalists used them. Following Tzvetan Todorov in his useful article 'Some approaches to Russian Formalism' (*Twentieth Century Studies*, nos 7 and 8, 1972), I prefer to use the English words 'fable' and 'subject' because of their etymological resemblance to the Russian, but with the strict proviso to the English-speaking reader that the terms as used here by Tynyanov do not have the meanings that they traditionally have in English.

By 'fable' the Formalists meant the non-literary or pre-literary aspects of a work, e.g. the bare narrative bones of a story, or the 'real-life' situation (in Shklovsky's words 'the table of events'), on the basis of which a work might be constructed. The 'subject' of the work is produced by the play on the fable of all the artistic devices specific of the particular medium. Thus Tomashevsky: 'These events must be *distributed*, they must be constructed into a certain order, and from the story material a literary construction must be made. The artistically constructed distribution of events in a work is called the *subject* of the work.'

As this text makes clear, for Tynyanov the term 'subject' has strong connotations of style and form. An understanding of the actions of subject (style, form, internal distribution, etc.) of a work gives access to an understanding of its fable. Indeed, the fable is best understood as itself an aspect of the subject.

It is perhaps more common for '*syuzhet*' to be rendered as 'plot', as for instance in the classic textbook on Russian Formalism, Victor Erlich's *Russian Formalism* (revised edn, The Hague, 1965). But while the pair 'fable' and 'subject' are difficult, the pair 'fable' and 'plot' seem positively misleading in that in English 'plot' traditionally means the outline of the narrative of a story, and this meaning is actually closer to what the Formalists meant by 'fable'.

20 'Sie war liebenswurdig, und Er liebte Sie; Er war nicht liebenswurdig, und Sie liebte Ihn nicht' (from *Ideen, Das Buch le Grand*, chapter 1, English translation Leland, op. cit., p. 167). Heine adds the ironic 'source', *Old Play*.

21 Poems by Pushkin referred to in this text: *The Fountain of Bakhchisarai* (1823), *The Prisoner of the Caucasus* (1821).

22 The opening lines of Pushkin's poem *Eugene Onegin*. Literally: 'When my uncle, a man of the highest principles, fell seriously ill. . . .'

23 Ambrose Bierce (1842–1914?), American writer, poet and journalist. *An Occurrence at Owl Creek Bridge* appeared in his collection *Tales of Soldiers and Civilians* (1891). In 1961 it was filmed by Robert Enrico under the title *Incident at Owl Creek*.

24 Leo Perutz (1884–1957), born in Prague, spent most of his life in Vienna, settled in Tel Aviv 1938. Author of historical and fantastic novels.

25 V. A. Zhukovsky (1793–1852), Russian poet. His *Epistle to Voyekov* (1814) is a poem addressed to his fellow poet A. F. Voyekov (1778–1839).

26 Boris Pilniak (1893–1938/41), Russian novelist and short-story writer. Leonhard Frank (1882–1961), German novelist, best known for *Karl und Anna* (1926).

27 *The Nose* (1835).

28 Novels by Bely referred to in this text: *Petersburg* (1912), *The Moscow Eccentric* (1925).

29 Alexander I, Tsar of Russia from 1801 to 1825.

30 'Pre-Socratics' is the term normally used to discuss together the Greek philosophers who between 600 and 400 BC attempted to find universal principles which would explain the whole of nature, from the origin of the universe to the place of man within it.

31 *Middlemarch* (1872).

32 Ibid. (London, 1977), pp. 432–3.

33 *Klute* (USA, 1971) directed by Alan J. Pakula.

34 *The Grapes of Wrath*, novel by John Steinbeck (1939, film (USA), 1940), directed by John Ford; *The Sound of Music*, stage musical by Rodgers and Hammerstein (1959), film (USA, 1965), dir. Robert Wise; *L'Assommoir*, novel by Emile Zola (1877), film adaptation as *Gervaise* (France, 1956), dir. René Clément; *Toad of Toad Hall*, title of the stage adaptation of Kenneth Grahame's children's story *The Wind in the Willows* (1908).

35 Ambrose Bierce, *Fantastic Fables*, 1899.
36 S. M. Eisenstein, *The Film Sense* (Faber & Faber, 1968), pp. 14–15.
37 Ibid., p. 20.
38 In Tolstoy's novel *Anna Karenina* (1875–7).
39 Eisenstein, op. cit., p. 37.
40 Costa-Gavras (1933–   ), Greek-born director working in France, whose films include Z (1968), *The Confession* (1970), *State of Siege* (1973). *Cathy Come Home,* a television play directed (on film) by Kenneth Loach (BBC-tv, 1966).
41 Papers and journals quoted by Brecht in these extracts: The *Kölnische Zeitung* and *Frankfurter Zeitung* are both respected liberal daily newspapers; *Kinematograph* was a general magazine published from 1907 to 1935; *Reichsfilmblatt* was the official organ of the National Federation of German Cinema-Owners (1923–35).
42 Krupp's: industrial combine which produced iron, steel, machinery and arms. AEG (Allgemeine Elektrizitats-Gesellschaft): combine manufacturing electrical equipment.
43 Bruno Kastner (1890–1932), German actor.
44 Films referred to in this extract: *City Lights* (USA, 1931), directed by Charles Chaplin; *Road to Life* (USSR, 1931), dir. Nikolai Ekk.
45 Philippe Sollers (1936–   ), French novelist and essayist, a leading member of the editorial board of the magazine *Tel Quel. Nombres* (1968) is a novel.
46 Louis Althusser, *For Marx* (France, 1966), Allen Lane, 1969.
47 *Cinéthique*, no. 4, Paris, 1969.
48 Karl Marx and Friedrich Engels, *The German Ideology* (London, 1970, written 1845–6).
49 Films referred to in this text: *Un film comme les autres* (A film like the others, France, 1968), directed by Jean-Luc Godard; *Flins* (France, 1969), made by the Cinéastes Revolutionnaires Prolétariens (Proletarian Revolutionary Film-Makers group); *The Hour of the Furnaces* (*La hora de los hornos,* Argentina, 1968), dir. Fernando E. Solanas; *Octobre à Madrid* (October in Madrid, France, 1969), dir. Marcel Hanoun; *Méditerraneé,* (Mediterranean, France, 1963), dir. Jean-Daniel Pollet; *Le Joueur de quilles* (The Skittles Player /The Runaway, France, 1968), dir. Jean-Pierre Lajournade.
50 Jacques Derrida, French philosopher whose main position is that writing is an activity which radically alters speech rather than being a direct reflection of it. Main works: *De La Grammatologie* (1967), *L'Écriture et la différence* (1967).

Part IV
Aesthetics and technology

FROM WRITERS as different in context and content as Bazin and Tynyanov it is clear that the state of development of film technology plays a large, though often contentious, part in determining the kinds of films that are made and the ways they are thought about. Technology offers film-makers a range of choices in technique; on the basis of these choices (which may of course be quite restricted by the actions or conventions or ideologies as well as by the limitations of technique itself) the films are constructed. So the areas of aesthetics and technology are strictly speaking inseparable. But it cannot be said that the relationships involved have been clarified to any marked extent. It is difficult to write critically about technology; most debate in the area tends to favour short-term solutions by emphasising aesthetic and stylistic choices. The texts that follow illustrate the interplay between aesthetic and technological questions.

The French film-maker and theoretician Jean Epstein, writing in 1930 about camera movement and manipulation of time and the sound track:

It was and still is very important to make the fullest possible use of the camera, to put an automatic camera in a spiralling football, on the saddle of a galloping horse, on a buoy in the middle of a storm, to plant it in the basement and track it along at ceiling height. Never mind that on ten occasions such displays of technical virtuosity appear excessive, they are essential. The eleventh time we see just how necessary they are, and how, as yet, inadequate. Thanks to them, even before the revelations of cinematic depth still to come, we experience hills, trees, faces in space as a new sensation. Given motion or its appearance, the body as a whole experiences depth. A sharp sense of rapid change

193

comes with being inclined, now into the centre, now out of the curve. Always and forever we have been and will be propelled through space, propelled and propelling an infinity of other projectiles. The cine-camera, more than the car or the airplane, makes possible particular, personal trajectories that reverberate through the entire physique.

You may live in a town, but you only know it when you have caught sight of it reflected in a radiator, when you have approached, penetrated and elaborated it in space and time, had it first in front of you, then left behind, to one side, above and below, in a constantly changing order. You have not really seen the earth or anything to do with it until you have seen it without breaking out of its movement. Your rotation must be faster, slower, other; you must let that tower recede, pursue it, displace and replace it among the unfolding hills, in a round danced by poplar trees playing at hide and seek.

The film camera reproduces movement, allowing us only those temporal experiences that are already accessible. The relativity of space is accepted almost as readily as the relativity of time, and within this general relativity we exist at varying speeds. We sense this intuitively in a thousand ways and nothing can invalidate the sense since no fixed point of comparison is ever imaginable. The hope that we will discover the means for a partial exploration of time as we have for space is not an absurd one, and mathematicians do not discourage it.

The cinecamera treats time within a perspective, giving a variable notion of this fourth dimension of existence which is closer to the truth than the banality of appearances. The playwright has as yet hardly ever explored the device of recording varying time scales to achieve a psychologically truer expression of human existence. And so it is not yet fully appreciated how much this technique would extend the moving image's propensity for generating meaning. Already, moving images so seriously modify appearance that they break down the barriers between laws of nature. Once we have seen a family presented within a temporal perspective which shows births and deaths for the sequence they are in reality, heredity steps forward like a visible character, wilful, whimsical, pitiless or benevolent. And this is but one, the first evoked, of an uncountable reign of angels. Perhaps even tomorrow, the cinema will offer a form more sensitive to the entities which obviously give life its continuity, beyond man, in what is conventionally called the scale of being, within the mystery of that insoluble contradiction – hierarchy and infinity. . . .

For the sound cinema as practised today ignores fifteen years of progress towards independence achieved by the cinema in general, of which it is a part. It has forgotten entirely that, as cinema, it is the reproduction of movement. It is repeating in a fatuously juvenile way all the mistakes the silent cinema has long since repented of. There was a time, it's true, when the camera equipped with simultaneous sound recording was not mobile, when it was locked up, strapped up and paralysed. That difficulty was easy to overcome and it has been overcome. Not only can the camera resume its mobility, whenever and as much as is desired, but the microphone which captures sound can also move, either in the track of the lens, or along an independent path. It is therefore possible to inscribe movement of forms and movement of sounds simultaneously, a sychronism which has no existence outside the intention of the film-maker and no value other than the dramatic. There is nothing to stop one from mounting a microphone on an axle controlled from a distance so that a rotation of a few degrees can create any distance between sounds. When I was directing some scenes from *La Fin du monde*[1] I went as far as using a hand-held microphone and had the results let me down I wouldn't be mentioning it.

But what's the use of dreaming of a movement of sounds! All films speak with a single voice, asexual and static. And this monotony is what the sound engineers are congratulating themselves upon. Their ideal is that the S should emerge from the speaker distinct from Z, without producing a whistle. What do they care if we can't make out whether a cry is made in anger or in joy? And perhaps they're right. They are the technicians, not the pilots of the machine. We would be more justified in reproaching many of them for not letting themselves be guided, for taking the routine as the law, and for carefully excluding any possibility of the random factor without which the greatest genius and the smallest talent alike will starve to death. The attitude isn't new; we have met it often enough and it will be met a few times yet among former cameramen with their ritual 'it can't be done!' Today we joke about their kind of impossibilities and about the camera lens at the obligatory 80 centimetres off the ground (neither the top nor the underneath of the table should be visible) and five metres from the actors, just as we will soon be joking about the clumsy way we manipulate the microphone.

It was an event more in the area of scandal than miracle when a film-maker with the necessary competence tried to take control of the photography himself; and the sound engineers part with their head-phones only at the price of a dispute over your right to wear them.

Listing all these obstacles brings a feeling of shame at their pettiness: an unworthy enemy gives a poor impression of the opposing case, except that his forces are bolstered by the weight of the weak, and theirs is often the winning number.

It is not in the simplified acoustics of the studio that useful experiments will be made in future. Microphones will have to be spread across the sound fields of the wide world so that we can devise sound deflectors and selective filters for them. The rare photogenic successes so far have been restricted to the impure sound of the news event. It is easy to imagine how these recordings must have been made, hurriedly, with no chance of any preliminary testing. In looking for one thing you find another. The important thing is to place yourself in conditions which do not exclude novelty, and chance will do the rest. The photogenicness of camera angles, travelling shots, and of so many mechanical, vegetable, cosmic, collective movements, was not discovered by method. Newsreel cameramen accepted millions of images indifferently and we learned to distinguish those which were exclusive to the cinema. Only after such a preliminary testing of the ground, which is still going on since we are far from knowing all the ins and outs of what constitutes photogenicness, could we think of organising the first works of the new art in a precise way. It will be no different for the sound film. The rhythmic tramp of passing troops, the inarticulate voice in the crowd at a match; feet, hands, roars of applause, and ten thousand gasps that raise a deceptive gale, to die away immediately, letting us hear in that almost impossible silence, the sharp laugh of a child; and because a man's double speaks to us from the screen, he breaks free of his legend, offering each one of us a chance to experience him in the resonance of his voice; taken by surprise he accepts the risky challenge of trying to make us like him as he is, warts and all. A few hundred metres of this sort of thing are really all we have that is good in sound production. There is reason to fear that we may not hear any more of this minimum for a while. Under the – deplorable – influence of radio which, like the sound camera, has its own characteristic voice, it was decided that the direct sound recording of news events – always a tricky business – should be cut out. In its place came the commentator's voice, backed up by a few fabricated sounds. I might add that on occasions, and doubtless to complete the illusion of past times, the commentator presented the scenes from a kind of tasteful box shaped like a frame. Such an evasion in the face of difficulties carries the danger of a major delay in the development of the art of sound. I don't really believe that it even represents any economic advantage, except of the most temporary kind, while audiences are still prepared to be entertained by the mere fact that the mechanism works without wondering what other pleasure or surprise it might offer. It ought to be borne in mind that a similar policy lost the interest of virtually the entire French audience to the phonograph. The manufacturers reasoned that it didn't matter very much if French recordings were the worst in the world – they were the cheapest. So the recordings barely sold and they dragged the phonograph machines with them into financial failure.

It is not that sound has eventually to become a copy of reality. The property of an art is to create a world of its own out of our world. Hearing everything just as it is heard by a perfect human ear is just the preliminary function of the microphone. After that we want it to let us hear what the ear does not hear, just as the camera lets us see what escapes the naked eye. Let nothing remain mute anymore! Let dreams and fantasies be audible. There are murmurs which can burst the eardrum and cries whose melody our ear never tires of. Let the secrets of their eloquence be snatched from the leaves and the waves, let them be broken down and reconstituted into voices more true than the natural. The human world has accents which have not yet been discovered; out of these the cinema will construct its style. Suspect speeches will be drawn out and swelled up until they reveal the lie in them. Cyclones will roll out like lullabies and all the children will hear the grass growing (Epstein, 1930).

Epstein's rhapsodic vision of the potentialities of technique has much in common with Vertov's a year or two earlier. But Epstein is writing in the context of the arrival of sound, and he takes a nuanced position about it typical of many who knew that it was inescapable but resented it because it might impose naturalistic flatness or the kind of representative, narrative characteristics they associated with the theatre. Sound will be acceptable on condition that it is manipulated; that it creates rather than reproduces. It is worth noting that the phenomenon of movement has often been isolated as one of the basic specifics of cinema, in the context of realist and anti-realist argument.

As we have seen (pp. 36–52) André Bazin placed a strong emphasis on depth-of-field cinematography in the construction of his realist aesthetic. The device had been prominent in the early silent cinema but was widely felt to have resurfaced in the late 1930s and early 1940s. The American researcher Patrick L. Ogle offers a technically-oriented account of this 'second coming':

A matter of continuing concern and some puzzlement to the author is the matter of the range and weight of relative emphases in film scholarship. Film is, as seems readily apparent, an art form and communications medium that has arisen from, and continues to be dependent upon, a relatively high level of technology. It is therefore surprising that most critical and scholarly work on film seems almost consciously to eschew any concern for film technology and the relationship it bears to many aesthetic and historic trends in the cinema. Just as aesthetic-communicative desires on the part of film-makers have tended to affect the direction and aims of research and problem solving in film technology, so has the ever-changing state of the art in film technology tended to define the 'band-width' within which the visual and aural styles of film art and communication could operate. Deep focus cinematography, the subject of this paper, furnishes a particularly good example of the degree to which the style of film-making can be dependent upon both aesthetics and technology.

Deep- or pan-focus cinematography as a recognised visual style in film-making first came to critical and public attention with the release of Orson Welles' film *Citizen Kane* in early to middle 1941. Unusual for the time, much note was taken of the contributions of Gregg Toland,[2] ASC, who directed the photography of the film. Toland's name has become synonymous with deep focus cinematography even though some other cameramen were working along similar lines at the time, and one of them, James Wong Howe, ASC, seems to have produced a proto-deep focus film in his photography of *Transatlantic*[3] ten years earlier. As practised by Toland and others, deep focus cinematography constituted perhaps the first coherent alternative seen in American films to the editing-centred film theories of Eisenstein, Pudovkin, and Kuleshov.[4] Whereas to the Russians the content of a given shot was subordinate to the feelings generated by its juxtaposition with those preceding and succeeding it, in deep focus cinematography the individual shot and the action recorded within it came to be of primary importance. In this sense the American deep focus school may be thought more cameraman-oriented than editor-oriented, and shared in common certain qualities with the German silent film tradition (not surprising, considering the number of old UFA cinematographers such as Karl Freund who were enjoying influential careers in the American industry) of concern with camera angle, camera motion, set lighting, and actor positions and movements within a take. Deep focus cinematography tended toward long duration sequences, the avoidance of cutaways and reaction shots, the employment of a meticulously placed camera that only moved when necessary, and the use of unobtrusive, virtually invisible editing.

The most noticeable quality of deep focus cinematography, however, was, as its name implies, the cultivation of crisp focus throughout an unprecedented depth of field in the scene photographed. In reviewing *Citizen Kane*, the *American Cinematographer* (house organ of the American Society of Cinematographers) commented:

The result on the screen is in itself little short of revolutionary: the conventional narrow plane of acceptable focus is eliminated, and in its place is a picture closely approximating what the eye sees – virtually unlimited depth of field, ranging often from a big head close up at one side of the frame, perhaps only inches from the lens, to background action twenty, thirty, fifty, or even a hundred feet away, all critically sharp. The result is realism in a new dimension: we forget we are looking at a picture, and feel the living, breathing presence of the characters.[5]

While succumbing to the lingering misconception that the human eye as a lenticular system possesses extreme depth of field (for this is not the case, the eyes and brain have instead a remarkable ability to follow focus on various points of interest almost instantaneously without normal conscious awareness on the part of the viewer), the *American Cinematographer* reviewer did properly emphasise the startling crispness of focus and sense of presence conveyed by the technique. It is in this conveyed sense of presence (to be usefully distinguished from the general concept of realism – for in the light of thirty years *Citizen Kane* is seen to be anything but realistic in style) that the chief distinguishing characteristic of deep focus cinematography may reside, for in providing the viewer with visually acute high information imagery that he may scan according to his own desires without the interruptions of intercutting, deep focus in André Bazin's words 'brings the spectator into a relation with the image closer to that which he enjoys with reality'.[6] In one way then, the deep focus aesthetic was an attempt to achieve a simulation of certain effects of theatre performance both by the elimination of certain film characteristics that pointed up the fact of there being an intermediary between viewer and performance, and by the employment of other inherently filmic characteristics that enhanced the theatrical sense of presence while simultaneously preventing any occurrence of the wretched 'canned theatre' effects of some early sound films. Chief among these latter characteristics was that of composition in depth, for the common deep focus 'all in one' shot of the type described in the *American Cinematographer* review involved spatial relationships impossible to experience in the theatre. Deep focus cinematography foreshadowed, in a sense, the development of the wide screen formats of a dozen years later, techniques that, while using different technology and composing in breadth instead of depth, shared with deep focus the goals of sense of presence and many other qualities of the long duration take aesthetic.

While not all examples of deep focus cinematography were necessarily realist in nature or style, the primary influences upon the
development of deep focus were strongly involved with the concept of
realism as a proper means of expression and communication. There
had always been a tradition of sharply focused and realistic American
film camera work, especially in outdoor footage, as much of Billy
Bitzer's work for David Wark Griffith will attest. While largely
eclipsed by the heavily diffused photographic style of the later 1920's
and 1930's, the realistic style was still to be seen in certain genre films
(such as westerns and gangster films) whose subject matter had a
certain adamantine quality inconsistent with the softness of the
prevailing camera style. (It is not surprising that the director for whom
Gregg Toland filmed the partially deep focus *The Grapes of Wrath*
and *The Long Voyage Home* in 1940 and for whom Arthur Miller,
ASC, filmed the deep focus *How Green Was My Valley* in 1941 should
be John Ford, whose experience with raw and realistic film-making
had gone back to *The Iron Horse* of 1924 and before. Ford's
Stagecoach of 1939, as photographed by Bert Glennon, ASC, looked
forward very much to *Citizen Kane* in its use of ceilinged sets, wide
angle lenses, and distinctly 'un-Hollywood' lighting.) Thus in the
controversy surrounding the visual style of *Citizen Kane* it was
possible for intelligent and presumably fair-minded cinematographers of such eminence as Leon Shamroy, ASC, and Gaetano
Gaudio, ASC, to take the extreme position that there was really
nothing new about deep focus, and that it consisted essentially of a
return to practices of a quarter century earlier.

Probably more important to the development of the deep focus style
were influences toward realism that came from outside Hollywood
and, to a large extent, from outside motion picture making. The
1930's saw the rise of the documentary film as an international
movement. Some of the better American examples such as Pare
Lorentz' *The Plow that Broke the Plains* of 1936 (cinematography
directed by Paul Strand, widely known as a still photographer) and
The River of 1937 were to prove enduring examples of crisp *plein air*
photography. The work of Jean Renoir in France during that decade
was also of a very realistic sort, even looking forward – in his *Toni* of
1934 – to post-war Italian Neorealism. Renoir's filming style tended
toward the preservation of a greater depth of field than usual for
the time, and toward the use of compositions that exploited this
somewhat expanded depth by the inclusion of realist background
activities often dispensed with by more theatrically influenced
directors. Renoir's actors usually moved about in evenly lit natural-

istic settings, and takes tended to be of rather long duration. Significant actions were highlighted by judicious use of the moving camera, but one which moved only for good reason, not in the wilful and near-gratuitous fashion of the German silent era 'camera as actor'.

The attitudes toward realism and practices in filming of Jean Renoir provide an important link with some non-cinematic factors that were tending to move American cinematographic styles in a more realistic direction. One of Renoir's assistants during the middle 1930's was Henri Cartier-Bresson, who has become world-renowned in his own right as a still photographer of the unposed and candid 'decisive moment'. Cartier-Bresson's photographs . . . were seen by millions of people, along with the similarly realistic work of other photojournalists, in magazines such as *Life* and *Look*. James Wong Howe, whose lifelong interest has been in the cultivation of realism in cinematography, made a perceptive remark in mid-1941:

There is one thing about modern cinematography which I feel no one has emphasised sufficiently. This is the profound influence the photographic and picture-magazines which have become so popular during the last ten years have had on styles in studio camerawork.[7]

Howe felt that the tendency towards crisper definition, greater depth, and occasional use of higher contrast was primarily due to a change in public taste 'directly traceable to the growth in popularity of miniature camera photography, and to the big picture magazines' in which the public saw the stark realism of miniature camera photojournalism every week. This change in public taste, Howe considered, had evoked a change in cinematographic style 'so slowly and subtly that we ourselves had scarcely been conscious of it . . .'.

The popularity of miniature camera photojournalism may have had more effect on changes in cinematographic style than just changes toward 'slice of life' realism. For reasons that have never been clear, the so-called 'normal' lenses for motion picture cameras (those which supposedly give the most natural perspective effects and which are consequently used in the majority of picture-taking situations) have always been of approximately twice the focal length of normal focal length lenses for still cameras of similar negative size. A 35mm (film gauge) motion picture camera has a normal lens of 50mm focal length, the same focal length as that of a 35mm still camera such as the Leica, whose negative size area is twice that of the motion picture camera frame. The fact that the Leica normal lens focal length is (relatively speaking) half that of the motion picture camera means that most pictures made with the still camera take in an angle of view twice as wide as that taken in by a motion picture camera filming the same event from the same distance. For cinematographers to duplicate on film the perspective and foreground-background image size relationships normally seen in the picture magazines, they would have to use what were considered in motion picture terms distinctly wide angle lenses. As this was precisely what the deep focus cinematographers did, much of the 'realism' attributed to deep focus may be due to the unconscious awareness on the part of the viewer that the object sizes and spatial relationships correspond more closely to those of still photography (and, in truth, to the way one's eyes tend to see) in deep focus than in conventional cinematography.

While the tendencies toward realism mentioned in the preceding paragraphs had a noticeable effect both on the general American cinematographic style and upon the development of the deep focus style, it should not be thought that the appearance of deep focus was either entirely inevitable or predictable on the basis of those tendencies alone. A number of changes in motion picture technology were necessary to provide the range of capabilities from which Toland and others chose those suitable for synthesis into the mature deep focus style. The significance of these changes can perhaps best be appreciated by a brief historical survey of the evolution in film stocks and developers, lenses, and lighting from the early 'hard edge' style of circa 1915, through the heavily diffused 'fuzzygraph' era of the later 1920's and early 1930's, to the coming of the deep focus style in 1914.

The era of silent film-making that extended from the time of David Wark Griffith's *The Birth of a Nation* (1915) until the coming of sound in the later 1920's has often been painted as one of great art prevailing over woefully deficient technology. Such a viewpoint may be based excessively on hindsight. Many a contemporary student of film history will dutifully shake his head in thinking of the agonies doubtless suffered by cinematographers confined to the use of orthochromatic film. What he will likely not be aware of is that orthochromatic film (a type sensitive to green, blue-violet, and ultra-violet light[8]) constituted a very real improvement over the 'ordinary' or non-colour-sensitised emulsions[9] (sensitive only to blue-violet and ultra-violet) that had been the basic material of even earlier film-making. (Blue-sensitive film, semi-ironically, was to reappear in modified form in 1939 as Fine Grain Release Positive film, an important ingredient in the deep focus technique.) As panchromatic film emulsions (a type reasonably sensitive to the entire visible spectrum rather than just the shorter wavelengths) had been first introduced in 1913 but had not proved popular, it would appear that cinematographers of the era may have preferred to use orthochromatic film. Most of this preference may have been due to the innate conservatism of many cinematographers (upon whose heads much wrath would inevitably descend in the event of photographic mishap), but some of it may have been due to the conduciveness of ortho-chromatic film to the crisp contrasty style of cinematography (which had its parallels in the 'f-64' school of still photography) that prevailed until sometime into the 1920's. While orthochromatic film was an intrinsically slow (ie not particularly light sensitive) emulsion type, this factor may not have been very obvious at the time as the extremely strong and contrasty developers then in use compensated in large measure for the deficiencies in film speed, albeit at a great cost in excessive graininess. Cinematographers often found themselves having to stop their lenses down to f-45 for filming exteriors, indicating that the violent developing chemicals of the time gave the film an effective speed of over 160 ASA,[10] similar to that of medium to fast black-and-white panchromatic emulsions of today. An f-45 lens aperture set on a normal 50mm motion picture camera lens provided an extreme depth of field, such that objects would be rendered sharp at distances from just under two feet to infinity. The full deep focus potentials of this great depth of field seem rarely if ever to have been explored at the time, however . . .

Lighting during the era of orthochromatic film was chosen for compatibility with the green-blue-violet sensitivity of the stock. As this was the era of the silent film, much filming was done outside, where sunlight and skylight provided rich and free sources of light concentrated toward the shorter wavelengths of the visible spectrum. At one time indoor filming had been accomplished largely by the use of studios with glass skylights, but as time went on production companies began to eschew the vagaries of weather by turning exclusively to the use of artificial illumination. Banks of mercury vapour lamps (identical in concept and similar in spectral distribution to modern street and highway lamps) were used for broad, general lighting, and provided the suitable bluish light needed with high electrical efficiency. The other primary light source at the time was the carbon arc lamp (which in later improved form was perhaps to be the crucial element in deep focus cinematography). The carbon arc lamp produced a very blue light (similar to that emitted by a contemporary electric arc welder) of high intensity per watt of electricity consumed. Unlike the mercury vapour lamp, the carbon arc lamp emitted light from a very small area. This point-source lighting tended to bring out textures and cast very sharp shadows, adding strongly to the sense of crispness and contrast already evoked by the film and lens types.

Some time into the 1920's the extremely hard and sharp look in cinematography began to give way to a softer, more diffused style, paralleling a similar trend in still photography. This was first achieved by the optical means of fitting layers of gauze over the camera lens and placing optical diffusers called 'silks' over the lights. Some visual softening appeared with the introduction of a number of newer and more complex motion picture lenses, the designs of which traded off a degree of lens correction in order to achieve greater light-gathering power. These lenses, with maximum apertures of about f-2.3, also possessed intrinsically less depth of field at maximum aperture (which came to be used as the normal filming aperture) than had the older, simpler lenses. This increased softness was optical rather than tonal, for orthochromatic film remained contrasty by nature. As part of the trend toward softening of shadows and lowering of contrast, Lee Garmes, ASC, began experimenting with the use of 'Mazda' incandescent lamps for lighting films during the mid-1920's. The Mazda lamp was initially at a disadvantage when used with orthochromatic film as much of its light was in the yellow-orange region to which orthochromatic film was blind, and its electrical efficiency was significantly lower than that of either arcs or mercury vapour lamps. The initial value of the Mazda lamp was in the non-point-source quality of the light, for it cast significantly softer shadows and tended to suppress textures. This single advantage of the Mazda lamp would probably not have been enough to ensure its success had not other events intervened, however, for 'as late as 1927 the majority of motion picture productions were made using orthochromatic negative with mercury vapour and arc lamps . . .'.[11]

Nineteen twenty-eight was a pivotal year for the American film industry, witnessing as it did the first significant amount of sound film production, the introduction of the soft-looking finer grain Type 1 panchromatic film by Eastman Kodak, and the beginning of the metamorphosis from arc to Mazda for studio lighting. Panchromatic film stock and Mazda lighting proved well matched to each other, the film being sensitive to the longer wavelengths of visible radiation in which Mazda illumination was particularly rich. Intensive testing by the American Society of Cinematographers definitely proved the Incandescent to be superior for use with Panchromatic film; but I doubt if the innovation would have been accepted so readily had not sound arrived to force the issue. The 'Inkie' was the only really silent lamp available, and it naturally sprang overnight into general use.[12]

With the at least temporary discontinuance of the use of arc lamps due to noise problems on the newly-built sound stages, American film-making entered a period of heavily diffused images, soft tonality, and shallow depth of field that was to characterise Hollywood films until into the later 1930's. While softness and diffusion was the prevailing aesthetic style of cinematography, it must be admitted that for much of the period it may not have been possible to achieve the earlier crispness even if cinematographers had wanted to, so encumbering were the demands of early sound film-making. The soft tonality panchromatic emulsions, while intrinsically more light-sensitive than orthochromatic, came to be processed in milder, more fine-grain borax-type developers (such as D-76) that greatly improved picture resolution quality but reduced effective film speed and contrast. Soft shadow Mazda lighting, crucial to sound film-making due to its silence, was less efficient electrically than arc and available only in lighting units of comparatively low power. The newer and faster lenses had almost by necessity to be used at maximum aperture, further softening the image and reducing depth of field.

   While the coming of the sound film had had a strong influence on moving cinematography away from the crisp, contrasty, depthy style of much of the silent era, another new film type and technology had a similarly strong influence in making possible a return to more realistic cinematography styles in the later 1930's and in furnishing much of the technology crucial to the deep focus style. This was Technicolor (which also, in a McLuhan[13] sort of way, may have given monochrome cinematography the possibility of becoming an art by supplanting it as the basic medium of mass popular visual entertainment). If the silencing of cameras and lights in order to record speech and music satisfactorily had been one of the major efforts of sound film technology, one of the primary problems in developing the three-colour subtractive Technicolor process was to maintain the silence of lighting equipment while enormously increasing its power and significantly shifting its colour balance. As the film stocks used in the Technicolor process had a very low effective speed and were balanced for the predominantly green-blue of daylight, Mazda incandescent lighting could no longer be relied upon as a primary lighting source. Consequently a new generation of arc lamps appeared, incorporating a number of improvements that rendered them quiet and flicker-free. Changes in the chemical formulas for the carbons used shifted the spectral distribution of the light produced such that arc could match daylight with only mild filtration by means of a straw-coloured Y-1 filter. The modern arc lamp of the middle to later 1930's retained the crisp shadow-casting and texture-revealing point-source light of its forebears, and models of remarkable intensity and carrying power began to appear. While much of the Mazda incandescent lighting equipment commonly used in black-and-white production after 1935 dated back (in design and often in construction) to the beginning of the sound era almost a decade earlier, virtually all arc lighting developed for Technicolor work was of 1934 or later vintage and possessed substantial advantages in uniformity, controllability, and power. Confined initially to use in colour production work (due both to scarcity and – one thinks – to power beyond that needed by most workers in monochrome), the new arc lights later began to be used in black-and-white production with fair frequency, the arrival of faster Technicolor film stocks in 1939 having allowed a sizeable reduction in colour lighting power requirements (and having even sparked something of a resurgence in the use of filtered Mazda lighting in Technicolor sets).

Developments in filmstock technology proceeded apace. The soft and fine grain (in comparison to orthochromatic) Eastman Type 1 panchromatic emulsion of 1928 was followed later the same year by the slightly faster and even softer Type 2 emulsion. February 1931 saw the introduction of the first super-sensitive panchromatic emulsion, Eastman Super Sensitive Panchromatic Negative, a stock at once materially faster, finer-grained, and softer than its predecessors. Rather than stopping down lens apertures (and thus risk losing the then-fashionable softness of image), cinematographers initiated a trend toward ever-lower key light levels on the sets (a trend that, in some quarters, continues to the present day). The introduction of Eastman Super X Panchromatic Negative in March 1935 continued the trend toward somewhat higher speed with much lower grain and improved picture quality. Super X film remained an inherently soft, low contrast emulsion, as indicated by the recommendation of the manufacturer that the film be developed to the comparatively high gamma of .70 for normal results. This characteristic of tonal softness in film stocks was abruptly reversed in late October 1938, however, when Eastman introduced Plus-X Panchromatic Negative as a new general use film, an emulsion with twice the speed of Super X, finer grain, similar developing characteristics, but with such noticeably higher contrast that many cinematographers, having grown accustomed to working with soft tonality films, were to experience real difficulty in lighting sets properly for the new film.

Two weeks after the introduction of Plus-X came the announcement of Eastman Super XX, a film possessing grain characteristics comparable to those of the standard Super X previously used, but with a film speed four times as great. Developed initially for newsreel work and other specialised and realistic filming done under difficult lighting conditions (and also developed, one suspects, to regain first place in the film speed derby from Agfa-Ansco, whose Agfa Supreme Negative and Agfa Ultra-Speed Negative emulsions had been introduced eleven months previously and had won a Class 1 Academy

Award for the manufacturer), Super Double X film quickly came to be used in ways far different from those intended or envisaged by Eastman Kodak. A few cinematographers such as Victor Milner, ASC, became immediately aware that the high speed film widened the potential expressiveness of the medium in that:

It makes it possible for us to run the scale between extremely soft, naturalesque low-level lightings (50 foot candles or less), shot with full lens apertures, to the opposite extreme of higher level illumination (perhaps as high as 200 foot candles or more) exposed at greatly reduced apertures for a new and greater depth and crispness.[14]

Only a very small number of cinematographers opted for the possibilities of increased crispness and depth of field, however. A greater number followed the path of James Wong Howe in maintaining full aperture filming while further lowering set lighting levels almost to those of conventional roof lighting, thus providing more naturalistic settings within which the actors could perform. By far the greatest number of cinematographers (Milner included), however, utilised Super Double X film in a strange (but fully explainable) way. Conservative by nature and distressed by the increased contrastiness of the new general use Plus-X emulsion, these cinematographers began to employ Super Double X as a production film with deliberate underdevelopment, a procedure that gave them lowered contrast similar to the old Super X film they had been used to, and fine grain similar to the new Plus-X emulsion. The great loss of film speed entailed in underdevelopment was desirable to them, as it permitted the use of lighting levels and lens apertures little different from those of previous practice. The armchair paleontologist would find this a classic example of the evolutionary principle that, within a modified environment, new or changed behaviours or forms in an organism arise in the organism's attempt to return to the homeostasis of the previous environment. Ironic indeed is the realisation that while Super Double X film was to prove an important ingredient in the development of the crisp, deep focus style, the main impetus toward its use as a production filmstock was the desire to preserve the soft tonality and low depth of field of the older type of cinematography!

A final important development in film technology occurred in 1939 with the introduction of a new emulsion type in the relatively unglamorous category of release print[15] stocks. This film, Fine Grain Release Positive, was an extremely slow stock sensitive only to blue-violet and ultra-violet light, and required printing by means of modified high pressure mercury arc light sources. To offset these inconveniences, Fine Grain Positive had the major advantage of being virtually grainless, and thus free from the problem of successive image degradation common to printing stocks before it. Picture quality improved noticeably, and the new freedom from grain multiplication through the various print generations from camera to release print allowed cinematographers to use high speed films such as Super Double X without the fear of excessive graininess. Sound quality improved even more than did picture quality on Fine Grain Positive Film: high frequencies were reproduced far better and emulsion ground noise was reduced 6–8 decibels, factors that would be highly important to films in which the sound track was to play a strong role.

In contrast to the relative flux that had been occurring in the areas of lighting and film stocks, the field of camera lens design had changed little since the introduction of the fast and relatively soft lenses of the late silent era. Small incremental improvements had been made in lens correction and sharpness, but a ceiling seemed to have been reached, dictated largely by the design compromises that had to be struck in dealing with the conflicting requirements of lens speed and optical quality. Revolutionary, therefore, were the implications of the announcement by two independent researchers in 1939 of the principle of lens coating, by which a microscopically thin layer of magnesium fluoride was deposited on the lens surfaces with resulting improvements in light transmissions of more than 75 per cent under some conditions. As might be expected concerning a process that promised much more efficient use of light, the lens coating principle proved of great interest to Technicolor Corporation, and the first commercial application of lens coating techniques was by Bausch & Lomb in delivering coated projection lenses to twenty-five Loew theatres in the larger cities for the first showings of *Gone With the Wind*,[16] where improvements in screen illumination, image contrast, and sharpness of focus were noted. Similar benefits were noted when coatings were applied to camera lenses. A typical uncoated high-speed motion picture anastigmat lens such as the Astro Pan-Tachar suffered light losses in excess of 41 per cent due to reflections from the eight air-to-glass surfaces comprising its lens formula. Such light losses were reduced to negligible proportions with the application of optical coatings. In addition internal reflection and fog-producing scattered light within the lens was largely eliminated, allowing the lens to capture a great deal of shadow detail normally lost. William Stull, ASC, noted that lens coatings produced

> . . . a practical increase in speed of virtually one full stop. . . . Thus a normal f-2.3 lens, when treated is the equivalent in speed of an f-1.6 objective, but still retains the depth of field, definition, and optical quality of the f-2.3 design!

The elimination of the internal reflections gives a marked increase in the apparent definition of scenes photographed with treated lenses. . . . The picture as a whole is visibly more crisp, and details not previously evident are suddenly revealed.
In the same way depth of field is apparently considerably increased by the treated lens. It is quite possible that the circle of confusion is affected, since the resolving power is known to be increased.[17]
A point not made by Stull is that another great increase in depth of field became possible with coated lenses simply because the greatly increased efficiency of light transmission demanded a physically smaller lens diaphragm aperture to transmit the same amount of light as a larger aperture had previously. This smaller aperture increased both depth of field and lens sharpness.

Looking back at the technological state of the movie-making art in 1940, a determinist could well argue that the conjunction of powerful point source arc lights, fast film emulsions, and crisp coated lenses rendered inevitable the emergence of deep focus cinematography. The argument has some merit, for, indeed, a number of cinematographers seem at the time to have looked over their newly improved tools and commenced semi-independent investigations into increased-depth photography. Aware as he is of the crucial importance of much of this technology to the deep focus style, the author nevertheless feels that for deep focus to appear and develop as it did, a number of essentially aesthetic choices and creative syntheses had to occur. These choices and syntheses seem largely to have been made by one man, Gregg Toland, for while other cinematographers may have been working rather haphazardly toward a cinematographic style of increased depth, crispness, and contrast, Toland was the first person to draw together and elaborate the series of attitudes and technical tool usages that became the coherent body of filming practices constituting the deep focus style. The matter of timing and opportunity also seems very important, for without the fertile creative environments provided by William Wyler, John Ford, and especially by Orson Welles, the deep focus style might never have come into being. . . . The coherence of *Citizen Kane*'s visual aspect (a coherence shared by the dialogue, sound, and music of the film) is due in large measure to the conditions under which the film was produced, for the making of *Citizen Kane* constituted a major coming together of technological practice with aesthetic choice in an environment highly conducive to creativity.

Judging that therein lay an unusual opportunity for photographic innovation, Toland actively sought the assignment to shoot the film, and brought his veteran operative crew with him to the RKO studios to do so. Unusual in a Hollywood production of the time, Toland was on the job for a full half year, including preparation and actual shooting. The importance of Orson Welles, both in terms of his own creative contributions and his encouragement of innovative behaviour in others, cannot be overemphasised. Toland was later gratefully to acknowledge Welles' willingness to let him experiment with photographic effects that often took weeks to achieve, remarking that 'such differences as exist between the cinematography in *Citizen Kane* and the camera work on the average Hollywood product are based on the rare opportunity provided me by Orson Welles, who was in complete sympathy with my theory that the photography should fit the story'.[18]

Coming to his first turn at film direction from a notoriety-filled period of work in radio and live theatre, Welles was determined to give *Citizen Kane* the kind of unique imprint that he had made upon his efforts in the other media. Whether due to his theatrical experience (in which action occurs within specific spatial bounds primarily within real-time duration) or that in radio (in which events take place in a fluidly homogeneous 'field' very different from the discrete segmentation of visually perceived space), Welles became strongly desirous of creating a film in which actions were to flow smoothly into each other by means of imperceptible transitions, with intercutting and inserts to be eliminated as completely as possible. In achieving this, according to Toland:

> We arranged our action so as to avoid direct cuts, to permit panning or dollying from one angle to another whenever that type of camera action fitted the continuity. By way of example, scenes which conventionally would require a shift from close-up to full shot were planned so that the action would take place simultaneously in extreme foreground and extreme background.[19]

Citizen Kane was one of the first important productions filmed with the Mitchell BNC motion picture camera, a device whose quiet operation was achieved by means of internal sound dampening measures. The elimination of the bulky external blimp[20] previously required had important consequences for filming in the deep focus style. Simply dispensing with the need for shooting through the optical glass plate of the blimp sharpened up the photographed image and increased light transmission over ten per cent. Lens focus, depth of field, and photographic composition could easily be checked without having to open up a blimp. The relative compactness and light weight of the self-blimped Mitchell BNC must have proved of distinct value under the conditions of use imposed by the generally small, deep sets within which *Citizen Kane* was filmed, allowing the camera to be raised, lowered, panned, and dollied[21] (no doubt often by means of an hydraulic tripod and dolly-track system previously developed by Toland) with comparative ease. An additional psychological advantage may have accrued in the use of this camera, as its comparatively small size surely rendered its presence less intimidating to the actors, who often found themselves having to perform only two or three feet away from it.

While the twenty-five millimeter focal length wide angle lens was a standardised item in most cinematographers' inventories of equipment, it was normally used only in situations where the camera could not be moved back far enough to capture all the relevant action within the field of view of the normal 50mm lens. The distinguishing feature of Toland's wide angle lens was in the way he used it. Like Howe and Glennon before him, Toland was both aware of the inherently greater depth of field of the wide angle lens (following the rule of thumb that depth of field varied inversely as the square of the magnification of the lens) and of the fact that the different perspective given by the lens could be used for dramatic effect. Where Toland went beyond Howe and Glennon's occasional semi-standardised use of the wide angle lens was in using his stopped down to f-8, f-11, or even f-16, extending depth of field in some cases from less than two feet to infinity! With Toland's small aperture wide angle lens, a cinema aesthetic of non-intercut compositions in depth became fully realisable.

The use of a coated lens (the 'Vard' opticoating system, developed at CalTech) was highly important to the deep focus cinematography of *Citizen Kane*, for the minutely thin chemical deposit (amounting in thickness to a fraction of the wavelength of light) on the air-to-glass surfaces of the lens doubled light transmission, sharpened the imagery and contrast, and made possible filming practices previously considered quite unattainable. As a coated lens at f-8 transmitted the same amount of light as an uncoated optic at f-5.6, scenes could be filmed with the increased depth of field of the former aperture, but with the halved lighting requirements of the latter. The most noticeable new filming technique afforded by the use of coated objectives was that of shooting into lights, examples of which are seen in the several sequences dealing with Susan Alexander's[22] opera debut in *Citizen Kane*. Without lens coatings such shots would have been unusably washed out and diffuse.

Employment of Eastman Super XX film as a production stock joined with coated lenses in helping permit the use of the small lens apertures necessary to Toland's compositions in depth. Unlike most cinematographers, Toland used the stock at full rated speed, developing time, and contrast. While the film speed of Super Double X (128 ASA for daylight or arcs, 80 ASA for tungsten-Mazda) may not seem remarkable by contemporary standards, the two points should be borne in mind that Super Double X did constitute an enormous advance over the Super X stock (32 ASA for daylight, 20 ASA for Mazda) that for all practical purposes had preceded it, and that the American Standards Association criteria for determining film speeds have been modified since that time such that by the current measurement system Super Double X would have a daylight ASA film speed of slightly over 250 – reasonably fast even by today's standards. The relatively new (and by no means universally used) Eastman Fine Grain Release Positive film stock was utilised for the final release prints to motion picture theatres, insuring protection of the Eastman Super Double X footage from grain multiplication or other image degradation and significantly improving the reproduction fidelity of *Citizen Kane*'s sound track, itself as revolutionary as the film's photographic style.

Granting that camera, lenses, and film stocks played important roles in the deep focus cinematography of *Citizen Kane*, nevertheless the true *sine qua non* of the style seems to have involved the lighting equipment and its method of employment. Faced with the desire to film at diminished apertures within narrow, deep, roofed-over sets, Toland had to rely entirely on floor-level lighting of very considerable intensity and carrying power. 'The answer, of course, was to use arcs very extensively. It is safe to say that *Citizen Kane* could not have been made without modern arc lighting.'[23] As the spectral distribution of arcs resembled that of daylight in that the preponderance of energy was to be found among the shorter wavelengths of visible radiation, all the inherent light sensitivity of the Super Double X emulsion could be utilised, for the stock was half again as fast under daylight-arc conditions than when exposed to Mazda-incandescent illumination. While also electrically more efficient in terms of lumens per watt, the primary advantage of arc lighting as used on *Citizen Kane* was in terms of sheer power. Toland's general practice was to use arc broads (specifically, the Mole-Richardson 'Duarc' developed for colour work) set back about twice as far (20–30 feet) from the players as incandescent broadsides would have been, thus increasing the depth of field of uniform illumination. Toland commented that:

> . . . the use of arcs permitted us to light this way [floor lighting from front of set] and yet to avoid the unevenness of exposure which might normally be expected under such circumstances. . . . With the [Mazda-type] lamp nearer the action, its depth of illuminative field might be a matter of two or three feet. With an arc placed further back your subject can move freely over an area of ten feet or more in depth without undesirable changes in exposure value. Arc illumina-

tion, in a word, gives you depth of field in lighting to match the optical depth modern technique affords. . . .[24]

Another (and final) way – besides allowing deep focus compositions – in which Toland's lighting for *Citizen Kane* furthered Welles' desire to avoid direct cutting or traditional transitions occurred in the lap dissolves that provided most transitions in the film. A pair of dimmers were used so that an overlapped sequence – (1) background of first shot dims; (2) players in first shot dim; (3) background of second shot fades in; (4) players in second shot fade in – could occur in which both imagery and lighting worked together in smoothing the transition almost to imperceptibility. This sense of various elements working smoothly together seems to characterise all of the film, and in intelligently blending compositional and tonal desires with technological capabilities, Gregg Toland created mature deep focus cinematography.

Considering Orson Welle's own flair for publicity and the pseudo-exposé qualities of the film's screenplay, *Citizen Kane* could hardly help attracting much notoriety and controversy upon its release. Part of this notoriety and controversy surrounded the cinematography and the cinematographer, a most unusual occurrence in the American film industry. Gregg Toland's name came closer to becoming a household word than any other cameraman's before or since. Mass circulation magazines published photo stories demonstrating the principle of deep focus and featuring its creator. Controversy raged among cameramen: some hailed it as a breakthrough, other considered it a slightly silly retrogression to the early days of film-making. . . .

The coming of the Second World War submerged the deep focus cinematographic style (as it did so much else) in the flood of mundane but important matters having to do with fighting and winning a global conflict. Many cinematographers spent the duration in military service, filming real events with sixteen millimeter equipment that gave inherently greater depth of field than had the thirty-five millimeter studio cameras. Thus, though deep focus cinematography did not reappear as a specific style after World War II, many of its qualities found their way, in modified form, into standard Hollywood usage by way of these returning cinematographers. In the postwar years, as today, crisp deep focus cinematography came to be seen for what it finally is – one possible visual means of conveying experience, just as is diffused shallow focus cinematography. The primary contribution of Gregg Toland and others in developing deep focus may have been in demonstrating that such a range of choice exists (Ogle, 1972).

The most interesting aspect of Ogle's work is his correlation of information about lenses, methods of lighting and film stocks. Though the article does not suggest any method for relating questions of film technology with developments in other arts or with wider issues of society and history, the connection Ogle implies between the realist style and the photojournalism of the 1930s is also interesting. The very weight of detail in the article makes it clear that film styles emerge out of a conjuncture of differentially-paced technical developments. The film-maker Jean Renoir corroborates some of Ogle's descriptions in his account of his turn from ortho- to panchromatic film stock in the 1920s:

I abandoned my search for exaggerated contrasts, the desire to pass without transition from absolute black to the most dazzling white, on the day I discovered the existence of panchromatic film. You see how ignorant I was! I had made my first films without knowing that every cameraman in the world used orthochromatic film for interiors – that is to say, film almost without shading, of absolute black and white. But the moment they went out of doors they substituted panchromatic film which has a great many shades, so that reds, blues and yellows, all the colours of the spectrum, are conveyed by greys of varying density. The fact was that the lighting equipment of the studios dated from the earliest days of the cinema and consisted chiefly of mercury-tubes which did not suit panchromatic film. Real sunlight possesses a different quality to which its shading reacts.

It did not take me long to adapt my taste to shaded photography. My reversal was complete. I saw the possibility of close-ups of a magical softness. Unfortunately there was no system of lighting equipment suitable for panchromatic interiors, and two years went by before it occurred to me to make it myself. . . .

The use of panchromatic film entirely was, for me, a step in the direction of colour film, which I was not to use until twenty years later, in *The River*.[25] The need for panchromatic film occurred at almost the same time to the film technicians across the Atlantic, and before long they, too, were using panchromatic film for interior shots. There was no plagiarism in this: ideas spread like epidemics. The harsh contrasts of orthochromatic film were suddenly relegated to the past; they became one of our memories of the pioneering stage, along with accelerated motion to produce comic effects. This new kind of photography, because it better expressed reality, paved the way for a different kind of script and a new style of acting – in fact, for that dream of the lover of realism, the talking film.

Artistic developments are in practice the direct outcome of technical improvements. The most striking example of this known to me is the Impressionist revolution in painting. Before Impressionism painters used colours contained in small cups which were difficult to carry about. The paint ran out of them, and this made outdoor work impracticable. But after someone had had the idea of storing paint in tubes with screw tops the painters of the new school could take their colours with them and paint directly from nature. It is true that the Impressionist revolution was conceived in the minds of the painters, but it would not have taken the same form if they had not been able to take their paintboxes into the Forest of Fontainebleau. Although it did not have all the repercussions of paint in tubes, the use of panchromatic film represented an immense forward step. Most of the screen masterpieces were made in black and white on panchromatic film (Renoir, 1974).

Renoir expresses the same kind of naïve belief in 'better expressing reality' that Ogle has already commented on; but his films themselves are more complicated. Rossellini, too, has been prepared to further his commitment to 'show reality' (see above, pp. 31–34) by experimenting with camera technology. Here he describes the system of the Pancinor lens which he developed in the late 1960s to enable a combination of the effects of panning and zooming[26] simultaneously:

In il generale della Rovere *you experiment with a moving lens for the first time.*

I had used one before, but here I was taking it seriously. It's now my usual method. *Atti degli Apostoli* and *La prise de pouvoir par Louis XIV*[27] were filmed entirely with moving lenses. I always defended the hand camera as a means of de-mystifying and de-dramatising the cinema. You have to make films simply and directly, and use the clearest possible language. I chose hand cameras to free myself from big industrial organisation. Since then they've been so much abused that going to the cinema is like boarding a ship, you come out feeling sea-sick. To avoid this but still have the same mobility, I made a camera that could be optically mobile but still remain in a fixed position, which would make these eccentricities impossible. I began by thinking out how to transform the zoom camera, in particular the controls. My system has two interlocking motors, and one of them acts as a counterweight to stop the lens oscillating as it moves, so that you don't get a zoom effect. This gives me great mobility – for example, I can zoom from an angle of 25° to one of 150°, and this opens up enormous possibilities. I operate it myself, it's a very easy thing to use and you can improvise with it during shooting. If an actor isn't quite in the right spot, for example, you can follow him with the zoom lens. It saves a lot of time and it may improve the actor's performance—if he loses the rhythm during the scene usually it's much less convincing. These slight adjustments show him more closely. The camera works more like an eye, and so you can develop a system of constant direct participation, because when you have organised the scene and begun shooting you can see if it's going well, and if not you can stop.

You sometimes use the zoom to give distance.

That shows how varied its potential is. We always shoot in sequences, which reduces montage to a minimum. This optical mobility makes it possible to base it all on organising the scene, and this means you have to know the set very well. You have to establish it. Normally you take a shot showing the set as a whole, then the actor comes on, you cut in nearer to the actor, follow him etc. With the travelling lens you don't need to alter the distance. It's all linked in the context of the scene, which has to follow a certain pattern and bring over a particular meaning. I have to know exactly where the actors are and make the meaning very clear. With this kind of mobility I can do that. I was tending to do this even before: in *Europa '51* there were many very difficult moving sequences, which had to be shot with the camera on a dolly following the actors around the whole time. In Hitchcock's films the moving shots are very important and he has to have special sets built that the actors can appear and disappear in, which is extremely complicated. But the travelling lens simplifies all this enormously (Rossellini, 1970).

'The camera works more like an eye, and so you can develop a system of constant direct participation.' Though Rossellini here means principally participation and control by the director, he states two of the central concerns of film realism. In two short extracts from an interview with Alan Rosenthal, the Canadian documentarist Allan King focuses first on the related question of how the camera crew affects the performers. The film referred to is *A Married Couple*,[28] in which a middle-aged couple perform as themselves in an apparently documentary account of their real lives. The film was produced through the normal *cinéma-vérité* method of shooting off a very large amount of material, and, for the finished film, keeping only the sections that best suited the structure of the film itself. In the shooting stage the camera crew more or less moved in with the couple for long periods:

Q. How much does the camera interfere? How much do people put on for the camera?

A. It depends on the cameraman. If you get a dumb, insensitive, obstructive cameraman, the interference is enormous. If you have a sensitive, intelligent, quiet, responsive, unobtrusive and unjudging, impersonally critical cameraman or camera crew, then not only is the camera not inhibitive, but it stimulates the couple to talk, in the same way an analyst or therapist does. You can talk if you want to; you don't have to talk if you don't want to; you do what you want. If you choose to put up smoke screens, or you choose to put on a dialogue, or you try to hide something, this would be evident to anybody with any sort of sensitivity. It isn't possible for people to produce material out of thin air irrelevant to their character. Whatever occurs is relevant to the character, and it gives us that overall sense we have of the person. So I felt for a long time that we were not concerned with the question, 'Is it the real person?' or those kinds of questions. These are really ways in which an audience or some elements of an audience tend to evade the actual feelings they are getting from the film. 'Is that really real?' – what the hell does that mean? Either the film means something to you, or it doesn't. On the question again of interference, I think it is well to allow the person to express stuff in perhaps a little more concentrated period of time.

Q. Did you sense that anyone was putting on an act for the camera?

A. There were various places in the film where they do, but there are two kinds of acting. If you ask, 'Are they acting for the camera?' you can say, 'no,' and a little while along you would have to say, 'yes.' It depends on how much space you have in which to explain. They performed for the camera in the same way they perform for friends. Friends come together, and often they would get into fifteen minutes of bantering back and forth, teasing each other; they'd have a mock row, or they'd set up a whole line of dialogue which they could carry for fifteen or twenty minutes as a way of entertaining themselves and their friends. You can see them do that in the film. . . .

Q. Let's move on to editing and structure. You shot seventy hours, and you use an hour and a half. Were the choices difficult regarding what to omit?

A. I can't remember – my memory is a bit foggy. I have a bad time once I've cut a sequence out; by and large, I forget it even existed. Yet when you're looking at a rough cut and you argue about what's to come out, you say, 'I can't take that sequence out; I've got to have that sequence'; but once you take it out, you very seldom miss it. However, I can't remember very much; I can't remember sequences, but there must be some which we had in and then took out. It was really much more a question of tightening sections and making them work as sequences and, more than that, making the overall structure work.

Q. Is the final film in chronological order?

A. No. The opening of the film was shot about two-thirds the way through; the breakfast scene was shot halfway through. Basically, the main arch of action is at the end of the film when they wake up – after they have had that moment of intimacy when she's sitting on his lap crying, and they wake up the next morning and have a great fight and he throws her out of the house. That whole passage happened the week before we finished filming, and it was what we were waiting for. Not that it had to be a fight; it might have been a very happy episode. But you wait for one significant arch of events that hang together and give you a core. The holiday, and when they're at the lake and so on, and the party around that – they all occurred very early in the filming and are actually unrelated to the rest. All I do is take episodes and put them into a dramatic structure that works for me.

Q. So you are aiming towards a kind of emotional fiction?

A. Yes. It is very often the case that episode *a* is put together with episode *b* to produce a feeling of *c*, when in reality they don't have that connection. However, if feeling *c* doesn't have a feeling relationship or isn't true of the characters, then it won't work. What I'm doing is finding conjunctions of events which create for me the feeling I have about that couple and about life, and what I want to express (King, 1971).

King's admission that *A Married Couple* works as a structured fiction can usefully be set alongside Rossellini's statement[29] that each scene has to 'follow a certain pattern and bring over a particular meaning'. Another version of the same point is made by Ed Pincus, discussing his film *Black Natchez*[30] with George Roy Levin:

On one hand we had this early SDS[31] political philosophy of let the people decide, don't manipulate people. The role of the organizer was to put people in condition to decide their own future, but he wasn't to coerce them. The worst thing was to manipulate. That was a real crime. Somehow this fits in very nicely with the kind of cinéma-vérité philosophy where the film-maker goes in, doesn't manipulate reality, tries to capture reality as if he weren't there. So for example in the American tradition of cinéma-vérité the interview is considered not cinéma-vérité because what's an interview but a kind of camera-created reality? The interview wouldn't exist without the interviewer or the camera crew. Well, during the editing, where we felt our presence hadn't affected the action, that it would have occurred even had we not been there, we saw ourselves as non-manipulators, capturing the reality in which, for example, somebody like Charles Evers[32] gets judged harshly because he tries to manipulate the crowd, because he doesn't let people make up their own minds for themselves.

G.R.L. Your point of view about that is you like to keep yourself clear of making judgments about what happens?

E.P. Yeah.

G.R.L. In the shooting or the editing, or both?

E.P. Both. There are lots of choices of shots that we could use. This is a really good example, I think: it was very crowded, and some of the shots were taken of Evers – this is in a particular scene – where I would stay two feet away from him, and I could hardly move. Now there's one part where his head is partially out of the frame and he's saying, 'We're going to tell you when to march and how to march.' Now, as he says 'how to march,' his head comes down full on the frame. Well, because he's so close and the wide-angle lens distorts his head, he seems like a very powerful figure – and it comes not through ideas but through authority itself that he's convincing people to do something. There's a kind of happenstance of my position. I didn't have a choice – it worked at what we were trying to say. Yet, we had a choice in editing of using that or not using that.

There's another time when he tells people who disagree with him that they should leave and he points his finger. The camera goes down his arm and it fills the frame with his finger. Well, behind his finger is the Catholic church, and then the camera pans down just as a police car goes by. There are these three symbols of authority coming into the frame at the same time. There in the shooting was the consciousness of it, but there was also the choice of using it or not, and we had a discussion about whether to use that even though the ideas were just what we wanted, because it seemed manipulated to have these three elements in the picture though it comes out of a continuous shot. It looked heavy. That was the phrase we used to use, too heavy. That was partially because we were playing two things against each other, I guess. On one hand we recognized the cinema as illusion, but we knew people didn't take it to be illusion, kind of took it to be hard and fast fact. We wanted to prod, to encourage those feelings of this is objective fact. At the same time we wanted to take advantage of the illusionistic aspects.

   An example of the kind of illusionistic aspect I'm talking about is that every time you use one camera – and we've only used one camera, on some level we're committed to that – when you make a cut within a sequence you've actually cut out time. Whenever there's a cut that means real time has been cut out. Well, we always used to be very careful that in the sequences all our cuts were matched cuts, meaning they appeared as though time wasn't cut out, they seemed to be a continuous flow of reality. As a matter of fact, we've always looked at the cut in a cinéma-vérité sequence as a way of emphasizing or pushing forward time, to hasten the pacing. That's us manipulating the way things happened to say what we want to say – to make people take it to be continuous. Lots of film-makers who saw the film said, 'You shot that with more than one camera, didn't you?' And we hadn't. It was because we were very careful about that level of editing, making all those cuts appear to be continuous, cuts where we change angles, stuff like that (Pincus, 1971).

So the impression of reality in film is produced by manipulation, and given the number of technical processes that have to be gone through, the manipulation must be conscious. We are a long way from the mystique of realism as seen in Frances Hubbard Flaherty (pp. 89–90).

   Another of the technical devices which have been seen as either inherently more realistic or else as 'promoting more realism' is the sequence-shot, derived from the French *plan-séquence*, and meaning the use of a single shot, whether still or moving, without cutting, for the entire duration of a section or scene of the film. The Italian semiotician Gianfranco Bettetini considers the device and draws attention to some of its other properties. Its very 'artificiality' (in comparison with more traditional methods of editing) can allow the director to entertain by playing openly with the communicative structure of the film-making process (i.e. to acknowledge that the film is part of a language-system), while still retaining the 'earlier', more documentary-style connotations of the long-lasting take:

The advent of the long-held shot and the tendency to move away from splitting up the action into fragments shot from different angles should not . . . be interpreted merely as a facile return to the reproductively designative origins of the film instrument. The 'sequence-shot' of Godard, Antonioni, Losey, Rosi, and Bertolucci[33] does not (despite certain statements by these authors to the contrary, especially Godard) in any way abandon considering the image's representative powers from the point of view of its sign function,[34] nor does it reduce its significant function to a simple and total identification with the object which anyway cannot be accomplished. Cutting is above all brought into question as a fictional instrument, potentially capable of evocatively involving the spectator's attention, but the expressive and linguistic lesson that it offered has been re-absorbed into other dimensions of film composition. Camera movements and 'cinematographic' movements of reality (the ones, that is, that have been pre-arranged with their distorting translation onto a two-dimensional surface in mind) result in the cinematographic narration developing by virtue of a rich series of explicit connotations of a technical and linguistic nature, even when whole actions, whole scenes, or indeed whole sequences are absorbed into a single shot.

In the sequence-shot, reality is revealed according to parameters that appear to be rather more its own, and less invented than is the case in narrative situations codified by classical cutting – but even in this instance is one not, as always, concerned with a pre-arranged reality, or at any rate with one that has been selectively translated into images so as to signify something that invariably differentiates itself from its purely denotative aspect? Cutting revealed itself to be an inadequate cultural instrument once the attention of directors had become oriented towards a critical examination of the film's linguistic characteristics and, above all, once the urgent desire for truth that had been establishing itself throughout contemporary thought, anchoring its values to the physical aspects of reality and renouncing all possibility of re-elaborating them in some fanciful or mythical form, had impregnated the various types of research taking place in the sphere of audio-visual expression as well.

A film using the sequence-shot is still a communicative instrument that signifies on other levels as well as that of direct representation (which in itself is already incomplete and intentional); it is still a work in which the place occupied by the signifiers is the support and root of the place occupied by the signifieds, by the diegesis.[35] The sequence-shot of the contemporary cinema is therefore governed by expressive intentions that transcend the impersonal value of the continuous spatio-temporal photographing of a certain action or object. In informative films concerned with current affairs, the sequence-shot is often the natural way of translating reality into images – but there, as in the most normal television program, the sign on screen is attempting, in cases of considerable expressive richness, to connote the same connotations that are revealed by the direct manifestation of the object concerned, the hints of meaning that the phenomenon in front of the film camera itself gives rise to, irrespective of its translation onto film.

In the case of a film composed by virtue of a narrative fiction, on the other hand, the sequence-shot tends to increase the moving image's credibility (which is, by its very nature, already considerable), and hence the indirect persuasiveness of its dialectic positioning between the author and the receiver of the message. It also tends to lower the threshold of suggestivity beyond which the normal spectator finds his powers of critical reaction fade away. But one is always confronted by a significant fiction, by a deliberate representation of reality that is subordinated to creative, or at any rate interpretive, interests. Or rather one might say that the choice of a sequence-shot or of a type of cutting that makes use of shots of great length reveals a desire on the author's part to free himself and the spectator from the risk of projecting themselves into the film, the danger of a total identification between the perceptor's psychic existence and the action taking place on the screen, which often implies the suffocating of such effective catharsis as may be derived from the perception of the work.

The sequence-shot ensures that the director will do without the various expressive tricks and effects that the medium offers him, and that, at the same time, his entire interest will be oriented towards setting out a sign, whose iconic nature may not be reduced to a simple figurative relation (or a relation between formal percepts), but also involves the whole spatio-temporal development of the phenomenon translated into images or of the action invented as the dramatic root of the event on screen. This expressive tendency can at times overcome straightforward reference to a natural or invented reality outside the camera: it can, that is, imply connotations as to the very way in which the cinematographic work is formed and the linguistic techniques that condition its realization. The director's 'realistic' interests are, in this case, directed towards the behaviour of film material, the actors' spontaneous reactions to a certain dramatic proposition, the dialectic between the interpreter and the scenery around him, the ephemeral and finalized life of all the elements that go to make up a shot, and on the other hand they lead him to consider the narrative development of the work as a simple heuristic pretense. Rather than concern himself with the truth of facts, he chooses to concentrate on the truth of the dramatic reactions determined by using them as the model for a certain situation; the only part of them that he makes use of is the stimulating function of a certain linguistic reality. So the sequence-shot presents itself as the ideal setting for this kind of research, as the semantic space within which the fortuitous, aleatory and accidental elements that may accompany the making up of the scene find room to expand naturally.

In such cases, the director's search for expressive means draws close to the principles that lay behind Bertolt Brecht's concern with creating an epic theatre, as revealed in all of his plays and productions. Openly displaying to the receiver of the film message the means by which the dramatic action has been structured does, in fact, tend to estrange him from any possibility of suggestion, revealing at every moment the presence of a dramatic fiction and a mediating instrument of communication. To gain this end, the cinema resorts to making the actor look straight into the camera lens (Bergman, Godard), inserting evidently documentary material (Brass, Godard, Straub in *Nicht Vershohnt*),[36] a direct relation between actor and spectator (in the narrative form of an unseen voice, or in the more aggressive one of apparent dialogue), sub-titles (Godard, Pasolini); but it can also resort to the well-calculated use of the sequence-shot, choosing from among the various takes those that make clearer the constructive and compositional effort lying behind the many elements that go to make up the film.

Once again, the example of Jean-Luc Godard is particularly interesting from this point of view: his films very frequently show traces of a certain degree of improvisation and of being made rather quickly. In his determination to 'gather the definitive almost by chance', Godard does not attempt to put pressure on the actors in their interpretive game; he leaves them free and responsible for their own gestures, aiming more at the truth of their condition as actors than at that of the characters they represent. When cutting, he often makes use of shots that have not turned out well, according to the traditional praxis of film expression, but which better reveal the elements discussed above. Godard is perhaps an extreme example of a linguistic game that may appear gratuitous, but that draws its *raison d'être* from the necessity of re-thinking the ways in which the film message, supported and elaborated by the forms of cinematographic narration themselves, is put into effect.

Even in these apparent exceptions to contemporary production, however, one can always make out a signified that goes beyond the image's mere denotation, and that finds its place as a connotative element within a representation of reality which is rendered dialectic from its earliest stages by intentionally presenting an account of the linguistic elements that make it up. In the sequence of the domestic squabble between Angela (Anna Karina) and Emile (Jean-Claude

Brialy) from *Une femme est une femme,* Godard resorts to lengthy shots, which reveal by direct representation a certain milieu, certain of the two characters' attitudes and modes of behaviour, a certain segment of the film's narrative evolution, and at the same time place before the spectators the two actors' efforts at interpretation, their uncertainty (the alternation of crying and laughing on Karina's face after she has dropped the eggs), and the ways in which their attempts to communicate with the public become established. Introducing the spectator into the compository secrets of the film image in this manner has no purely informative and documentary aim; it is not an end in itself. On the contrary, it is precisely from the simultaneous and superimposed reception of the two narrative levels (the story and the data regarding its formation) that the spectator may deduce the complex meaning of the message: the director's critical attitude to a certain familiar reality, the sense of intellectual fun that pervades the whole work, a parodying glance at the Hollywood musical comedy.

So one can state that the use of the sequence-shot and the abandonment of cutting by the most interesting directors of the present generation do not in the slightest invalidate an approach to the cinematographic image in terms of its sign function (Bettetini, 1973).

The most interesting developments within modern documentary film have been in the diffuse, but much discussed, area known alternatively as direct cinema or as *cinéma-vérité*. In their original senses, direct cinema seems to have implied direct access to life, while *cinéma-vérité* allowed or encouraged the intervention of the film-maker as part of the 'truth' being presented. In practice the two terms became rapidly confused with each other. In the article which follows, Jean-Louis Comolli of *Cahiers du Cinéma* attempts to explore these confusions, basing himself on the inevitable difference between the filmed image of the object and the object itself. The difference is seen as also making manipulation inevitable; but for Comolli this manipulation (admitted by some documentarists, see King and Pincus, pp. 217–20) adds to the richness of the documentary material by allowing a 'greater instability of meanings and forms'. Fiction and documentary interpenetrate each other; documentary takes on an 'aura of fiction', fiction becomes documentarised. Instead of film trying to copy life by reproducing it, film and life produce each other, 'reciprocally':

1. A certain tendency of modern cinema is becoming more and more plain: namely, an increasingly apparent recourse – in the 'fiction' film – to the modes of *direct cinema*.

Rivette's[37] *L'Amour fou*[38] comes naturally to mind. But so too, does *Partner* (Bertolucci), *La Collectionneuse* (Rohmer) and the films of Godard and Garrel: and *L'Enfance nue* (Pialat) and *Faces* (Cassavetes) of course. And, more paradoxically, *The Chronicle of Anna Magdalena Bach* (Straub) and *Silence and Cry* (Jancso). These films have their complement in others, coming straight out of *direct cinema* in the first instance, only to turn into narrative and to spill into the domain of fiction, with fictions they produce and organise. *La Règne du jour* (Perrault) for example, but also (already) all of Rouch's films; certain of Warhol's; and even, again at the limits of the paradox, *La Rosière de Pessac* (Eustache) and *La Rentrée des usines Wonder* (a May 68 film[39]).

In aesthetic terms it would seem that for a particular (experimental) fringe of contemporary cinema, the traditionally separate and even opposing fields of 'documentary' and 'fictional' films were interpenetrating more and more and intermingling in innumerable ways. It is as if they were involved in, and involved, a vast process of exchange, a reciprocal system where reportage and fiction alternate or conjugate within one and the same film, react upon, break down and modify each other, until finally it is perhaps impossible to choose between them.

2. *Such interplay calls for a redefinition* of *direct cinema*. If it can both embrace the fictional and be implicated by it, if it can equally well be the instrument and the effect of narration, *direct cinema* overflows at all points the bounds originally set for it by strict reportage.

(In this first section [paras 1–20] I shall limit my concern to such a redefinition and to the analysis of the function and influence of *direct cinema*. The second part [paras 21–35] will give more precise consideration to the various degrees and modes by which *direct cinema* is integrated into contemporary 'fiction' films).

We know where *direct cinema* begins, but not where it ends.

Actually, it begins with the most elementary reportage film (the newsreel genre) and the most minor sound-film document. This is really the level of its widest use, by television, sociologists, ethnologists, educationalists, and the police.

But the fact that *direct cinema* in its 'pure state' is to be found in any filmed interview or survey, in any bit of reportage or newsreel, doesn't mean that these are therefore to be seen as its exemplars and ideal locations, or the representations of its aesthetic absolute.

The reportage film can hardly represent anything more than the minimum definition of *direct cinema*. And rather than its most complete form, its perfect illustration and example, it is in fact its degree zero, the most rudimentary of its roots.

In its raw form *direct cinema* is present in every scrap of reportage filming, just as the cinema in its raw form is present in any sequence of images.

3. That degree zero seems to me to apply to the majority of reportage films calling themselves 'objective', non-interventionist (with a few exceptions considered in paragraph 7). They are good (or less good) reportage in which what Louis Marcorelles[40] calls the 'magic of immediacy' (*la magie du direct*) operates. All the same, they cannot, it seems to me, stand as *models* of *direct cinema* to which other films might be compared and related.

This is not due to any lack of honesty or 'respect for the material filmed', but rather to a lack of boldness – an excess of such respect. In a sense they represent an under-use of the potential and paradoxes of *direct cinema*, a neglect of the principle of 'perversion' which is fundamental to it, its essence in fact.

4. The basic deception of *direct cinema* is really its claim to transcribe truly the truth of life, to begin the position of witness in relation to that truth so that the film simply records events and objects mechanically. In reality, the very fact of filming is of course already a productive intervention which modifies and transforms the material recorded. From the moment the camera intervenes, a form of *manipulation* begins. And every operation, even when contained by the most technical of motives – starting the camera rolling, cutting, changing the angle or lens, then choosing the rushes and editing them – like it or not, constitutes a manipulation of the film-document. The film-maker may well wish to respect that document, but he cannot avoid manufacturing it. It does not pre-exist reportage, it is its product.

A certain hypocrisy therefore lies at the origins of the claim that there is antinomy between *direct cinema* and aesthetic manipulation. And to engage in *direct cinema* as if the inevitable interventions and manipulations (which produce meaning, effect and structure) did not count and were purely practical rather than aesthetic, is in fact to demand the minimum of it. It means sweeping aside all its potentialities and censoring its natural creative function and *productivity* in the name of some illusory honesty, non-intervention and humility.

5. A consequence of such a productive principle, and automatic consequence of all the manipulations which mould the film-document, is a coefficient of 'non-reality'; a kind of fictional aura attaches itself to the filmed events and facts. From the moment they become film and are placed in a cinematic perspective, all film-documents and every

recording of a raw event take on a filmic reality which either adds to or subtracts from their particular initial reality (i.e. their 'experienced' value), un-realising or sur-realising it, but in both cases slightly falsifying and drawing it to the side of fiction. Within *direct cinema* a whole range of exchange, reversal and inversion activity is set up between what might be called the reality effect (the impression of the experienced, true, etc.) and the fiction effect (sensed for instance in common expressions like 'too good to be true', etc.). Following the paradox through to the end, it might be said that *direct cinema* only asserts itself as such once a crack appears in the reportage – the rift through which fiction surges in and through which also, the basic deception presiding over reportage betrays itself – or is admitted. In other words, manipulation lies at the very heart of non-intervention.

6. Every reportage film contains a *certain threshold*, dependent on the nature and degree of the manipulations which stake out its ground and manufacture it. The more manipulation there is involved, the more firmly fiction takes hold and the stronger the mark of the (critical/aesthetic) distance taken, which modifies the reading (and nature) of the event recorded.

Thus the transition is ensured, from report to commentary, from commentary to reflection – from sound-image to idea. But there is a notable consequence of this self-'perversion' on the part of *direct cinema*. The movement which takes it across the threshold where it begins to be affected by fiction provokes a contrast effect such that the film-document, even as it takes on an overlay of fiction and is thereby slightly denatured, immediately gains a new value on another level. It responds to the flight from reality with a new lease of meaning and coherence and emerges from the dialectic endowed with perhaps greater conviction, its truth reinforced by and because of this detour through the 'fictitious'.

7. Inversely, in the case where absence of manipulation is as great as possible (i.e. when intervention is limited to simply being there to film), the overspill into fiction may be total and irrevocable. *La Rentrée des usines Wonder* consists of one take lasting the length of one 120 metre reel. No other editing or manipulation, just the event utterly raw. It shows the day of return to work at the Wonder factories, a woman worker being urged by boss, trade-union representative and fellow workers to go in and start work and to give up the objectives of the strike. She resists and weeps. Those around reassure and encourage her. No, the strike wasn't for nothing, the return to work represents a victory for the workers, etc. And, apparently 'by some miracle', the total situation of worker-boss-union relations of May and June is crystallised and symbolised, and all in one take. Every

actor plays his role to perfection, enunciating the key phrases of that strike to the point where an irresistible sense of unease is set up. We know as clearly as it is possible to know it that nothing here is 'faked'. Nevertheless everything is to such a degree exemplary, so much 'truer than the truth', that the only possible reference is the most Brechtian of *scenarios*; the effect of the film-document is equivalent to that produced by the most controlled of fictions.

The same with *La Rosière de Pessac*. It too contains the surest guarantees of hyper-objectivity and absolute non-intervention: three cameras film the sequence where the girl who is to win the garland of roses is chosen, the editing obeys the chronology of the discourse and the action. And little by little, the extreme reality effect changes into a dream impression. The exemplary nature of characters, language and behaviour fuses with that of the heroes of fairy tales, myths and parables. Fiction triumphs over the real, or rather it gives it its true dimension, relating it back to archetypes and constantly recalling the moral of the fable. The passage from the particular to the general comes about quite naturally.

8. The role of manipulation in *direct cinema* is thus to control such slides and switches. In other words to provoke them while gauging their scope and effect.

The (always highly relative) absence of manipulation, however, can have some unforeseeable and uncontrollable consequences, effects which can equally well (but rarely) be extraordinary as in *Usines Wonder* and *La Rosière*, or (frequently) simply null as in everyday reportage films, that dull wasteland ruled by the non-signifying and the formless.

Proof (via the absurd) that, outside manipulation, *direct cinema* shrinks to degree zero is provided by Warhol's 'film' on the Empire State Building. For the duration of a day, a camera was planted in front of the building, filming what was in front of it with no intervention other than the reloading of film. The event was thus recorded and reconstructed just as it was, mechanically, with a total degree of purity. The result is a film completely devoid of signification or form in which the confusion between the documentary and fictional dimensions is total. As a whole it passes beyond the 'experienced' and the 'fictitious' into the realm of pure dream.

9. There is yet another paradox, by no means the least. The border-line separating what is received as 'experienced', 'real', 'raw event' from what is experienced as fictional, fairy tale, parable – a transition which reverses perspectives and values – is crossed more often and apparently more easily in *direct cinema* than in films located within the fictional from the outset.

It is as if fiction were never closer nor more available than when it is not inscribed as a project within the film and not envisaged in its programme; that is, when the film in some sense overflows into fiction, either abruptly and apparently accidentally in certain 'pure' reportage films (*La Rosière, Usines Wonder*) or concealing and manufacturing it at the same time as it manufactures itself (which is the case in highly manipulated *direct cinema* products such as those of Perrault and Rouch).

On this basis it is possible to arrive at a definition of *direct cinema* based on the inverse ratio linking manipulation of the film-document (the film event) with its signification (its reading). The latter gains in richness, coherence and conviction in proportion to the extent that the impression of reality produced is impeded and falsified by manipulation – in other words, the degree to which it is drawn either towards the exemplarity of fiction or to the generality of the fable. These are no doubt obvious facts, but they are forgotten, even, and precisely, by the present 'theoreticians' of *direct cinema* because they have long been buried in the furthest reaches of cinema history.

10. Let us therefore go back to the origins and 'history' of the development of *direct cinema* – origins repressed by the sound revolution and masked by its reign.

It took only three years (1929–31) for the cinema as a whole to change its nature and accomplish a technical mutation – a measure of the violence of the upheaval provoked by the talkie, but also of its explosive, universal victory. Under pressure from the mass audience (from money), in three years – instantaneously, that is – the silent film was wiped out, passing from the superior status of a complete art to the inferior one of a technical development. Its manifold aesthetic and technical achievements (montage, cutting continuity, movement) were abruptly occulted by one defect, the lack of speech.

There were of course numerous film-makers who baulked at such a mutation. But the most highly 'endowed' among them (in the Darwinian sense) adapted as quickly as possible to the new medium. And it is not altogether accidental that the most backward in this sense were the Soviet film-makers (Mikhail Romm's silent version of *Boule de Suif* dates from 1934; in that year, according to Sadoul,[41] only 772 of the 26,000 cinemas in the USSR were equipped for sound).

Patents and equipment belonged to the Americans. But it was also from the USSR that the most vigorous protests against the talkie came, from as early as 1927 (the 'Manifesto' of Pudovkin, Eisenstein and Alexandrov). For with Vertov and Eisenstein, Russian silent cinema had advanced further than any other avant garde of the silent film with basic research on the possibilities and methods of cinema, its formal procedures and their results at the level of meaning and emotion (a research which was simultaneously theoretical and practical, an exemplary union since suspended).

11. The astonishing (but logical) thing is that at that time *direct cinema* (Kino Pravda = cinéma verité) and montage cinema were being experimented with *jointly*. This was true of Vertov's ideas: no actors, no heroes, just people or the masses; no fiction, but reportage or (in *October* and *Potemkin*) reconstruction in the newsreel genre. And inseparably, from this use of elements from 'real life', documentary and *direct cinema*, came manipulation through montage and the search for formal rhymes and rhythms. Both aspects (direct/manipulation) were explored as modes of a *political and revolutionary cinema* which would no longer owe anything to the forms established under capitalism, that is, to the bourgeois arts.

And of course, researches such as these could not but be totally barred by the triumph of the talkie, in America because this meant the triumph of the dominant ideology, in the USSR because there too, speech was amply sufficient to ensure (and control) the dissemination of the doctrine and ideals of Communism via the cinema.

This *repression* was to last thirty years. That is, until the first manifestations of the *direct cinema* revolution on the one hand and the renaissance of montage on the other (without one necessarily being the correlative of the other) in modern cinema (Resnais, Godard, Straub).

12. Unlike the sound revolution, that of *direct cinema* was not a violent and irreversible upheaval. It was, rather, a diffuse operation, a subtle reversal, an insidious change. Its first discreet appearances did not inaugurate any exclusive reign and its first manifestations did not render the earlier modes of cinema null and void. The signs of its emergence even passed completely unnoticed, except perhaps by a few specialists – film-makers, critics, privileged users (in television, sociology, the police).

The question is therefore to determine in what way the advent of *direct cinema*, in spite of appearances, clearly marks the occurrence of a revolution, the realisation of a break and the inscription of a difference within the conception/manufacture of cinema.

13. Putting *direct cinema* into orbit was first of all a question of technical advance. The 16mm. format was disseminated and perfected by the amateur film-maker market, then by that of television. The latter (through news and war reporting) trained quicker, more flexible and bolder techniques. At the same time an advance was made in the sensitivity of film stock which made costly and cumbersome artificial lighting equipment more and more redundant. Cameras

became considerably lighter and, at the same time, more compact and simpler to operate. It became possible to film anywhere, quickly and more discreetly. And more people were capable of operating cameras without the need for extensive training. Above all, cameras were synchronised and silent, so eliminating the need for either a studio or post-synchronisation (which on the one hand is costly and on the other conditions the reconstruction – that is, the *re-presentation*).

Thirty years after his time it had become possible to apply Dziga Vertov's injunctions without any loss between the idea – to film every-thing, record everything, to be *in* life without disturbing or falsifying it – and its realisation. (Vertov had been restricted to filming public manifestations, crowds, ceremonies, etc., and was unable to seize everyday life because his equipment could not pass unnoticed.)

True Kino Eye was thus realised at the level of the recording of the image; but it was now reinforced by an ear since, for the first time, speech became inseparable from lips and life. It was no longer the laborious product of a reconstruction, an approximate re-making (of necessity theatrical because written and recreated). In the same sense as the visible, speech now belonged to the first level of the filmable. In the case of the talkie it was *the language of the ruling class* and the dominant ideologies which conquered the cinema. With synchronised sound it was *the cinema which conquered* speech, all speech, the speech of both sides, workers and bosses.

14. But the mere existence of this technical advance did not in itself render the other processes of the cinema unusable or peripheral (as distinct from what happened in the case of the sound/silent advance). Not only did it not cancel them out, it could not even *replace* them, whether completely or partially. The techniques of *direct cinema* were suited to neither the industry nor the aesthetic of re-presentational cinema.

Direct cinema did not make for the filming of the *same things* in a newer and better way, it opened the way to filming *something other*. It opened up a new horizon for cinema, made it change its objective – and therefore its function and its nature.

Direct cinema thus left cinema, such as it was made and has continued to be made ever since the talkies, undisturbed. Because its techniques are not adapted to the aims, practices or content of classical cinema (so-called for the sake of simplicity), it was of hardly any interest to classical cinema, or as a result to the industry which nourishes (is nourished by) it.

The industry was therefore content to let it be, somewhere on its margins, serving its sub-products: television from the outset, docu-mentary and educational films, advertising, etc.

15. Nevertheless, on the level of distribution, *direct cinema* encountered a number of resistances from the power points of cinema. The industry of spectacle in no way encourages techniques which are *more economical* than those already in use; manufacturers of film stock and cameras, the laboratories, the technicians' unions, hostile to a reduction in crews; the technical castes, terrified by the greater ease of operation of the new instruments which puts them within the scope of a greater number of people, and does away with the need for systems of induction and training, and hierarchies of control over cinema technicians.

Finally, the public authorities are (justifiably) afraid that it will no longer be so easy to control the cinema (as an ideological agent), once it ceases to be so constrained by questions of costs and can go anywhere, film anything, more cheaply and discreetly. Once freed from its capitalist chains, the twofold precaution of script and studio and the supplementary, *a posteriori* controls of release into the commercial cinema circuits, the cinema becomes dangerous. At least capable of being so.

Direct cinema thus enables us to look at the industrial/commercial system of the cinema as a system of repression, within which the economic cycle has a political function. The ideological control of the cinema is masked by and exerted through economic pressures. *Direct cinema* breaks out of that vicious circle. Not surprisingly therefore, its aesthetic investigations have a political value.

16. Such economic/ideological censorings help to keep *direct cinema* on the *periphery* of cinema. But while they may hold it outside the commercial arena and deflect it from the cinema circuits, they do not actually kill it. They force it *to develop* within a mind of clandestinity. By repressing it for political reasons, they give it reason to be political. This is what shapes the film-makers/pioneers who practise it and forces them to question its political nature.

The conditions of work and the economic pressures set *direct cinema* in a *political situation*, even if the majority of films which put it into practice do not claim to be and are not primarily political. Through direct cinema the cinema is renewing links with the political function assigned to it by Eisenstein and Vertov. The eclipse is entering its final phase. With direct cinema alienation is ceasing to be the simultaneous condition and function of the cinema.

17. Deprived by the system of any temptation towards '*embourgeoisement*', *direct cinema* is developing in a slightly unhousebroken fashion. It is that part of cinema where cinema is invented as and while it is manufactured. Film-makers turn cameramen, cameramen film-makers. The technico-aesthetic capacity to turn a hand to everything

fills the gaps in the industry and the lack of tradition. In the field of *direct cinema* experimentation goes on as nowhere else at the level of image/sound, documentary/fiction and speech/editing relationships. Actors are abandoned, and so begins one of the major adventures of modern cinema (the silent film adventure all over again). Because of this ascendance of non-actors and triumph of the non-professional (where, moreover, the pre-eminence of unknowns demonstrates the untenability of stars), *there are now only characters* – whether film-characters or living characters, 'real' or 'fictional'. A new and powerful link binds the cinema to the experienced, binds them and articulates them into one and the same *language*. Life is no longer 'represented' by the cinema. The cinema is no longer the image – or the moral – of life. Together they speak to each other and produce each other through and within that speech.

So many breaks on so many levels (technical, aesthetic, economic, ideological) with the modes of manufacture and utilisation of the classic cinema confirm the fact that a *direct cinema* revolution is taking place. But is it possible to speak of a revolution like the one brought about by sound in relation to such a marginal, hyper-specialised cinema, practised quasi-clandestinely by, in the last analysis, very few 'real' film-makers?

18. The existence of *direct cinema* compels the cinema to redefine itself. *Direct cinema* seems to have acted on the cinema as a whole like a photographic developer. Within its difference, a double transformation, in nature and in function, is inscribed for the whole of cinema. Through *direct cinema* the point is reached when the cinema is linked to life according to a system, which is not one of reproduction, but of reciprocal production, so that the film (e.g. Perrault, Rouch) is simultaneously produced by and produces the events and situations. (And through this double linking it constitutes their reflection – reflection of and upon those events and situations – and *their* critique, in other words, their language). From this point the other (greater) part of cinema, where innumerable definitions and contradictions seemed inextricably entangled, closes ranks within a single definition and reduces to a single dimension – that of re-presentation, the socially codified play aimed at constituting a spectacle which runs parallel to life, obliterating it by superimposition. In other words a substitution of the thing by its re-construction.

But such re-presentation is always (to a greater or less degree) manipulated by the dominant ideology, both on the level of manufacture (not just economically, but through the interplay of social conventions which make up, which *are* the totality of all narrative), and on the level of utilisation, as a spectacle.

In part at least, *direct cinema* escapes this triple ideological dependency (economy, convention, spectacle). Moreover it *manipulates* the ideology itself and is the producer of political meaning.

19. The rift between *direct* and *non-direct* therefore separates, in aesthetic and ideological terms, production from re-presentation, transformation from transposition. But that rift, although categorical in nature, seems curiously to become less and less clear the closer one gets to contemporary cinema. As if it continued to associate what it separates, to merge what it distinguishes, *direct cinema* has cor- and dis-rupted re-presentational cinema, changing it by influence and contact. And the effect of this proximity is largely what has brought about the *direct cinema* revolution.

20. First on the economic level: 'independent' film-makers (generally speaking = 'auteurs',[42] the young film-makers) more or less rejected (or not accepted) by the commercial system are resorting more and more to the less onerous techniques of the direct method. Either they film in 16mm. (still rather rarely) or (more frequently) they use very small film crews, documentary material, natural locations and no stars, or even no 'actors'. The utilisation of the processes of *direct cinema* by the fiction film in this case does not work in favour of the former; rather it is *direct cinema* which is influenced towards fiction. Thus at the aesthetic level direct techniques open up a new formal domain (and a new thematic domain, as we have seen): this is a duty-free zone open to experimentation, innovation and manipulation of the sound/image, life-document/fictional and random/structured relationships whose apparently infinite possibilities of variation and combination (to be reviewed in the next section of the text) are attracting the attention of more and more film-makers.

On the ethical level: the problem of the role of cinema in society, its political function, so long obscured, is once again posed as essential.

The *direct cinema* revolution has overturned perspectives already overturned once by the advent of the sound film. (A primary meaning of revolution is 'complete turn', in this instance a complete rotation on itself by the cinema.) At the end of this rotation, which is both a detour and a divergence, certain advantages have been achieved on the practice and the theory of silent cinema: notably, on the level of the motor role of editing, the importance of manipulation, and the political aim of cinema.

21. [. . .] We have already seen that direct cinema is always a cinema of manipulation and that in certain extreme cases (*Usines Wonder, Rosière de Pessac*), the accidental or deliberate quasi-suppression or reduction of manipulation brought in its train some surprising effects, which worked counter to the documentary principle of those films:

that is, an irresistible slide on the part of the film-document – when not controlled by manipulation – towards the fictional, a reversal of the 'experienced' into the 'fictitious'. As a result it seems that it is not just the simple fact of filming 'real' events which automatically produces the impression of 'realism' in *direct cinema*. On the contrary, it is all the aesthetic operations (which are more or less de-realising since they affect the filmic material), the whole play of manipulation, which produces the impression of 'pure documentary record' – as a forceful effect of artifice.

22. This observation already indicates how arbitrary it would be to mark a strict dividing line between direct and non-direct. The two can easily be opposed on the level of concepts, broken down and resolved into differences for comparison. In cinematic works, however, while they may not merge together, they can assert a value simultaneously, intervene with and replace each other in a reciprocal process which relativises and in some sense perverts the terms of the duality. The 'fictional' and the 'documentary' are not always either autonous or impermeable to each other. It could even be said, since, whether *direct* or not, it is always cinema we are dealing with, that everything shown by film is fiction, the fiction of a fiction, or the fiction of a film-document. 'The work is a tissue of fictions: it does not, properly speaking, contain anything true. Nevertheless, because it is not pure illusion but a declared lie, it demands to be considered as factual; it is not just any illusion, it is a particular illusion' (Macherey).[43] In film *too*, fiction is as 'true' as document; and in return, document is as 'true' and as 'false' as fiction. By right, their value in film is equal; in practice, it is determined by the intention in the usage – by what makes them the 'particular illusion' which is the film.

It should be made clear that while we may distinguish fiction and document in the same film, we do not, on the one hand, lose sight of the fact that both are subject to the same filmic 'reality' (or 'non-reality'). And on the other hand, we look not at the truth or falsity of their nature (since for fiction and document alike, that nature is cinematic), but at the effect and impression they *produce* – not independently of one another (within an absolute which would belong to the realm of logic but not to the field of film), but precisely within their contact and relationship, their values of contrast and exchange.

It is the function of the film-document for fiction, and fiction for the film-document, which needs to be examined. Better still, the way in which they call each other up and *produce* themselves for each other, the way they pass on and reflect back to each other film's twofold dimension of deception and truth.

23. This means that as the analysis of the interaction between *direct* and *non-direct* advances, the very notion of the specific nature of *direct cinema* evaporates. And this disappearance at the theoretical level corresponds closely to what takes place in actual cinematic practice. The different techniques of *direct cinema* (from material means to methods, taking in non-actors, and the production of the events to be filmed by the film itself), which are the sum total of its 'specificity', serve fiction and documentary filming indifferently. The important role on the level of theoretical and political responsibility assigned to *direct cinema* in this text cannot act fully except in terms of the cinema as a whole, engaged with and against the non-direct, not just through a relationship, but on the inside, precisely as one of its techniques. As such it could only be more important than other techniques used because of its instrumental and productive potential (including its defects), and not because of any specific natural virtue or quality immanent to it. The whole specificity of *direct cinema* lies in its techniques (means, methods, tools). It defines itself as technique.

24. The illusion of some other specificity is doubtless owed to the circumstances in which *direct cinema* developed (cf. paras 13, 14, 15). From the 'Golden Age' of the great Russian silents, to the present, the evolution of cinema seems to have clearly traced an immense ellipse, with *direct cinema* resurging after decades of occultation. During this period it was reduced to underemployment by the various documentary schools, but it also ranged through their techniques, strengthened in its political determinations by such banishment. The censorship erected as a defence against it also served as a protection and in its state of isolation it was both preserved and refined. Thus it would be possible to elaborate a view of film history as going from the *direct* (Lumière *and* Méliès, Vertov *and* Eisenstein), to the *direct* (Perrault, Godard, etc.) once the detour via fiction was accomplished. . . . But this teleological perspective has the drawback of posing *direct cinema* as the end of cinema – i.e. reintroducing into the definition of *direct*, elements of an idealistic/theological concept of cinema, so that there would be *one* true cinema, a state of nature or perfection to which all films would tend in a more or less pertinent and perfect way. . . . All terms and themes which the practice of *direct cinema* has, precisely, banished from its theory.

25. Taking the point further, *direct cinema* is not a particular condition (or domain) of cinema which might be regarded as its absolute and ideal. It canot even be defined in terms of 'a particular condition' of cinema in so far as what characterises it is not the submission of film to things or a search for the greatest possible transparency to the world. Quite the contrary (cf. paras 4, 5, 17, 18), it is

characterised by the mutual modification of the cinema and the world, and the extreme manipulation of the elements of the film-world. *Direct cinema* is not therefore the place where meanings or forms are fixed, rather that of their greatest *instability*, their ceaseless experimentation, with all that that entails of tentative groping in the dark, reversals, surprises and paradoxes. *Direct cinema* is the place where cinema is manufactured: within the manufacture of any film (and any filmic action), there is a moment which is dependent on the *direct*. And the question of whether the system of re-presentation is transcended or not depends on the importance given or refused to that moment (which, for the film, is the moment of *its* truth).

26. Let us take an example of this precisely where it seems least likely that a trace of some interference by the *direct cinema* would be found. In Jancso (although, wasn't it just where it 'should not' have been, i.e. in *La Rosière de Pessac*, for example, that fiction took hold, at a divergence by and a deflection of the documentary?).

In Jancso's films, and especially in *Silence and Cry* (in which the 'system' functions in the clearest and most rigorous way) everything – that is, recourse to actors, post-synchronisation of the dialogue, the important role assigned to the *mise en scène* in setting into operation complex movements by camera and actors, the dominance of formal elements (framing, black/white contrasts), and the very project of the film, which is to redirect historical traces/pre-texts towards metaphor – everything thus tends to lead the work away from *direct cinema's* immediate methods and concerns. But that tendency is contradicted by the modes of filming themselves, i.e. on the one hand the relation of the action filmed to the scenario or project of the film, on the other, the relation of the camera to the action which it films.

We know that most of the time and for the essential part of the film Jancso does not *pre*pare, *pre*-envisage, *pre*-design (or, with all the more reason, *pre*-destine) his shots. He shoots them.

In other words, the action that is to be filmed does not have an existence prior to its filming but is strictly contemporaneous with it: the question ceases to be one of action *to be filmed* and becomes *action filmed*.

27. A location is chosen, for example a farm courtyard. There are thousands of ways of filming scenes equivalent to those filmed by Jancso in such a location. In other words, the location in question does not contain in itself anything absolutely predetermining for the film – except of course in being the location of that film. It 'expresses' nothing in advance or in its own right, it does not anticipate the film or what the film will do with it.

Jancso, the camera, the dolly tracks,[44] the technicians and the actors move into place. The script (the few pages officially standing in for a script which in any case do not give any categorical instructions or precise information) is put away *for good.*

Jancso organises this or that travelling shot – a movement from right to left, or from left to right – in accordance with the disposition of the set and its spatial coordinates alone (lengths, breadths, depths, angles and configurations). So far none of these operations, choice of location, arrangement of travelling shots, is in itself productive of the least meaning. Nothing 'productive' has happened before the camera comes into play.

28. The scene is then executed like a ballet. It is not, above all, regulated independently or in advance of its shooting, but during the shooting itself, and by it. Installed on the dolly next to the cameraman, Jancso directs – imperatively – during the very moment of recording the image and scene, that is, the conjunctional or disjunctional movements of the camera and the actor-characters. The entries and exits, meetings and separations of the actor-characters among themselves and in relation to the camera are accomplished together and simultaneously with the filming – it would be closer to say they are accomplished by the filming.

The action is thus not what conditions the manufacture of the film. On the contrary, it is the consequence – the product of that manufacture. The traditional division between 'the action to be filmed' and 'the action of filming' resolves itself into action filmed.

Not only is the shooting of the film contemporaneous with the filmable event, but it is itself that event, which therefore films itself. There is no 'pre-filmic world' (reconstructed, 'true' or immediate, it makes no difference) before which the cinema might take up a position and from which it would draw the film. There is exclusively a filmic world, produced by the film and within the film, simultaneously and in conjunction with the manufacture of the film.

This contemporaneousness of the film with itself, of the film as event and the film as recording, is accentuated – reduplicated – by the fact that the basis and essential elements of the dialogues subsequently synchronised are there in the orders thrown out by the film-maker to camera and actors in the course of filming (and in order to produce that filming): orders such as 'left', 'right', 'forward', 'back', 'come in', 'go out', etc., whose function it is to organise 'on the spot' both the factual content of the shot and its spatio-temporal balances, and therefore the play of signs and meanings. Orders from the film-maker to the camera and the actors, and orders from a particular character to the rest have the same formulation and the same function – they arrange the shot in terms of action. This is still the film filming itself, imposing order on itself through the intermediary of the ordering speech of which, as a whole, it is – and reflects back – the echo.

29. In the first part of this text we spoke of the phenomenon of interproduction of the event and the film by each other as one of the main contributions (aesthetic, theoretical, political) of *direct cinema*. Proof that this involves more than just a convergence of elements from fictional and direct cinema at the level of the conception/manufacture of the film is provided by the fact that Jancso does not, precisely, use any of the specific techniques of direct cinema. *We are therefore dealing with a particular practice of fictional cinema which is equivalent to a particular practice of direct cinema.* We are in fact looking at a film fiction being produced 'live'.

(The argument by which the fact that Jancso does not film with synchronised sound would rule out any analogy between his system and *direct cinema* does not stand up since, as we saw, the film dialogues are simply the echo within the shot of orders and instructions which make the shot – and are therefore necessarily synchronic with it.)

Clearly then, even when for stylistic-technical reasons, the *direct* element seems 'repressed' from a fiction film, the fiction may prove to function 'like' the direct. This again most decisively blurs any existing trace of a frontier between *direct* and non-*direct*, or perhaps even shows quite simply that *the direct is just one of the methods and modes of the non-direct*.

30. For all cinema is, if you like, non-direct. The cinematic image is precisely an 'image' when it is projected, a 'spectacle' in other words. In fact one should say that re-presentational cinema is the only cinema. But the fact that re-presentation is inescapable is aggravated or attenuated to a greater or lesser degree by the modes of manufacture of the film. In the films which come out of what I have called the 're-presentational system' (which includes the majority of films made on the Hollywood model), this inevitability is reinforced, indeed multiplied, by the battery of successive stages in the manufacture of the film, each of which is the re-presentation and re-production of the preceding one.

Thus the project of the film is repeated for the first time in the scenario, which is repeated by the cutting continuity which is in turn itself repeated by rehearsals (appropriately so named). The latter are then reproduced for the filming, the editing of which is simply its reconstruction with post-synchronisation, finally closing the cycle of re-presentations.

This process of reduplication, far from allowing (as one might wrongly suppose) for new and decisive interventions at each new stage, on the contrary imposes auto-fidelity of the most extreme kind (on pain of seeing the whole edifice crumble, as for example in cases of re-editing by producers). It permits only the most minor retouches or variations. Thus each new operation must really be a *false operation*, a quasi-mechanical recommencement of the preceding one, and therefore imitative and non-productive. Though a hundred times reworked, the film is not thereby changed a hundred times, but simply repeated a hundred times, each time a copy of itself.

In other words it is not just the duplicate of a pre-existent world or 'reality' (even though that world and that 'reality' are mediated by a script, the script is always *their* script) whose ideology it will almost automatically guarantee. It is also the duplicate of that first duplicate, its ideological reinforcement and perpetuation.

31. The cinema has, it seems (through a variety of film-makers), in numerous circumstances tried to escape the trap of perpetual re-presentation. In the face of the universal dissemination and domination of Hollywood models there has been a kind of vague and quite unformulated temptation towards the direct which manifested itself on two levels: a reduction in the number of operations which manufacture the film (i.e. suppression of the script, improvisation, etc., which culminated in the first experiments in direct fictional cinema: *Shadows*, Rouch); or the reinvestment of some productivity into these operations (revival of montage) and the reduction of the false innocence of re-presentation by the fiction of that re-presentation. Thus in Hollywood and elsewhere numerous films emerged which took as their object a spectacle already constituted as such, stage drama, show or even film itself.

In many musical comedies (*The Band Wagon* is the prototype), as in *The Golden Coach, La Règle du jeu*, numerous Bergman films, *The Patsy*, etc., the phenomenon of re-presentation becomes part of the fiction of the film, one of the motor elements on the dramatic level. This surplus dimension – since in the principle of film there is already re-presentation of a re-presentation – produces an effect of what might be called 'candour'. The film designates itself (if not 'denounces' itself) as illusion in one instance, and in another, as reconstruction or spectacle – in other words as what it is. An admission of some bad conscience in the spectacle about being a spectacle comes to the surface (hence no doubt the very widespread and apparently inexhaustible fascination with the theme of the theatre, etc.). But in addition, when the re-presentation admits as much, takes itself as an explicit theme and films itself, the re-presentation of that re-presentation (the film) becomes in some sense primary or 'live'. To film a spectacle is effectively an act of reportage or a reintroduction of documentary into fiction.

32. If the fiction is a fiction of re-presentation, as if filmed directly, that is, if the spectacle becomes a film-document, the effects of inversion and contrast already encountered in connection with certain works of direct cinema cannot fail to come into play. Designated as such, its artificiality admitted, the spectacle acts as a foil within the fiction, making the fiction seem more 'true' than itself. At the same time the spectacle itself assumes a dose of authenticity all the greater for its being presented as a genuine spectacle.

The more the spectacle is designated as spectacle (the authenticity and 'reality' of the spectacle being its artificiality) the more the rest of the film will pass for factual. It is to this process of contrast that musical comedies owe their ability to operate within fantasy, to remain credible in the midst of all sorts of excesses. This process is explored by *The Golden Coach* and makes it function: 'life' and 'theatre' exchange value, everything is re-presentation, the spectacle successively betrays itself and triumphs.

33. The high point of this dialectic – re-presentation/re-presentation of a re-presentation, fictional spectacle and fiction of a spectacle – is reached in Rivette's *L'Amour fou*. High point in the sense that the spectacle re-presented and the fiction of a spectacle are *effectively* filmed as reportage, i.e. as 'live'. All the 'rehearsals' of *Andromaque*[45] on stage are, we know, filmed by a documentary crew, itself filmed by the 35mm. camera which has charge of the film fiction. (The documentary crew is directed by Labarthe[46] – an occasion for Rivette and myself to render homage to a man who, more than anyone else, has put into practice the mutual perversion of documentary and fiction in his 'Cinéastes' programmes on television, in which extracts from the fiction films acquire the status of 'documents', while interviews with film-makers acquire that of narratives and fictions, open to any fantasy: Ford, Fuller, Sternberg, Cassavetes.)

A very subtle reversal thus takes place. Since the spectacle is being filmed directly, re-presented as both 'real' spectacle and raw document (especially through the 16mm. grain of the image), it alternately takes on and sheds the 'reality effect' and itself assumes in places the coefficient of authenticity spoken of earlier. The contrast effect is set in play not only between the spectacle-in-the-fiction and the fiction itself, but above all within the re-presentation of the spectacle. On the one hand it reveals itself and films itself, designating itself as spectacle and therefore (as in musical comedies) as of a false order, as 'non-reality'. On the other hand and at the same time, since it is filmed as reportage, it acquires an immediate, raw reality, annulling the false character which constitutes the authenticity of the spectacle. The truth of the spectacle as artifice is substituted by a truth of the spectacle as event.

At the extreme, the contrast effect acts in reverse. It is the scenes of non-spectacle (everyday life, the flat, meetings between the couple, scenes of loneliness) which are struck with a certain artificiality in the face of a strong coefficient of reality in the theatre scenes. Thus it is the fiction which designates itself as fiction, 'life' as fictional. The theatre is emptied of all artificiality, which passes instead into 'life', and all fantasies are transferred from the re-presentation of the play to the re-presentation of 'life'.

34. Coming back to the problem of the image as the 'double' of the 'world' we quote Macherey again: 'The image which conforms absolutely to the model merges with it and loses its status as image: it remains such only by virtue of the gap separating it from what it imitates.'

In observations on the duplicatory nature of the cinematic image the cinema has been reproached (Marcelin Pleynet[47]) with being 'the double of the world', its natural ideological accomplice. By only 'reproducing' reality, film unites with its ideology or at least is charged with it.

On the one hand it should be noted that the cinematic image as such mechanically reproduces only a fraction of the world. Precisely that fraction *designated* by the camera. This selection process does not entail modification of that part of the 'world' selected. But it is possible to say that that fragment of reality, as soon as it is designated by the camera for filming, no longer equals itself, but itself plus camera. It is precisely that 'dislocation' which ensures that the image is not quite the model. But such a dislocation does not prevent the image from, if not conforming to the model, at least being 'faithful' to it, representing it without really transforming it and so remaining subject to it.

On the other hand, film is only very rarely a sequence of cinematic images. It is the product of a particular *work* operating on images as its basic material, but also on meanings, rhythms, devices, etc. It is therefore on the level of the modes of re-presentation that the duplication or otherwise of the 'world' takes place – either repeating its ideology or on the contrary, 'transforming it' with a production of new meaning (cf. para 30). The action of the 're-presentational system' is thus the re-duplication of the phenomenon of mechanical duplication of 'reality' through a chain of reproductions (especially through the script which itself stands in the position of model in relation to the film, although in almost all cases it is not the expression of an 'auteur' but of ideology, since it is not a finished work, either film or novel, and the only voice that can speak in it is 'life'.) As such the re-presentational system is incapable of achieving what *direct cinema*, whether fictional or documentary can – namely, deposing the world from its position as model of the film by depriving the film of any 'model'.

35. In *direct cinema* – and this is equally true for documentary (Leacock, Eustache, etc.) and fiction (Perrault, Rouch, Cassavetes, Baldi), filming is never a moment of repetition or reconstruction of 'reality'. Nor is it quite that of a selection inside a pre-filmic reality (as the re-production and elaboration of the script is in re-presentational cinema). Rather it is a moment of *accumulation*. Often without any fixed 'programme', a whole quantity of film is shot, the ultimate end of which is neither determined nor known. What this involves is of course images of 'reality', filmed events, but in some sense these are floating images without a referent, divested of any stable significance and open to all-comers. It is on the other hand at the editing stage – the true 'filming' of the film and the real moment of its manufacture (which is why I don't believe in the celebrated 'contact' with 'reality' which Marcorelles makes the touchstone of the direct) – that not only the choice and the ordering and comparison of images, but above all the production of meaning is achieved. In *direct cinema*, if you like, the filmed event does not pre-exist the film and the filming, but is produced by it. It is not therefore possible to speak of a 'reality' alien to the film of which the film would be the image, but only of material shot which is all the reality the film will have anything to do with. Editing begins with the material shot, just as the shooting script of a classical film starts from the 'reality' it deals with. *Direct cinema* rejects all *a priori* form or signification, and all pre-determination and aims, not to reproduce things 'as they are' (as they are intended by the scenario of the film or of 'life' – i.e. of ideology), but positively to transform them, to take them from an unformed, uncinematic stage to the stage of cinematic form. As such, *direct cinema* emerges in the best instances, not as a model, but as a *practice* of cinema (Comolli, 1969).

Comolli's argument has force as a stylistic description of the films he is involved with, but it also has notable weaknesses. The greatest of these is the potted account of film history which offers the modern direct film-makers as descendants of Lumière, Eisenstein and Vertov, with the concomitant image of sound as the manipulated (manipulated so as to appear 'natural') voice of the ideology of the ruling class. Here Comolli is making a confusion between the power of language as the system which regulates and makes possible human communication and the (relatively restricted) powers of spoken sound on a film soundtrack. The different technical processes in 'conventional' film-making do not endlessly repeat the same meaning, though they do quite often co-operate on a partial basis to establish one particular range of meanings. A similar naïvety about language seems to be present in his account of what he calls the 'Director's ordering speech', as though this speech did not itself constitute a form of preparation. There is also a certain vagueness in Comolli's remarks about style – terms such as rhythm, figures, meanings are used but not gone into – and a corresponding passivity about his use of the term 'ideology'. Ideology is everywhere; but what exactly does it do? He is using the term in the same spirit as some of the texts in Part III (pp. 164–86), but without articulating any particular function for it in the play of 'truth' and 'fiction'. The belief that the process of editing is the real 'moment in which the film is made' reunites us with an old tradition, but not a helpful one. Why should meaning be produced only in the editing? Its resurgence in this context owes something to the simple notion (formulated by Godard in relation to some of his more recent films) of correcting 'bad' ideology (captured in the 'scenes' of 'life') by 'correct' ideas.

But Comolli's insistence on the play between notions of 'fiction' and 'reality' – a play which happens in the films themselves as well as in our ideas about them – is valid not merely for the films he is discussing but perhaps also for all films except the most deliberately abstract (explorations of kinetics, scratching exercises, etc.). We end with an extract from the discussion between Eric Rohmer and Comolli, Pascal Bonitzer, Serge Daney and Jean Narboni. The interview first appeared in *Cahiers du Cinéma* and refers to many of the issues and problems which have been discussed throughout this book. What is remarkable about the discussion is that the interlocutors agree about nothing at all:

Cahiers: Let's talk about your overall conception of the cinematic medium. To us, like any other aesthetic medium, the cinema does not hover above History and Ideology, but is totally inscribed within them.

Rohmer: I don't quite get this word 'ideology'. Could you ask me the question in a more precise way?

C: You say that you don't intend to make films with a 'message'. But it is not necessarily at the level of the 'message' or the 'thesis' that the ideological determination operates: the general conception of cinematic means is itself already completely determined.

R: That is your historical materialist point of view. I can quite agree that, yes, we are determined. But can we be conscious of this determination? Can the film-maker himself answer such a question or is it up to the critic to answer it? The question may not even be terribly interesting.

C: This brings us back to our previous conversation[48] where you counter-posed the notion of cinema as an end – an end-in-itself – to the notion of the cinema as a means. According to you, the cinema must record and fix realistically pre-existing situations: a conception of the cinema as transparency, pure reflection. Can we talk again about this?

R: I certainly have ideas on the cinema, but these ideas have not changed.

There are two distinct stages in the conception of the *Moral Tales:*[49] in the first stage, the story is invented, and in the second stage, it is adapted filmically. Some tales were fully written whilst others were just sketched, but still, they all had a pre-cinematic existence. Their *mise en scène* seemed to me above all an act of transmitting something – though it could also be an act of creation: but it is not for me to judge.

C: You told us then: what is interesting is what is shown: the cinema is a means. But you did not specify the end to which this means is put. It seems that, in your films, two answers are possible: one is to be found in your educational films, and the others in your *Moral Tales*. In your educational films, one thing and one thing only must be taught to children. But in the *Moral Tales*, things are more complex. However much one would like to go on thinking of cinema as being transparent, the very fact of putting a camera in front of an object and doing all the work of the *mise en scène* forces one to arrive at the opposite conclusion. Even if 'things speak for themselves', the very fact of looking at them for a length of time will eventually make them say increasingly different things. So we are left confronting 'the concrete of the film', and not the 'concrete of the world'. This negation of transparency is precisely what happens in the crane scene of *Les Métamorphoses du paysage industriel*. The cinema is a means of production: but the product is in the film itself, and not the world.

R: There is nothing I can say to that. I did not say that the film, the work, was a means, but that the cinema was, as a technique, as a 'language'. Just as some would say that in poetry language is itself the end whilst others would take language to be the means to express poetry, but this doesn't imply that language is degraded or that this poetic means serves any value other than a poetic value. For example, in the extreme case of the Lettrists,[50] language is an end in itself, since for them, the pure act of articulation is not bound to any meaning. In Baudelaire, language is less of an end than it is in certain *Illuminations*,[51] or in Mallarmé, etc. I was in fact criticising the kind of cinema which indulged in the sort of procedures said to be 'procedures of cinematic language', which it made a great deal of, while ignoring dramatic, plastic content, etc.

C: On the whole, would you subscribe to a definition along the lines: the cinema is a technique whose aim is to help us see *better* – see better things which are right under our noses?

R: I would say what Astruc[52] made Orson Welles say at the *Objectif 49* Film Society. He was interviewing Welles, and he freely translated one of Welles's answers with a formula I find rather beautiful: 'Cinema is poetry.' Given that cinema is poetry in the realm of forms (and sounds), it widens out perception: it makes us see (and hear). This is a point that I've made in an awful lot of articles, so forgive me if I take it up again: a film does not deliver a translation of the world for us to admire, but rather, through the translation, it delivers the world itself. The cinema, even in its works of fiction, is an instrument of discovery. Because it is poetry, it reveals, and because it reveals, it is poetry.

C: So, it boils down to a conception along the lines of Bazin's; that is, the cinema is like a window, the widest possible, opening out onto the world, with the frame operating like a mast. We are absolutely opposed to such a conception. If we find your films interesting, it is, on the contrary, because a strong process of 'making opaque' happens in them: a process which gives us the film to see, and not reality – or rather, a work which gives us the film as the only reality.

R: I still think Bazin was right. However, I associate the idea of a 'window' more with 'opening' than 'transparency'. Transparency is too static, and I take opening in its active sense: the act of opening rather than the mere fact of being open. If it is true that the other arts have driven us away from the world, then the art of the cinema has brought us back to it. It has forced us, in the course of its history, to take the world into consideration – and it still does now. That, I presume is what Bazin thought, and, at any rate, it's what I think. And you can't possibly think otherwise. Bazin's merit is to have turned some aesthetic values (some of which were normal in any case) upside-down. He put imitation before invention and submissiveness before independence – to begin with, at least. The scorn the contemporary artist had for the world was replaced by respect, for it is above all through respecting its models that the genius of the cinema comes into its own. Whether we like it or not, this is imposed on us by the very nature of photographic representation. Bazin had thus put his finger upon what was *unique* in cinema, what distinguished it from all other art forms.

C: You referred to the cinema as 'a means to make us admire the world better'. But this already implies that we have in the first place a conception of an essential world as Beauty, as Order, of which 'concrete reality' and 'appearances' are the visible manifestations. Consequently, the objectivity you are seeking will turn out to be non-absolute, non-eternal – it will be situated precisely in history and will be determined ideologically. So, is it still possible to talk about 'the world' or 'nature' after having made 'what we see' in the cinema inseparable from 'what we know', after admitting that our knowledge directs and determines what we see? An observed object is just as 'treated' as it is observed by the means of observation (the cinema itself also appeared at a given point in history in response to a social requirement) and the person who handles these means (the film-maker). So is it not true that reaching the objective world means reaching *your particular* idea of the world, *your particular* idea of the objectivity of the world?

R: It is quite true that, as a work of art, a film fits your description: a film is a reconstruction, an interpretation of the world. But of all the arts, the cinema – and this is its paradoxical character – is the one where the reality of the thing filmed is of the greatest importance, where the 'interpretation' aspect seems sometimes to disappear entirely. This, in other words, is the miracle of Lumière's first films. With these films we are left with the impression of having seen the world with different eyes. They make us admire, as Pascal says, things that we did not know how to admire in their original form. People walking in the streets, children playing, trains going by: nothing out of the ordinary. But this – the first feeling of wonder – is, to my mind, the most important. In so far as my own films are very elaborate, very constructed, this impression tends to disappear, but it persists none the less, tied to the fact, common to all films, of using actors, for instance, their physical presence. Take *La Carrière de Suzanne* for instance: what is specifically cinematic here is to bring into play a real girl, one who exists, and even to feel uneasy about making remarks on the film, since any judgment passed on Suzanne will automatically be a judgment on the person who played her.

C: Let us go back to Pascal's phrase: in *La Carrière de Suzanne*, it is not the Suzanne of before and after the film who will be 'seen better' thanks to the film, but Suzanne as a filmed-being, between the beginning and the end of the film. In other words, Suzanne-outside-the-film is neither the discourse nor the subject matter of the film: the spectator's reading can only bear upon Suzanne-in-the-film, Suzanne the 'filmic being'.

R: Yes, in a sense. There is no doubt that Bazin's attitude was polemical: there was a need, in the 1950s, to insist on this character of the cinema, to recognise that a Lumière was, in the last analysis, more important than any existing or future avant-garde film. Bazin was reacting against theorists (like Arnheim[53] and Bálazs) who saw film as interpretation. Since this has been secured, I find it perfectly normal that you should now go back to building a 'linguistic' theory of the cinema — adopting the manner and terms of linguistic research, because the process of criticism has always been dialectical. But Bazin's theory of cinematic objectivity still retains all its truth and vigour.

C: So far as we are concerned, we are not trying to go back to 'film-language'. One can apply linguistic methods to the cinema without, however, falling into some reassuring codification or turning the object of these methods itself into a language. Nowadays, linguistics are being applied to molecular genetics, but that does not mean that molecules are being turned into a language.

R: Certainly, but we are still talking about a study of signification, which is somewhat more abstract than the more direct position we had in the Bazin period: the cinema as an instrument of discovery. The contribution of our critical output in the 1950s had sought to establish a more profound relation with nature, to help discover natural objects whose beauty was revealed to us through the cinema. You don't agree with that. . . .

C: You always insist on referring to the 'outside' of the film — the 'world' which exists before and after it — as though it were a concrete reality. Does not this indicate that, after all, you are not seeking the 'natural', but rather that you are really after a *guarantee*? Now, is it the fundamental realism of the cinematic image (to use Bazin's expression) that guarantees the 'presence' of the world? Or is it not rather the real world itself which could be taken to guarantee 'cinematic realism'?

R: Well, since you're pressing me, I will go further; not only is there a beauty and an order to the world, but there is also no beauty or order that are not *of the* world. Otherwise, how could art, a product of human effort, equal nature, a divine creation? At best, art is the revelation, in the universe, of the Creator's hand. True enough, there can be no position more teleological or theological than mine. It is also the position of the spectator. If the spectator had not found beauty in this world, how could he seek it in its image? How could he admire an imitation of life if he did not admire life itself? That is the position of the film-maker. If I film something, it is because I find it beautiful; therefore, there must *exist* beautiful things in nature. This is the position of any artist, any art-lover. If I did not find nature beautiful – the sky, the air, light, space – I would not find any painting beautiful – not a Leonardo, not Turner or Hartung.[54] But enough generalities; could you not ask me more precise questions?

C: When you say that cinema puts us in touch with the beauty of the world, even after a detour, we would agree with you as far as Lumière is concerned. With him, at least, one has the firm impression that things are filmed for the first time. But fifty years on, if you want to get the same effect, you need to make an enormous detour, because nothing is automatic any more, because anyone's relationship with a film or a shot is no longer the same at all: the pure wonder of recognition is disappearing fast, so that, if you still want to produce it, you now need a lot of care, subtlety, plus an absolutely diabolical intelligence. Since this trend is growing inexorably, why not consider your cause an increasingly lost one?

R: No, because I think that, fundamentally, this feeling of wonder will remain, but to arouse it is a little like Lumière's train coming into the station:[55] today it no longer has any effect. The beauty of Lumière's films is more obvious to people of our generation than to Lumière's contemporaries who reacted, above all, by being strongly impressed. But I find it difficult to discuss this, because there are fundamentally two attitudes to the cinema, and both these attitudes are justified. In our days, ours was justified, and I hope that now yours is.

C: We must perhaps question the famous cinematic 'transparency' of classical cinema, its concern to erase the evidence of its own work, the criticism it gave rise to, or rather, tended to give rise to. We would agree to dismiss some 'external signs' of work as vain showing-off which, more often than not, serves to camouflage the fact that no real work has been going on. But, on the other hand, to erase deliberately any sign of labour, does not this point to a very specific ideological project – a theological one? Does not a film that presents itself as cut off from its own process of production aim at being read as an epiphany, as a miraculous event? And it certainly is read like that.

R: Yes, but why not, since everything is a miracle? Everything is a miracle: 'That Pascal was born, that two friends separated since their school-days meet again in the street' (Alain: *Propos de littérature*).[56] . . . Before television one could make an absolute value of the natural. This was true in Bazin's time, but less true today. As far as I am concerned, I'm still on the side of the natural, the telly, etc., but without being completely on that side. Could you ask a precise question on this?

C: For example, it would seem that, between *La Carrière de Suzanne* and *Ma Nuit chez Maud*, your technique was moving closer to direct cinema. . . .

R: Post-synchronisation does not, you know, imply a less natural approach; quite the opposite, really. In *La Carrière de Suzanne* people did not know their lines. I had to whisper their lines for them, and did it so well that they weren't acting any more. . . . The fact that work, organising, etc., go into the film does not mean that the film cannot legitimately be claimed by its author, including those parts he cannot control. On the other hand, the cinema cannot live without constant reference to 'photographic realism'. I think you will easily agree that in the cinema, the mark left by the work of the artist is something *shocking* – much more shocking than in other artistic fields. The film-makers I admire are those who conceal the means they use, like, first of all, Lumière of course, or Renoir. The greatest danger to the cinema is the pride of the film-maker who says: I have a style, and I want to draw people's attention to it.

C: It is not so much a matter of 'style' as the fact that one is working a material and that one knows this fact. Whereas you think that the work must be concealed. . . .

R: In fact, it must conceal itself. This is what we admired so much in American films: the neutrality, the transparency, the apparent lack of stylistic research.

C: But that does not apply much to Hitchcock, for instance, or to Renoir, whose films you have just quoted as examples of total transparency.

R: Not so much transparency as humility towards the model. I am here talking of this attitude so often adopted by Renoir. 'I am not quite sure what I want to do, I let people do what they want', etc. . . .

C: But is this not affectation? Is there really any point in promoting such a mystifying conception of the artist? And don't you think, for instance, that there is more vanity in erasing the evidence of one's labour, than in letting it be seen? Are not the natural and the effect of naturalness the most extreme forms of ostentation?

R: Whether labour can be seen or not, does not really matter. It is not my labour that I put on show, but things, whether through my labour or through no labour. My initial project is always to show some thing *as it really is* with as little alteration as possible. For instance, in *Le Signe du Lion* I wanted to show the Seine, its banks, the impression of the sun playing on the water, etc. I started from this intention, this desire, this need: need to show things rather than manufacture them. It is the truth of things which interests me, rather than the labour I use to reach that truth. The question is not whether I succeed in reaching it or not: I have no pretensions. My attitude is not born from any pretension, but out of respect for things themselves, and, because of my love for them, from a legitimate desire to embrace them. And this applies to the *Moral Tales* too.

C: Let us take, for example, the night scene at Maud's. Now, there is a place, the place where you filmed; this place pre-exists. However, what is striking when one sees the film, is that, as the film develops, because of the scenario, the interplay of looks, the rhythm of the shots, a filmic place emerges which no longer has anything to do with the pre-existing place; the outcome of genuine work, this filmic place is much more interesting.

R: For the first time in my life, I didn't shoot the film in a flat, but used a set instead. Why? Because the subject matter demanded very precise direction of the actors' positions and movements in relation to the shape of the place. But once the set was built according to my specifications, it became endowed with the same quality of existence, autonomous and real, as any 'natural place'. And I felt I wanted to show it, not as something I had invented, but as something I had discovered. If I had shot in a real apartment, I would have had to cheat, move the furniture, etc. This manufactured décor existed much more objectively than a natural décor. So what do you mean when you say that this décor ends up by being 'something else'?

C: One could, of course, by the end of the film, reconstitute Maud's apartment, make a drawing of it; but that's not where the interest of the film lies. . . .

R: But it was very important for my *mise en scène*, since if I'd had to cheat, I wouldn't have felt certain about my characters' movements. My characters were guided by the real moves they had to make.

C: So, we come back then to the idea of the pre-existent real as a guarantee, not as an object. We quite accept that this 'filmic place' could not have existed if this place had not been filmed. All the same, through the development of the scene, the created filmic place substitutes itself totally for the filmed place.

R: Here, I find it difficult to agree with you. On the contrary, I felt very strongly the presence of the filmed place — an artificial one in this case, but it could be natural — so much so that the only thing that dictated the position of my camera was the topography of the place.

C: What we mean to say is that the time-factor is very important: this décor that you built becomes increasingly invested by the drama. It thus becomes loaded with meanings which are no longer those of its topography. Its filmic functioning can no longer be equated with its functioning as a film-set.

R: Of course, since architecture is a functional art, any décor must clearly be functional. It's also evident that I built this set to meet dramatic requirements. However, let me say again that once this décor was created, it existed for me like a real being, in the same way as my actors. My *mise en scène* was born out of the contact between the actors and this décor. For your information, that's how things in fact happen.

C: But is there not some confusion here between what, for you, is an essential means to any film (the necessity of a pre-existent place) and what, in fact, one finds – or should find – at the end of the film?

R: Listen, I'm not looking for explanations, I'm telling you a fact. Maybe some of my colleagues don't find it important to work from pre-existent things. Me, I'm one of those who need to work on living matter, not in abstraction. That's all I can say.

C: It's not a question of 'abstraction', but of an 'imaginary real'. To begin with, there is a real and concrete décor, but one which, through the film and the relation between the characters and this décor, becomes gradually *a décor of fiction*, purely dramatic – a décor of the imaginary. So we can no longer say that the film is a document about the décor. On the contrary, it would seem that the décor says something about the film. Take your film on *La Place de l'Étoile*: although it was absolutely necessary for the Place de l'Étoile to exist in order that the film could be made, it could be said that, once the film is made and whilst it is being seen, there is no Place de l'Étoile except the one in the film.

R: Of course. What interests me about décor is that it relates to the characters, although it must have an *a priori* existence as well. In the case of *La Place de l'Étoile*, if there had been no image, in the spectator's mind, of what the Place de l'Etoile is in space, then the film would have lost quite a lot of its force. But some films are very hard to get a sense of, and sometimes even the director himself tries to disorient you. My idea was to show a real journey: having said this, I would point out that the feeling of continuity is the most difficult one to suggest in a film. We all know that cinematic time is not the same as time in real life. Films that have tried to show in an hour and a half an action supposed to last an hour and a half – *Rope* or *Cleo from 5 to 7*[57] – seem to run much longer. It's the same thing in *La Place de l'Étoile*: I have certainly failed to capture the continuity of space and time. Nevertheless, I think I am right to set out wanting to be a realist, even though at the end of the road one is likely to run into the abstract and the fantastic. What would be bad would be to set out with the intention of being anti-realist. That's what frightens me in Eisenstein.

C: You talked about the inevitable gap between filmic time and filmed time, between filmic space and filmed space – then you said that you did not manage to master time and space in *La Place de l'Étoile*, as if the perennial vocation of the cinema was to bridge this gap. Don't you think, instead, that a film-maker's real work should be inscribed within this gap and should make use of it? Does not the fact that in the last account there will inevitably be infidelity lead you to question the absolute belief in the concept of cinema as mimesis?

R: No, I think the opposite is true. I think the aim of the cinema is to keep tightening its hold on reality, and one could easily envisage a history of the cinema which would show that the cinema has never stopped discovering nature and moving towards the natural. It hasn't got there yet completely, there are loads of things it can't show yet, but it will eventually manage to do it. Very simple things, like two people passing each other in the street. Undoubtedly, the way actors act in films today is much closer to life. If the camera is hidden, the way people behave in front of it looks increasingly like what you see in fiction films; whereas the further you go back in the history of the cinema the greater you find this gap to be. I am not scared of being too close to life. I am trying to eliminate what still draws me away from it, though I do know that I will never achieve my aim completely. I know there will always be a fringe area, but I don't try to work within it, nor to emphasise it, though I think it is possible that, by wanting to go further, I may reach what you called abstraction. In the *Moral Tales* what I want to do is to go further towards the concrete. I think it is very sterile and dangerous to believe that the cinema has gone far enough in the direction of realism, and that it should now turn its back to it. To me, the interesting thing about the cinema is that it has potential powers of investigation. Let's take photography. Is a photograph out of a current magazine any more real than a daguerreotype? Yes and no. Let's say that each reveals a different aspect of nature. A daguerreotype is closer to the vision of a painter, whereas the current photo is the outcome of possibilities that painting ignored: the possibility of capturing a fleeting moment, for instance. And the more techniques develop, the greater will be the increase in photography's powers of investigation. A soft-focus, halated or tricked photograph which helps us achieve a better knowledge of things would be more realist than a *trompe-l'oeil* painting, but without that better knowledge, and if you use a soft focus, a halation or a trick for their own sakes, you're not a photographer any more, but a painter (more often than not, a bad painter). You would be painting with a camera, as others paint with a brush or a flame-thrower (Rohmer, 1970).

Notes

1 *La fin du monde/Finis Terrae* (The end of the earth, France, 1929), directed by Epstein.

2 Cameramen (cinematographers) mentioned in this text: Gregg Toland (1904–48); James Wong Howe (1899–1976); Karl Freund (1890–1969); Billy Bitzer (1874–1944); Arthur Miller (1895–1970); Bert Glennon (1893–1967); Leon Shamroy (1901–74); Gaetano Gaudio (1885–1951); Lee Garmes (1898–); Victor Milner (1893–).

3 *Transatlantic* (USA, 1931), directed by William K. Howard.

4 Film-makers mentioned in this text: S. M. Eisenstein (see Brief notes on contributors, p. 260); Vsevolod Pudovkin (1893–1953); Lev Kuleshov (1899–1970); John Ford (1895–1973); Pare Lorentz (1905–); Paul Strand (1890–1976); Henri Cartier-Bresson (1908–); Jean Renoir (1894–1979). Strand and Cartier-Bresson are better known as documentary still photographers.

5 'Photography of the Month', *American Cinematographer*, May 1941, p. 222.

6 This is a quotation from Bazin's single most important text, 'The evolution of film language'. It is not reprinted in this volume because of its wide availability elsewhere, e.g. André Bazin, *What is Cinema?*, vol 1, California University Press, 1967, pp. 23–40 (incomplete version) and Peter Graham, ed., *The New Wave*, Secker & Warburg, 1968, pp. 25–50 (complete).

7 Walter Blanchard, 'Aces of the Camera VII: James Wong Howe, A.S.C.,' *American Cinematographer*, July 1941, p. 346.

8 But not to red. Orthochromatic stock began to be used in the cinema during the first decade of this century.

9 Film stock consists of a cellulose base with a layer or layers of photo-sensitive emulsion. The image is formed by the exposure of this emulsion to the light, followed by the subsequent chemical treatment of emulsion and base together (the 'developing' process). Different emulsions possess different sensitivities to light. These different sensitivities are referred to as 'speeds', and measured on a numerical scale: the higher the speed, the more sensitive to light the stock.

10 ASA = American Standards Association, the body responsible for supervising many technical standards in the USA. In this context the initials refer to the Association's system for measuring the speeds of film emulsion (see previous note).

11 Emery Huse, ASC, 'The characteristics of Eastman Motion Picture Negative Film', *American Cinematographer*, May 1936, p. 190.

12 Walter Strohm, 'Progress in lighting means economy', *American Cinematographer,* January 1936, p. 16.

13 Marshall McLuhan (1911–), Canadian commentator on mass-media, author of *The Gutenberg Galaxy* (1962), best known for his belief that the form of a medium determines the content of its communication.

14 Teddy Tetzlaff *et al.*, 'Lighting the new fast films', *American Cinematographer*, February 1939, p. 70.
15 Release prints are the copies of films made available for public exhibition.
16 *Gone with the Wind* (USA, 1939), produced by David O. Selznick, directed by Victor Fleming.
17 William Stull, ASC, 'Non-Glare Coating makes lenses one step faster', *American Cinematographer*, March 1940, p. 109.
18 Gregg Toland, ASC, 'I broke the rules in *Citizen Kane*', *Popular Photography*, June 1941, p. 91.
19 Ibid., p. 90.
20 The blimp is a heavy device for enclosing the camera to prevent the sound-recording equipment from picking up the noise of the camera when filming is in progress.
21 The pan is a camera movement in which the camera is rotated in a horizontal plane to right or left to give a 'panoramic' impression of the material. The dolly is a mobile platform on which the camera and its operators are mounted in order to obtain moving-camera shots.
22 Susan Alexander (played by Dorothy Comingore) is Kane's second wife.
23 Gregg Toland, 'Using arcs for monochrome', *American Cinematographer*, December 1941, p. 558.
24 Ibid., pp. 558-9.
25 *The River* (India, USA, France, 1950) directed by Renoir.
26 The variable-focus zoom lens, introduced in the 1950s, allows the camera operator to give the effect of movement without actually moving the camera.
27 Films directed by Rossellini mentioned in this extract: *The Acts of the Apostles* (*Atti degli Apostoli*, 1968, for Italian television), *The Rise of Louis XIV* (*La Prise de pouvoir par Louis XIV*, 1966, for French television), *Europa '51* (Italy, 1952), *Il generale della Rovere* (1951).
28 *A Married Couple* (Canada, 1969).
29 Above, p. 216.
30 *Black Natchez* (USA, filmed 1965, released 1967), a documentary made by Ed Pincus and David Neuman, produced by the Centre for Social Documentary Films.
31 Students for a Democratic Society, an organisation of the American New Left founded in 1960 and prominent in the following decade.
32 Charles Evers, a black civil rights leader, brother of Medgar Evers (murdered in Mississippi, 1963).
33 Film-makers referred to in this extract: Jean-Luc Godard (1930–); Michelangelo Antonioni (1912–); Joseph Losey (1909–); Francesco Rosi (1922–); Bernardo Bertolucci (1940–); Ingmar Bergman (1918–); Tinto Brass (1933–); Jean-Marie Straub (1933–); Pier Paolo Pasolini (1922–75).
34 That is, as an element of film language.
35 According to Saussurean linguistics, the linguistic sign is a two-sided

entity comprising simultaneously the dimensions of *signifier*, or sound-image, and *signified*, or concept. Here Bettetini, like other film-semioticians, is attempting to use the terminology of structural linguistics in relation to film. In this context, signifieds = concepts conveyed by the film, signifers = filmic forms. In classical rhetoric, the diegesis is one of the divisions of a speech or oration, the section which sets out, in the speaker's own words (i.e. without any direct quotation) the facts of a case, the table of events or the development of a story. The term has been used loosely in some modern film criticism to signify 'that which pertains to the story, the narrative, or the plot of a film'.

36 Films referred to in this extract: *Nicht Versohnt* (Not reconciled, West Germany, 1965), directed by Jean-Marie Straub; *Une femme est une femme* (A woman is a woman, France, 1961), dir. Jean-Luc Godard.

37 Film-makers referred to in this text: Jacques Rivette (1928–   ), also a critic; Bertolucci; Eric Rohmer (see Brief notes on contributors, p. 261); Godard; Philippe Garrel (1948–   ); Maurice Pialat (1925–   ); John Cassavetes (1929–   ), also an actor; Straub; Miklos Jancso (1921–   ); Pierre Perrault (1921–   ), also a critic; Jean Rouch (1917–   ), also an ethnographer; Andy Warhol (1928–   ), also a painter; Jean Eustache (1938–   ); Mikhail Romm (1901–71); Grigori Alexandrov (1903–   ); Alain Resnais (1922–   ); the Lumière brothers, Auguste (1862–1954) and Louis (1864–1948); Georges Méliès (1861–1938); Bergman; Ford; Samuel Fuller (1911–   ); Josef von Sternberg (1894–1969); Richard Leacock (1921–   ); Gian Vittorio Baldi (1930–   ).

38 Films referred to in this text: *L'Amour fou* (Mad love, France, 1968), directed by Rivette; *Partner* (Italy, 1968), dir. Bertolucci; *L'Enfance nue* (Naked childhood, France, 1962), dir. Pialat; *Faces* (USA, 1968), dir. Cassavetes; *The Chronicle of Anna Magdalena Bach* (West Germany/Italy, 1967), dir. Straub and Danièle Huillet; *Silence and Cry* (Hungary, 1968), dir. Jancso; *Le Règne du jour* (Canada, 1966), dir. Perrault; *La Rosière de Pessac* (The rose-girl of Pessac, French television, 1968), dir. Eustache; *La Rentrée des usines Wonder* (Going back to work at the Wonder factories, France, 1968), a collective film produced by the États Généraux du Cinéma; *Empire* (USA, 1964), dir. Warhol; *Shadows* (USA, 1960), dir. Cassavetes; *The Band Wagon* (USA, 1953), dir. Vincente Minnelli; *The Golden Coach* (France 1952) and *La Règle du jeu* (France, 1939), dir. Renoir; *The Patsy* (USA, 1965), dir. Jerry Lewis.

39 Referring to and/or produced by participants in the French student revolt and worker occupations of that month.

40 Louis Marcorelles, French critic, champion of direct cinema and vérité, author of *Living Cinema*, London, 1973.

41 Georges Sadoul (1904–67), French film critic and historian.

42 Comolli here uses the term in the traditional sense of 'film-maker with a view of the world' rather than in the modern sense of 'structure of meaning within a body of work'.

43 Pierre Macherey, French theoretician, member of the group which

worked on Althusser's *Reading Capital*, author of *Pour une théorie de la production littéraire* (Towards a theory of literary production, Paris, 1966).

44 Pair of rails laid down on the ground to facilitate the movement of the dolly (see note 21 above).

45 *Andromaque*, tragedy by Racine (1667).

46 André-S. Labarthe, French critic and television director.

47 Marcelin Pleynet (1933–   ), French poet, essayist and art critic, now editor of *Tel Quel*; has contributed to *Cinéthique*.

48 *Cahiers* had previously interviewed Rohmer in no. 172, November 1965.

49 Films directed by Rohmer and referred to in this interview: The *Moral Tales (Contes moraux)* series, I *La Boulangère de Monceau* (The baker's wife of Monceau, France, 1962), II *La Carrière de Suzanne* (Suzanne's career, France, 1963), III *My Night with Maud (Ma Nuit chez Maud*, France, 1969), IV *La Collectionneuse* (France, 1966), V *Claire's Knee (Le Genou de Claire*, France, 1970), VI *Love in the Afternoon (L'Amour l'après-midi*, France, 1972); *La Signe du Lion* (The sign of Leo, France, 1959); *La Place de l'Étoile*, an episode of the compilation film *Paris vu par . . .* (Paris seen by . . ., France, 1965); *Die Marquise von O* (France/ West Germany, 1975); and eleven educational/cultural documentaries made for French television between 1964 and 1969, including *Les Métamorphoses du paysage industriel*.

50 The Lettrists, school of French poets active between 1945 and 1950, most prominent of whom was Isidore Izou (1925–   ).

51 *Les Illuminations* (1886), a collection of prose poems by Arthur Rimbaud (1854–91). Stéphane Mallarmé (1842–98), French symbolist poet, best known for *L'après-midi d'un faune* (1876) and *Un Coup de dés jamais n'abolira le hasard* (A throw of the dice will never abolish chance, 1897).

52 Alexandre Astruc (1923–   ), French critic and director, best known for his writings on film style and for the films *Une Vie* (1958) and *La Proie pour l'ombre* (1960).

53 Rudolf Arnheim (1904–   ), film theorist, author of *Film as Art* (Berlin, 1932, Faber & Faber, 1958); has also written on the psychology of art.

54 Hans Hartung (1904–   ), influential German-born painter who became a French citizen. His painting has been described as 'achieving autonomy and carrying a significance that cannot be revealed through any other medium' (Will Gehmann, in *Art since 1945*, Thames & Hudson, 1958), though critics have also seen his work as containing elements of commentary on previous art movements.

55 *L'Arrivée d'un train en gare de La Ciotat*, one of the earliest films (1895–7) made by the Lumière brothers, famous for supposedly having terrified its first spectators because of its realism; convinced that the train would leave the screen and mow them down, they are supposed to have left their seats in panic.

56 Alain (1868–1951) was a French essayist, teacher and critic. The *Propos de littérature* (1933) are a collection of his articles on literature.
57 *Cléo de 5 à 7* (Cleo from 5 to 7, France, 1962), directed by Agnès Varda.

Brief notes on contributors

André Bazin (1919–58), French critic, contributor to a wide range of journals, influenced by the 'personalist' Catholicism of the philosopher Emmanuel Mounier, co-founder of the magazine *Cahiers du Cinéma*, was a strong influence on the critics and film-makers of the French 'New Wave' movement. His writings were collected into book form after his death.

Gianfranco Bettetini (1933–), Italian theorist and television film-maker, Professor of Theory and Technique of Mass Communications at Rome University. Author of *The Language and Technique of the Film* (1968; English-language edition, 1973); *L'Indice del realismo* (1970); *Produzione del senso e messa in scena* (1975).

Bertolt Brecht (1898–1956), German playwright and poet, whose plays include *The Threepenny Opera* (1928), *The Mother* (1931), *Galileo* (1939), *Mother Courage* (1939), *The Good Woman of Setzuan* (1940), *Mr Puntila and his Servant Matti* (1941), *The Caucasian Chalk Circle* (1945). Founder of the Berliner Ensemble theatre company, 1951. In cinema he was involved as a writer with G. W. Pabst's film version of his own *Threepenny Opera* (his repudiation of which led to the *Threepenny Trial*, cf. extracts pp. 164–70), with Slatan Dudow's *Kuhle Wampe* (1932) and Fritz Lang's *Hangmen also Die* (1943).

Osip Brik (1884–1945), Russian formalist critic and editor, occasional film scriptwriter.

Jean-Louis Comolli (1941–), joined *Cahiers du Cinéma* as critic in 1966 and was editor-in-chief between 1966–71. He has made a number of films for the television series 'Cinéastes de notre temps', produced by Janine Bazin and André S. Labarthe, and two feature films – *Les Deux marseillaises* (1968) and *La Cecilia* (1975).

Helen van Dongen (1909–), Dutch-born film editor and assistant producer, worked on *Misère au Borinage* (1933), *New Earth* (1934), *Spanish Earth* (1937), *The 400 Million* (1937), all with Joris Ivens, and on *News Review No. 2* (USA, 1944–5).

S. M. Eisenstein (1898–1948), Russian film-maker, theorist and teacher, director of *Strike* (1925), *Battleship Potemkin* (1925), *October* (1928), *The Old and the New* (1929), *Alexander Nevsky* (1938), *Ivan the Terrible, Part 1* (1944), *Part 2* (1946, released 1958). Also worked occasionally as a theatre director. Visited Europe and America (1929–32).

Jean Epstein (1897–1953), French film-maker and theoretician, director of *L'Auberge rouge* (1923), *The Fall of the House of Usher* (1928), *Finis Terrae* (1929). Known as an experimentalist who attempted to work within commercial structures.

Jean-Paul Fargier (1944–), French critic and theoretician, member of the editorial board of *Cinéthique* (1969–74).

Frances Hubbard Flaherty (1883–1973), wife of the film-maker Robert Flaherty, played an important role as collaborator (editing, production, still photography) in many of his films.

John Grierson (1898–1972), Scottish film producer, critic and theoretician; director of *Drifters* (1929); headed the Empire Marketing Board Film Unit (1929); founded the National Film Board of Canada (1939); presented *This Wonderful World* for Scottish Television (1957–68). Grierson's organising and intellectual influence permeates British documentary film since the 1930s.

Allan King (1930–), Canadian film-maker, principally documentaries, including *Rickshaw* (1960), *Warrendale* (1966), *A Married Couple* (1969), though *Who has seen the wind?* (1977) adopts a fictional format.

Siegfried Kracauer (1889–1966), German-born theoretician, settled in the USA in 1941, author of *From Caligari to Hitler* (1947), and *The Nature of Film: The Redemption of Physical Reality* (1960).

Colin MacCabe (1949–), assistant lecturer in English at Cambridge University, member of the editorial board of *Screen* magazine, author of *James Joyce and the Revolution of the Word* (1978).

Léon Moussinac (1890–1964), French critic and journalist, author of *Naissance du cinéma* (1925).

Patrick L. Ogle (1944–   ), instructor in radio, television and film, University of Texas at Austin, author of an article on the beginnings of commercial motion picture sound, in *Film Reader 2*, Northwestern University, 1977.

V. F. Perkins (1936–   ), British critic and teacher, lecturer in film studies at the University of Warwick, member of the editorial board of *Movie* magazine, author of *Film as Film* (1972).

Ed Pincus (1939–   ), American film-maker and teacher, often working in collaboration with David Neumann: *Black Natchez*, (1967), *The Way We See It* (1970).

Jean Renoir (1894–1979), French film-maker, director of numerous films including *La Chienne* (1931), *Boudu sauvé des eaux* (1932), *Madame Bovary* (1934), *Le Crime de Mr Lange* (1936), *La Vie est à nous* (1936), *Une Partie de campagne* (1936, released 1946), *La Grande illusion* (1937), *La Marseillaise* (1937), *Toni* (1938), *La Bête humaine* (1938), *La Règle du jeu* (1939), *Swamp Water* (1941), *The Southerner* (1945), *The Diary of a Chambermaid* (1946), *Woman on the Beach* (1947), *The River* (1950), *The Golden Coach* (1953), *French Can-Can* (1955), *Le Déjeuner sur l'herbe* (1959), *Le Caporal épinglé* (1962). Author of a novel, *The Notebooks of Captain Georges* (1966) and an autobiography, *My Life and my Films* (1974). Contributed regular columns, on filmic and non-filmic matters, to the Communist evening paper *Ce Soir* in the 1930s.

Eric Rohmer (1920–   ), pseudonym of Maurice Sherer, French critic and film-maker, editor of *Cahiers du Cinéma* (1958–63), director of the *Moral Tales* series (see note 49, p. 257).

Roberto Rossellini (1906–77), Italian film-maker, director of *La nave bianca* (1941), *Roma, città aperta* (1945), *Paisà* (1947), *Germany Year Zero* (1947), *Stromboli* (1949), *Francesco giullare di Dio* (1950), *Viaggio in Italia* (1952), *Il generale della Rovere* (1959), *Viva l'Italia* (1960), *Vanina Vanini* (1961), and, for television, *The Rise of Louis XIV* (1966), *The Acts of the Apostles* (1968, with his son Renzo Rossellini, jr.), and *Socrates* (1970).

Viktor Shklovsky (1893–   ), Russian formalist critic and theoretician, who developed the idea of *ostranneniye* ('making strange') which has since had a wide influence, most notably on the theatres of Meyerhold, Piscator and Brecht. Books include *The Technique of the Writer's Craft* (1928), *On Mayakovsky* (1940). Wrote some film scripts in the late 1920s.

Sergei Tretyakov (1892–1939?), formalist then futurist poet and playwright, author of *Listen, Moscow* (1924), *Gas Masks* (1924, directed by Eisenstein), *Roar, China!* (1926). He was active in *Lef* and *Novy Lef*, wrote journalism in the 1930s, and perished in the purges of the late 1930s.

Yuri Tynyanov (1894–1943), Russian formalist critic and novelist, author of *Problems of Poetic Language* (1924), *Archaists and Innovators* (1929), *Death and Diplomacy in Persia* (1929), and *Lieutenant Kizhe* (1930, filmed by Alexander Feinzimmer in 1934).

Dziga Vertov (1896–1954), pseudonym of Denis Kaufman, Russian film-maker, director of the newsreel series *Kino-Pravda* (1922—5), *Stride, Soviet!* (1926), *A Sixth of the World* (1926), *The Eleventh* (1928), *The Man with the Movie Camera* (1929), *Enthusiasm* (1931), *Three Songs of Lenin* (1934).

Cesare Zavattini (1902–   ), Italian scriptwriter, critic and journalist, played an important part in the development of neo-realism, scripting *I bambini ci guardano* (1942), *Sciuscia* (1946), *Bicycle Thieves* (1948), *Miracle in Milan* (1950), *Umberto D* (1952), *Gold of Naples* (1954), *Il tetto* (1956), *Yesterday, Today, Tomorrow* (1965), all for the director Vittorio de Sica, and *Bellissima* (1951) for Luchino Visconti.

Checklist of readings

Place of publication is London except where indicated otherwise.

Bazin, A. (1948a), *Qu'est-ce que le cinéma?*, vol. 1, Éditions du Cerf, Paris, 1958. (See pp. 36–52.)

Bazin, A. (1948b), *Qu'est-ce que le cinéma?*, vol. 4, Éditions du Cerf, Paris, 1962. (See p. 53.)

Bettetini, G. (1968), *The Language and Technique of the Film*, Mouton, The Hague, 1973. (See pp. 220–4.)

Brecht, B. (1931), *Schriften aus Literas*, Suhrkamp Verlag, Frankfurt, 1967. (See pp. 164–70.)

Brik, O. (1928), *Screen*, vol. 12, no. 4, SEFT, 1971–2. (See pp. 121–7.)

Comolli, J.-L. (1969), *Cahiers du Cinéma*, nos 209, 211, Paris. (See pp. 225–43.)

van Dongen, H. (1953), in K. Reisz, *The Technique of Film Editing*, Focal Press, 1968. (See pp. 91–9.)

Eisenstein, S. M. (1929, 1934, 1939), *Film Form*, Harcourt Brace, New York, 1949; Dennis Dobson, 1963. (See pp, 18–22.)

Epstein, J. (1930), in M. Lapierre (ed.), *Anthologie du cinéma*, La nouvelle édition, Paris, 1946. (See pp. 193–7.)

Fargier, J.-P. (1969), *Cinéthique*, 5, Paris. (See pp. 171–85.)

Flaherty, F. H. (1960), *Odyssey of a Film-maker*, Beta Phi Mu Chapbooks, Princeton, New Jersey. (See pp. 89–90.)

Grierson, J. (1930/31/32), in F. Hardy (ed.), *Grierson on Documentary*, Faber & Faber, 1966. (See pp. 17, 89, 100, 104–6, 112, 113–15.)

King, A. (1971), in A. Rosenthal (ed.), *The New Documentary in Action*, California University Press. (See pp. 217–18.)

Kracauer, S. (1960), *Theory of Film*, Oxford University Press. (See pp. 101–3.)

MacCabe, C. (1974), *Screen*, vol. 15, no. 2, SEFT. (See pp. 152–62.)

Moussinac, L. (1925), in M. L'Herbier (ed.), *Intelligence du cinématographe*, Correa, Paris, 1946. (See p. 111.)

Ogle, P. L. (1972), *Screen*, vol. 13, no. 1, SEFT. (See pp. 197–213.)

Perkins, V. F. (1972), *Film as Film*, Penguin, Harmondsworth. (See pp. 69–79.)

Pincus, E. (1971), in G. R. Levin, *Documentary Explorations*, Doubleday, New York. (See pp. 218–20.)

Renoir, J. (1974), *My Life and my Films*, Collins. (See pp. 214–15.)

Rohmer, E. (1955a), *Cahiers du Cinéma*, no. 49, Paris. (See pp. 54–60.)

Rohmer, E. (1955b), *Cahiers du Cinéma*, no. 51, Paris. (See pp. 60–8.)

Rohmer, E. (1970), *Cahiers du Cinéma*, no. 219, Paris. (See pp. 244–53.)

Rossellini, R. (1952 and 1970), *Screen*, vol. 14, no. 4, SEFT, 1973–4. (See pp. 31–4, 215–16.)

Shklovsky, V. (1928), *Screen*, vol. 12, no. 4, SEFT, 1971–2. (See pp. 120–1, 127–9.)

Tretyakov, S. M., (1927), *Screen*, vol. 12, no. 4, SEFT, 1971–2. (See pp. 116–19.)

Tynyanov, Y. (1927), *Poetica Kino*, Moscow, 1927. (See pp. 130–51.)

Vertov, D. (1926), *Articles, journaux, projets*, Union Générale d'Éditions, Paris, 1972. (See pp. 23–8.)

Zavattini, C. (1953), *Sight and Sound*, vol. 23, no. 2. (See pp. 29–30.)

Suggestions for further reading

The following select bibliography is restricted to texts in the English language, except in a few areas where the paucity of material in English makes it necessary for us to indicate material in French or Italian. These exceptions are marked with an asterisk. Place of publication is London except where indicated otherwise.

Part I

Forsyth Hardy (ed.), *Grierson on Documentary*, Faber & Faber, 1946, revised 1966. A comprehensive selection from Grierson's theoretical and critical writings.

S. M. Eisenstein, *The Film Sense*, Faber & Faber, 1968, especially for the essay 'Word and Image (Montage in 1938)', which represents Eisenstein's revision of his earlier ideas about montage, and Appendix 2, 'Montage of Attractions', which sets out his earliest, theatrically-based concept of it.

S. M. Eisenstein, *Film Form*, Harcourt Brace & World, New York, 1949; Dennis Dobson, 1963. Basic texts of the 1920s and 1930s. The essays 'The Cinematographic Principle and the Ideogram', 'A Dialectical Approach to Film Form', 'The Filmic Fourth Dimension' and 'Methods of Montage' set out Eisenstein's 1920s ideas about montage in film.

S. M. Eisenstein, *Notes of a Film Director*, Lawrence & Wishart, 1959; revised ed., Dover, New York, 1970. Miscellaneous articles, including the important one on 'Organic Unity and Pathos in the Composition of Potemkin'.

S. M. Eisenstein, *Film Essays*, Dennis Dobson, 1968. Miscellaneous essays, including Eisenstein's appraisal of John Ford's film *Young Mr Lincoln*.

Vladimir Nizhny, *Lessons with Eisenstein*, Allen & Unwin, 1962. A useful account of some of Eisenstein's teaching exercises.

Andrew Tudor, 'Eisenstein: Great Beginnings', chapter in *Theories of Film*, Secker & Warburg, 1974.

Peter Wollen, 'Eisenstein's Aesthetics', chapter in *Signs and Meaning in the Cinema*, Secker & Warburg, 1968.

David Bordwell, 'Eisenstein's Epistemological Shift', article in *Screen*, vol. 15, no. 4, Winter 1974–5.

Norman Swallow, *Eisenstein: A Documentary Portrait*, Allen & Unwin, 1976.

Mash Enzensberger, 'Dziga Vertov', article in *Screen*, vol. 13 no. 4, Winter 1972–3. An excellent introduction to Vertov's work.

*Dziga Vertov, *Articles, journaux, projets*, Union générale d' editions, Paris, 1972. The best collection of Vertov's written work.

*Georges Sadoul, *Dziga Vertov*, Champ Libre, Paris, 1971.

Roy Armes, *Patterns of Realism*, Tantivy, 1971. A thoroughgoing account of the Italian neo-realist movement with some reference to its stylistic and social contexts.

George A. Huaco, *Italian Neo-realism*, Basic Books, 1965. Part 3 of *The Sociology of Film Art*, an ambitious attempt to chart the links of the movement with its sociohistorical preconditions.

Pierre Leprohon, *The Italian Cinema*, Secker & Warburg, 1972. Chapter 5 is a general account of neo-realism.

* André Bazin, *Qu'est-ce que le cinéma?*, vol. 4, *Une esthétique de la réalité*, Editions du Cerf, Paris, 1962. A few essays from this volume appear in English translation in *What is Cinema?*, vol. 2, University of California Press, 1971.

Screen, vol. 14, no. 4, Winter 1973–4, contains various material about neo-realism and Rossellini, including Mario Canella, 'Ideology and Aesthetic Hypotheses in the Criticism of Neo-realism', which locates the strengths and weaknesses of neo-realism in its dependence on the relatively unpolitical ideology of anti-fascism; and Christopher Williams, 'Bazin on neo-realism'.

*P. G. Hovald, *Le Néo-réalisme italien et ses créateurs*, Éditions du Cerf, Paris, 1959.

*Raymond Borde, André Bouissy, *Le Néo-réalisme italien, une expérience du cinéma social*, Cinématheque Suisse, Lausanne, 1960.

*Lino Micciche (ed.), *Il neorealismo cinematografico italiano, atti del convegno della X Mostra del Nuovo Cinema*, Marsilio, Venice, 1975.

Jose Luis Guarner, *Roberto Rossellini*, Studio Vista, 1970, an auteur account of Rossellini through his films to 1970.

Roberto Rossellini, *The War Trilogy: Scripts of* Rome, Open City, Paisà, *and* Germany Year Zero, Lorrimer, 1973.

Cesare Zavattini, 'How I did not make *Italia mia*', article in Robert Hughes (ed.), *Film: Book I*, Grove Press/John Calder, 1959. Interesting account of Zavattini's problems with de Sica, Rossellini and Carlo Ponti in 1951.

Cesare Zavattini, *Sequences from a Cinematic Life*, Prentice-Hall, NJ, 1967. Autobiographical essays which give the flavour of the man but are not very helpful about film.

Geoffrey Nowell-Smith, *Luchino Visconti*, Secker & Warburg, 1967, contains useful information about the neo-realist context.

*André Bazin, *Qu'est-ce que le cinéma?*, vol. 1, *Ontologie et langage*; vol. 2, *Le cinéma et les autres arts*; vol. 3, *Cinéma et sociologie*; vol. 4, *Une esthétique de la réalité: le néo-réalisme*, Éditions du Cerf, Paris, 1958–62. The fullest selection of Bazin's articles. The two entries that follow are both highly edited versions.

*André Bazin, *Qu'est-ce que le cinéma?* 'édition définitive' in one volume, Editions du Cerf, Paris, 1975.

André Bazin, *What is Cinema?*, vol. 1 (1967), vol. 2 (1971), California University Press.

André Bazin, *Jean Renoir*, W. H. Allen, 1974, a useful collection of all Bazin's writing on Renoir.

André Bazin, 'La Politique des auteurs', article in Peter Graham (ed.), *The New Wave*, Secker & Warburg, 1968. An article which, among other things, demonstrates something of Bazin's relationship with the magazine *Cahiers du Cinéma* and its author policy.

*Eric Rohmer, 'Cinéma, art de l'espace', article in *La Revue du cinéma*, no. 14, 1948, for Rohmer's early affinity with Bazin's idea of spatial realism.

*Eric Rohmer, 'De Trois films et d'une certaine école', article in *Cahiers du Cinéma*, no. 26, August–September 1953. The three films linked together in this text are Renoir's *The Golden Coach*, Rossellini's *Europa '51*, and Hitchcock's *I Confess*.

*Eric Rohmer and Claude Chabrol, *Hitchcock*, Éditions Universitaires, Paris, 1957; the celebrated 'religious' reading of Hitchcock.

V. F. Perkins, *Film as Film*, Penguin, 1972, Perkins's concise statement of a model for reading film on the basis of its coherence and credibility.

Ian Cameron (ed.), *The Movie Reader*, November Books, 1972. A selection of articles from the early period of the magazine *Movie*, including some by Perkins, which usefully illustrates the critical ambiance in which Perkins developed his ideas.

Siegfried Kracauer, *Theory of Film: The Redemption of Physical*

Reality, Oxford University Press, 1970. A far-ranging but heavily pedantic attempt to discover the essence of 'the normal black-and-white film, as it grows out of photography'. Kracauer's general tendency is to discover realism everywhere.

Erich Auerbach, *Mimesis: The Representation of Reality in Western Literature*, Princeton University Press, 1953. Literary realisms from Homer to Virginia Woolf, described through stylistic analysis of considerable brilliance. The most useful book about the general background of literary realism, though it does not talk about film at all.

Linda Nochlin, *Realism*, Penguin, 1971, especially for chapter 1, 'The Nature of Realism'. A useful account of how nineteenth-century painting developed realistic styles as part of its wish for concreteness, contemporaneity, and democracy.

Rudolf Arnheim, *Film as Art*, Faber & Faber, 1958, revised 1969.

Béla Bálazs, *Theory of the Film*, Dennis Dobson, 1952.

Part II

*Henri Agel, *Robert J. Flaherty*, Seghers, Paris, 1965.

'Robert Flaherty Talking', article in Roger Manvell (ed.), *The Cinema 1950*, Penguin, 1950. Chat, principally about *Nanook of the North* and *Moana*.

Robert Flaherty, *My Eskimo Friends*, Heinemann. 1924; Flaherty's account of his expedition to the Eskimos and the making of *Nanook*.

Part III

For general background information on Griffith and the Hollywood cinema of the 1920s and 1930s, the following may be helpful:

Lewis Jacobs, *The Rise of the American Film*, Harcourt Brace, New York, 1939, Teachers College Press paperback ed., 1974 (but beware of outdated critical opinions).

Iris Barry, *D. W. Griffith*, Museum of Modern Art/Doubleday, New York, 1940, 1965.

Harry M. Geduld (ed.), *Focus on D. W. Griffith*, Prentice-Hall, NJ, 1971.

Paul O'Dell, *Griffith and the Rise of Hollywood*, Zwemmer/Barnes, 1970.

David Robinson, *Hollywood in the 20s*, Zwemmer/Barnes, 1968.

John Baxter, *Hollywood in the 30s*, Zwemmer/Barnes, 1968.

Kevin Brownlow, *The Parade's Gone By*, Secker & Warburg, 1968.
The Velvet Light Trap, no. 1, 1971, special number, 'Warner Bros in the 1930s'.
Edward Buscombe, 'Notes on Columbia Pictures Corporation, 1926–41', article in *Screen*, vol. 16, no. 3, Autumn 1975.

On Russian cinema of the 1920s:

Jay Leyda, *Kino*, Allen & Unwin, 1960. The only serious attempt at a history of the Russian cinema in English.
Luda and Jean Schnitzer and Marcel Martin (ed.), *Cinema in Revolution*, Secker & Warburg, 1973.
Lev Kuleshov, *Kuleshov on Film*, California University Press, 1974. Kuleshov was one of the first conscious experimenters in synthetic montage and influenced Eisenstein and Pudovkin.
Vsevolod Pudovkin, *On Film Technique*, Gollancz, 1929.
Richard Sherwood (ed.), 'Documents from Lef', and Ben Brewster (ed.), 'Documents from Novy Lef', both in *Screen*, vol. 12, no. 3, Winter 1971–2.
Stephen Crofts and Olivia Rose, 'An Essay towards Man with a Movie Camera', article in *Screen*, vol. 18, no. 1, Spring 1977, stressing the relationships between Vertov and the modernist avant-garde.

On formalism:

Victor Erlich, *Russian Formalism: History-doctrine*, Mouton, The Hague, 1965. The best account of the Formalist school of literary criticism.
Fredric Jameson, *The Prison-House of Language*, Princeton University Press, 1972.
*Tzvetan Todorov (ed.), *Théorie de la littérature*, Seuil, Paris, 1965. A collection of formalist texts.
Twentieth-Century Studies, nos 7 and 8, 1972, 'Russian Formalism'. Includes an introductory essay by Tzvetan Todorov; Boris Eikhenbaum, 'Literature and Cinema'; and Viktor Shklovsky, 'Poetry and Prose in Cinematography'.
Boris Eikhenbaum, 'Problems of Film Stylistics', article in *Screen*, vol. 15, no. 3, Autumn 1974.
Osip Brik, 'Selected Writings' presented by Maria Enzensberger, in *Screen*, vol. 15, no. 3, Autumn 1974.
Lee T. Lemon and Marion J. Reis (ed.), *Russian Formalist Criticism: Four Essays*, University of Nebraska Press, 1965. Shklovsky on Art as Technique and Sterne's 'Tristram Shandy', Tomashevsky on 'Thematics', and Eikhenbaum on 'The Theory of the Formal

Method'.

Tynyanov's story 'Lieutenant Kizhe' is available in Krystyna Pomorska (ed.), *50 Years of Russian Prose*, vol. 1, MIT Press, 1971.

Viktor Shklovsky, *Mayakovsky and his Circle*, Pluto Press, 1972.

Containing material on the background to formalism:

Marc Slonim, *Soviet Russian Literature 1917–77*, Oxford University Press, 1977.

E. Braun (ed.), *Meyerhold on Theatre*, Eyre Methuen, 1969.

Linguistics:

Ferdinand de Saussure, *Course in General Linguistics*, McGraw-Hill, 1966.

Jonathan Culler, *Saussure*, Fontana, 1976.

Roland Barthes, *Elements of Semiology*, Cape, 1967.

Brecht:

John Willett, *The Theatre of Brecht*, Methuen, 1959, revised ed. 1967.

Walter Benjamin, *Understanding Brecht*, New Left Books, 1977.

Screen, vol. 15, no. 2, Summer 1974, special number on 'Brecht and a Revolutionary Cinema', including Colin MacCabe, 'Realism and the Cinema: Notes on some Brechtian Theses', and Stanley Mitchell, 'From Shklovsky to Brecht: Some Preliminary Remarks towards a Politicisation of Russian Formalism'.

Screen, vol. 16, no. 4, Winter 1975–6, record of the 'Brecht and the Cinema' event at the 1975 Edinburgh Film Festival.

Ideology:

T. B. Bottomore and Maximilien Rubel (ed.), *Karl Marx – Selected Writings in Sociology and Social Philosophy*, Penguin, 1963.

David Craig (ed.), *Marxists on Literature: An Anthology*, Penguin, 1975.

Working Papers in Cultural Studies, no. 10, *On Ideology*, CCCS, University of Birmingham, 1977. Contains Stuart Hall, 'The Hinterland of Science: Ideology and the "Sociology of Knowledge"', and useful articles on the concepts of ideology in Lukács, Gramsci and Althusser.

Stuart Hall, 'Culture, the Media and the "Ideological Effect"', article in J. Curran, M. Gurevitch, J. Woollacott (ed.), *Mass Communication and Society*, Edward Arnold/Open University Press, London, 1977.

Louis Althusser, *For Marx*, Penguin, 1969.
Louis Althusser, *Lenin and Philosophy*, especially for the essay on 'Ideology and Ideological State Apparatuses', New Left Books, 1971.
Stephen Heath, 'On Screen, in Frame: Film and Ideology', article in *Quarterly Review of Film Studies*, Autumn 1976.
Colin MacCabe, 'Theory and Film: Principles of Realism and Pleasure', article in *Screen*, vol. 17, no. 3, Autumn 1976.
Screen Reader, no. 1, SEFT, 1977.
Raymond Williams, 'A Lecture on Realism', article in *Screen*, vol. 18, no. 1, Spring 1977.
Christine Gledhill, 'Whose Choice? Teaching Films about Abortion', article in *Screen Education*, no. 24, Autumn 1977.
Peter Wollen, 'Counter-cinéma: Vent d'Est', article in *After-Image*, no. 4, 1972.
Christopher Williams, 'Politics and Production', article in *Screen*, vol. 12, no. 4, Winter 1971–2.
Jean Narboni and Tom Milne (ed.), *Godard on Godard*, Secker & Warburg, 1972.
Louis D. Gianetti, *Godard and Others*, Tantivy, 1975.
Leif Furhammar and Nils Isaksson, *Politics and Film*, Studio Vista, 1971; mainstream essays on 'films which have a clear political purpose, on the cinema as a weapon of political propaganda'.

Part IV

Technology:

Karel Reisz and Gavin Millar, *The Technique of Film Editing*, rev. ed., Hastings, New York, and Focal Press, London, 1968.
Charles Highams, *Hollywood Cameramen: Sources of Light*, Thames & Hudson, 1970. Interviews with Wong Howe, Cortez, Struss, Miller, Shamroy, Garmes and Daniels.
H. Mario Raimondo Souto, *The Technique of the Motion Picture Camera*, Focal Press, 1967.
R. Fielding (ed.), *A Technological History of Motion Pictures and Television*, California University Press, 1967. An anthology of papers presented to the US Society of Motion Pictures and Television Engineers.
Raymond Spottiswoode, *Film and its Techniques*, Faber & Faber, 1951.
Barry Salt, 'Statistical Style Analysis of Motion Pictures', article in *Film Quarterly*, Fall 1974.
Barry Salt, 'The Early Development of Film Form', article in *Film*

Form, no. 1, 1976.

Film language and semiotics:

Brian Henderson, 'The Long Take', article in *Film Comment,* vol. 7, no. 2, Summer 1971. A useful article which, after comparing the theories of Bazin and Eisenstein, considers editing as a *mise en scène* device.

Christian Metz, *Film Language,* Oxford University Press, 1974. This represents Metz's earlier critical positions and is largely concerned with realism. Includes the essays 'On the Impression of Reality', 'Cinema, *langue* or *langage*', 'Some Points in the Semiotics of the Cinema', 'Problems of Denotation in the Fiction Film', 'Syntagmatic Analysis of the Image Track', and 'The Modern Cinema and Narrativity'.

Jack Daniels, 'Metz's Grande Syntagmatique: Summary and Critique', article in *Film Form,* no. 1, 1976.

Noel Burch, *Theory of Film Practice,* Secker & Warburg, 1973. A study of the narrative practice of film through its temporal and spatial articulation.

Roy Armes, *The Ambiguous Image: Narrative Style in Modern European Cinema,* Secker & Warburg, 1976. Authorship essays bearing on the dissolution of narrative.

Stephen Heath, 'Narrative Space', article in *Screen,* vol. 17, no. 3, Autumn 1976. On the relations between space and narrative.

Renoir:

Jean Renoir, *My Life and my Films,* Collins, 1974.

Leo Braudy, *Jean Renoir: The World of his Films,* Doubleday, New York, 1972.

Raymond Durgnat, *Jean Renoir,* Studio Vista, 1975.

Documentary:

Erik Barnouw, *Documentary: A History of the Non-fiction Film,* Oxford University Press, 1974. Breathless and potted, but can serve as an introduction.

Lewis Jacobs, *The Documentary Tradition: From* Nanook *to* Woodstock, Hopkinson & Blake, New York, 1971. An anthology of opinions.

G. Roy Levin, *Documentary Explorations,* Doubleday, New York, 1971; a rambling but interesting collection of interviews with film-makers. The interviewer tries to pursue critical questions.

Alan Rosenthal, *The New Documentary in Action,* California University Press, 1971. More interviews, some of which are usefully complementary to those in Levin.

Alan Lovell's essay 'The Documentary Film Movement: John Grierson', in Lovell and Jim Hillier, *Studies in Documentary*, Secker & Warburg, 1972, is a good summary of the origins of British documentary.

Elizabeth Sussex, *The Rise and Fall of British Documentary*, California University Press, 1975. Its history narrated largely by the film-makers themselves.

Paul Rotha, *Documentary Diary*, Secker & Warburg, 1973.

Louis Marcorelles, *Living Cinema*, Allen & Unwin, 1973. A committed exposition of the truth of direct cinema, useful in comparison with the text by Comolli in this book.

Bill Nichols, 'Documentary Theory and Practice', article in *Screen*, vol. 17, no. 4, Winter 1976–7. An attempt to study documentary as a genre, with its own conventions, expectations and narrative devices paralleling those of the fiction film.

Rohmer:

*Eric Rohmer, 'Le Celluloid et le marbre', articles in *Cahiers du Cinéma*, nos 44, 49, 51, 52, 53, 1955.

Interview with Graham Petrie, *Film Quarterly*, vol. 24, no. 4, Summer 1971, describes Rohmer's critical background.

Martin Walsh, 'Structured Ambiguity in the Films of Eric Rohmer', *Film Criticism*, vol. 1, no. 2, Summer 1976.

Colin Crisp's article 'The Ideology of Realism', in the *Australian Journal of Screen Theory*, no. 2, 1977, sets *Le Celluloid et le marbre* alongside *My Night with Maud*.

16 mm film availability in Great Britain

The following lists are intended as a rough guide for teachers and others planning courses on realism and the cinema and associated topics. Potential users are reminded that film availability fluctuates from year to year. For other details, including country of production, date, director, running time and hire fees, you should consult *Films on Offer*, published annually by the British Film Institute.

Topics	Titles	16mm distributors
Grierson/British Documentary in the 1930s	*Drifters*	Central Film Library
	Industrial Britain	BFI
	Song of Ceylon	BFI
	Coalface	BFI
	Night Mail	Central Film Library
Eisenstein	*Strike*	Contemporary
	Battleship Potemkin	BFI and Contemporary
	October	BFI and Contemporary
	The Old and the New (The general line)	
	Alexander Nevsky	Contemporary
	Ivan the Terrible part 1	Contemporary
	Ivan the Terrible part 2	Contemporary
Vertov	*The Man with the Movie Camera*	BFI
	Three Songs of Lenin	Educational and Television Films

Italian neo-realism	*Rome, Open City*	Contemporary
	Stromboli	BFI
	Umberto D	Connoisseur
	Senso	Connoisseur
	Due Soldi di Speranza	Connoisseur
	I Vitelloni	Connoisseur
	Amore in Città	BFI
	Paisà	BFI
	Germany Year Zero	BFI
	Bicycle Thieves	Contemporary
	Viaggio in Italia	BFI
Bazin	*The Best Years of our Lives*	BFI
	The Little Foxes	BFI
	Citizen Kane	Harris
	La Règle du jeu	Contemporary
	The Magnificent Ambersons	Harris

(Neither *Sunrise* nor *Greed* is available, but

	The Last Laugh	BFI
	Foolish Wives	BFI

can represent some aspects of Murnau and von Stroheim.)

Renoir	*Boudu sauvé des eaux*	Contemporary
	Le Crime de Mr Lange	Connoisseur
	Toni	Contemporary
	Une Partie de campagne	Connoisseur
	La Grande Illusion	Contemporary
	La Marseillaise	Contemporary
	La Règle du jeu	Contemporary
	The Golden Coach	Contemporary
Perkins / mise en scène	*Letter from an Unknown Woman* (cut version)	Intercontinental
	Psycho	Rank
	Wild River (scope)	Film Distributors Associated

	River of No Return (standard print of a scope film)	Film Distributors Associated
	Rebel without a Cause	Columbia-Warner
	Party Girl	Harris
Rohmer /Cahiers/ mise en scène	*I Confess*	Columbia-Warner
	Suspicion	Harris
	The Wrong Man	Columbia-Warner
	Hatari!	Rank
	Only Angels Have Wings	Columbia-Warner
	Red River	Film Distributors Associated
	Rio Bravo	Columbia-Warner
	Adam's Rib	Harris
	Philadelphia Story	Harris
	La strada	Contemporary
	The Passion of Joan of Arc	Contemporary
	Day of Wrath	Cinegate
	Le Procès de Jeanne d'Arc	Contemporary
	Chikamatsu Mono- gatari	Cinegate
	Sansho Dayu	Cinegate
	Ugestsu Monogatari	Cinegate
Rohmer as author	*La Collectionneuse*	Connoisseur
	Le Genou de Claire	Harris
	Love in the Afternoon	Harris
	My Night with Maud	Artificial Eye
Flaherty	*Nanook of the North*	BFI
	Moana	BFI
	Man of Aran	Rank
	Elephant Boy	London Film Productions
	Louisiana Story	BFI
Griffith	*Birth of a Nation*	BFI and Cinegate
	Broken Blossoms	BFI and Cinegate

	Intolerance	BFI and Cinegate
	Judith of Bethulia	BFI
	Hearts of the World	BFI and Cinegate
	Way Down East	BFI and Cinegate
Columbia	*Mr Deeds goes to Town*	Columbia-Warner
	Mr Smith goes to Washington	Columbia-Warner
	It Happened One Night	Columbia-Warner
	Twentieth Century	Columbia-Warner
	The Whole Town's Talking	Columbia-Warner
Russian cinema of the 1920s	*The End of St Petersburg*	Contemporary and BFI
	Mother	Contemporary and BFI
	Storm over Asia	Contemporary and BFI
	The New Babylon	Contemporary

(Apart from films by Eisenstein and Pudovkin this area is poorly represented.)

British realist cinema of the 1960s	*A Taste of Honey*	Rank
	A Kind of Loving	EMI
	Billy Liar	EMI
	This Sporting Life	Rank
	The Loneliness of the Long-Distance Runner	Rank
	Saturday Night and Sunday Morning	Rank
	Poor Cow	EMI
	Kes	EMI
	Family Life	EMI
British television realism	*Cathy Come Home*	Concord
	Gale is Dead	BBC
Ideology	*Klute* (scope)	Columbia-Warner
	State of Siege	Rank
	Hour of the Furnaces	Other Cinema
	The Nightcleaners part 1	Other Cinema

	Cinetracts	London Film-Makers Co-op
	Six Cinetracts	Other Cinema
	Weekend	Connoisseur
	Le Gai savoir	Other Cinema
	British Sounds	Other Cinema
	Pravda	Other Cinema
	Vent d'est	Artificial Eye
	Tout va bien	Other Cinema
	Letter to Jane	Other Cinema
	Numéro deux	Other Cinema
	The Road to Life	Educational and Television Films
	Behind the Rent Strike	Other Cinema
	Coup pour coup	Other Cinema
	Whose Choice?	Other Cinema
Avant-garde	*Wavelength*	Cinegate
	The Bridegroom, The Actress and the Pimp	Artificial Eye
	Introduction to the Accompaniment to a Cinematographic Scene by Arnold Schoenberg	Artificial Eye
Early realism	*Lumière programme*	BFI
	A Visit to Messrs Peek Frean's Biscuit Factory	BFI
	The Great Train Robbery	BFI
Around the return of depth of field (cf. Ogle)	*Stagecoach*	Film Distributors Associated
	The Grapes of Wrath	Columbia-Warner
	The Long Voyage Home	BFI
Documentary (general)	*Listen to Britain*	Central Film Library and BFI
	A Diary for Timothy	BFI
	À propos de Nice	Contemporary

Farrebique	BFI
Misère au Borinage	BFI
Every Day except Christmas	BFI
Chronique d'un été	Contemporary
Le joli mai	Contemporary
A Married Couple	Contemporary
Seventy-nine Springs	Educational and Television Films
Black Natchez	
The Space between Words: Family	Concord
High School	Other Cinema
Essene	Other Cinema
Gimme Shelter	Harris

(In this area there is currently an almost total unavailability of the most useful *cinéma-vérité*/direct films. Nothing by Leacock, Pennebaker, or Perrault, almost nothing by Rouch or the Maysles brothers.)

Bettetini /the sequence-shot / changes in narrative style	*Deux ou trois choses que je sais d'elle*	Contemporary
	Une Femme est une Femme (standard print of a scope film)	Amanda
	Le Mépris (scope)	Contemporary
	Pierrot-le-fou	Connoisseur
	Sympathy for the Devil	Connoisseur
	Le amiche	Connoisseur
	L'avventura	Connoisseur
	La notte	Connoisseur and Contemporary
	L'eclisse	Connoisseur
	The Red Desert	Artificial Eye
	The Passenger	Harris
	Blind Date	Harris
	Accident	Harris
	Eve	BFI
	Figures in a Landscape	Film Distributors Associated

	King and Country	EMI
	The Servant	EMI
	Hands over the City	Contemporary
	The Mattei Affair	Cinegate
	Before the Revolution	Contemporary
	Partner (scope)	Contemporary
	Persona	Film Distributors Associated
	Not Reconciled	Artificial Eye
Comolli / interpenetration of fiction and documentary	Celine and Julie go Boating	Contemporary
	Chronicle of Anna Magdalena Bach	Artificial Eye
	Paris vu par . . .	Amanda
	Blue Movie	Vaughan-Rogosin
	Chelsea Girls	Connoisseur
	Kitchen	Vaughan-Rogosin
	La Maman et la putain	Harris
	Hiroshima Mon Amour	Contemporary
	Last Year in Marienbad	Contemporary
	Silence and Cry	Artificial Eye
	The Red and the White	Artificial Eye
	The Round Up	Contemporary
	My Way Home	BFI
	The Bandwagon	Harris
	The Pirate	Harris
	Cabaret	Rank
	For Me and My Gal	Harris
	42nd Street	Film Distributors Associated
	Singin' in the Rain	Harris

Index